W9-BSO-997

AMERICAN WOMEN'S FICTION
1790–1870

GARLAND REFERENCE LIBRARY
OF THE HUMANITIES
(Vol. 1110)

AMERICAN WOMEN'S FICTION
1790–1870
A Reference Guide

Barbara A. White

GARLAND PUBLISHING, INC. • NEW YORK & LONDON
1990

Library of Congress Cataloging-in-Publication Data

White, Barbara Anne, 1942–
    American women's fiction, 1790–1870: a reference guide / Barbara
A. White.
        p.   cm. — (Garland reference library of the humanities ; vol.
1110)
    Includes bibliographical references.
    ISBN 0–8240–6673–1 (alk. paper)
    1. American fiction—Women authors—History and criticism—
Bibliography. 2. American fiction,—19th century—History and
criticism—Bibliography. 3. American fiction—18th century—History and
criticism—Bibliography. 4. Women and literature—United
States—History—19th century—Bibliography. 5. American fiction—
Women authors—Bibliography. 6. American fiction—19th century—
Bibliography. 7. American fiction—18th century—Bibliography.
8. Women novelists, American—Biography—Bibliography. I. Title.
II. Series.
Z1231.F4W49   1990
[PS374.W6]
016.813009'9287—dc20   89–17213
                                                              CIP

Printed on acid-free, 250-year-life paper
Manufactured in the United States of America

For my father, Frank L. White,
who enjoys reading these authors

CONTENTS

PREFACE

This guide provides information about women who wrote fiction in the United States during the period 1790-1870. The book has two parts: 1) an annotated list of sources that discuss women's fiction in the period or comment on female authors who were born before 1841 and wrote some fiction before 1870; and 2) an alphabetical list of nineteenth-century writers who meet those criteria. Under each author's name I note the sources from Part 1 that discuss her. In other words, the parts are keyed to each other so that the researcher can determine which source (Part 1) treats which writer (Part 2).

USES OF THE GUIDE

The need for this reference work has arisen along with the rapidly growing interest in early American fiction by women. Until the 1980's women who wrote before the Civil War were generally dismissed as "sentimentalists" who produced inferior "domestic fiction." However, Nina Baym drew attention to these writers with her Woman's Fiction: A Guide to Novels by and about Women in America, 1820-1870 (1978), and literary critics and historians have begun both to read this neglected fiction and to question the standards for classifying and judging literature that led to its eclipse. The past few years have seen the publication of two important full-length studies, Mary Kelley's Private Woman, Public Stage: Literary Domesticity in Nineteenth-Century America (1984) and Jane P. Tompkins' Sensational Designs: The Cultural Work of American Fiction, 1790-1860 (1985), and the first two anthologies of this fiction, Hidden Hands: An Anthology of American Women Writers, 1790-1870 (1985), which I co-edited with Lucy M. Freibert, and Provisions: A Reader from Nineteenth-Century American Women (1985), edited by Judith Fetterley. In addition, in 1984 the

University of Massachusetts at Amherst began publishing
Legacy, a journal devoted to study of nineteenth-
century American women writers.

Each critic or historian new to the field quickly
discovers the lack of a satisfactory bibliography of
works on nineteenth-century women writers in general or
of works by and about individual authors. One must
rely on the brief bibliographies included in the works
mentioned above, and these are highly selective and
usually not annotated. Nineteenth-century women are
very spottily represented in standard sources like
Narda Lacey Schwartz's Articles on Women Writers,
1960-1975 (1977) and Articles on Women Writers,
1976-1984 (1986) and Carol Fairbanks Myers' Women in
Literature (1976) and More Women in Literature (1979).
My American Women Writers: An Annotated Bibliography of
Criticism (1977) can sometimes be useful but is
restricted to literary criticism and does not focus on
the nineteenth century.

Perhaps because of this lack of bibliographic
control, I have occasionally heard it said that "hardly
anything" has been written about early nineteenth-
century women writers. Not so, as the following pages
attest; but the quality of the work can certainly be
questioned. As I noted in a recent bibliographic
survey (#366), the two main types of commentary on
early women writers have been the patronizing survey of
literary curiosities and the biographical dictionary.
Both tend to be full of mistakes. Although a certain
amount of error must be expected in biographical
sources, the large number of wrong names and dates for
female authors seems to reflect the lack of importance
accorded the subject. The patronizing surveys err in a
different direction. Because they lump all women
together, labelling them "sentimental" or "domestic,"
they falsely classify satirists and realists like Fanny
Fern and Caroline Kirkland; Kirkland, a sharp observer
of frontier economic and social conditions, becomes
"primarily interested in domestic life" (#119). Time
sequences get blurred so that a critic can refer to the
"heavily freighted, melodramatic work of Catherine
Sedgwick, Lydia Child, and Mrs. Cheney. 'A damned mob
of scribbling women,' Hawthorne called them" (Ernest E.
Leisy, "The Novel in America," Southwest Review 22
(Oct. 1936): 88-99). These not-very-melodramatic
novelists gained prominence in the 1820's, whereas
Nathaniel Hawthorne made his famous remark in 1855
about an entirely different generation of women.

However limited some of the sources may be, they

contain a good deal of information that cannot be
obtained elsewhere. Only a few of the best known
writers, such as Harriet Beecher Stowe and Louisa May
Alcott, have been the subject of a biography, critical
book, published bibliography, or reference guide. For
information on most authors one still has to consult
the biographical dictionaries, and frequently the
nineteenth-century examples, such as John S. Hart's The
Female Prose Writers of America (#154), Ida Raymond
(Mary T. Tardy)'s Southland Writers: Biographical and
Critical Sketches of the Living Female Writers of the
South (#276), and the "Living Female Writers" section
of Sarah Josepha Hale's Woman's Record (#145).
Interestingly, the most inclusive and reliable modern
dictionary, Ungar's American Women Writers (#13),
contains entries on less than half the writers on the
author list in Part 2 of this guide.

The sources for the study of American women's
fiction, 1790-1870 provide information not only about
individual authors but also about the history of
criticism and literary politics, especially women's
place in the American literary canon. For instance,
Paul Lauter has made a valuable study of the
professionalization of the teaching of literature and
accompanying developments in the 1920's that "virtually
eliminated black, white female, and all working-class
writers from the canon" ("Race and Gender in the
Shaping of the American Literary Canon: A Case Study
from the Twenties," Feminist Studies, 9 (Fall 1983):
435-63). If one looks at earlier literary histories,
however, one finds similar exclusionary processes at
work. For every mid-nineteenth-century John S. Hart
who was busy promoting women writers along with the
men, there was a Rufus Wilmot Griswold (remembered
today as Poe's rival) relegating women to the margins
(#140). The same holds true in other decades, so that
one might compare in the 1890's Pattee, Richardson, and
Wendell (#262, 284, 362) with the more inclusive
Rutherford, Smyth, and Underwood (#293, 314, 345). Of
course, only the most inclusive literary histories and
anthologies will be found in this guide at all; the
majority either do not include women or mention names
only in passing and so are not represented here.
Female authors are more likely to be discussed in
histories of children's literature than in the better
known and more influential histories and anthologies of
nineteenth-century American fiction.

SCOPE

The sources listed and annotated in Part 1 of this guide fall into two categories. The first contains books, chapters in books, and articles directly about American women's fiction, 1790-1870; this means the fiction in general and not one individual author. Examples are "Why Their Success? Some Observations on Publishing by Popular Nineteenth-Century Women Writers" (#71) and Woman's Fiction: A Guide to Novels by and about Women in America, 1820-1870 (#28). The works included were written in English and for the most part originated in the U.S. I have included works published through 1985 and have tried to be comprehensive in my coverage of this type of source. I would be pleased to hear about any additions.

The second category consists of works that have a broader focus but emphasize either literature or women and discuss three or more women who wrote fiction in the period 1790-1870. Examples are Notable American Women, 1607-1950 (#239), a biographical source that covers women who were not writers and who lived in the twentieth century but obviously includes several authors from my time period, and "Patterns of Violence and Non-Violence in Pro-Slavery and Anti-Slavery Fiction" (#228), an article that discusses both male and female antebellum writers.

The second category, although it contains sources that can be extremely useful, is obviously more problematic than the first. Its breadth has led me to impose some rather arbitrary limitations. For instance, there are literally hundreds of biographical dictionaries and general histories of states that may include three or more of my authors; if this bibliography were ever to be completed, it was necessary to eliminate some of these possibilities. Thus I insisted on a literary or female focus-- Liberty's Women (#199) and American Authors 1600-1900 (#8) but not Webster's Biographical Dictionary; Virginia's Women from 1607 (#357) and Virginia Authors, Past and Present (#350), but not History of Virginia. (The one exception to this rule is the Dictionary of American Biography (#88), which is included because of its heavy use by researchers.) I have also excluded some classes of material that proved not very instructive: encyclopedias, outline surveys, digests of books and travel guides, except when specifically on nineteenth-century women writers. Dissertations are omitted because they can easily be located in

<u>Dissertation Abstracts International</u> and similar
sources.

Another issue raised by the second category is the
question of what it means to "discuss" authors and
their fiction. Many literary histories simply mention
names of authors, as in "Also writing fiction during
this period were _____, _____, and _____"; sometimes no
information is provided beyond a writer's dates and the
titles of her major books. I decided that a source
must provide more substantial information in order to
be included; the information does not have to be
presented discursively and may be in chart form, but it
has to go beyond a mere mention of a name and title.
Although this limitation introduces a greater element
of subjectivity than I consider ideal in a
bibliography, it will hopefully simplify the
researcher's task.

In some cases three or more women on my author
list are referred to in a source that does not discuss
their fiction. For instance, many novelists also wrote
poetry, which is described and analyzed in books
ranging from Thomas Buchanan Read's <u>The Female Poets of
America</u> (1849) and William T. Coggeshall's <u>The Poets
and Poetry of the West</u> (1860) to Joan A. Sherman's
<u>Invisible Poets: Afro-Americans of the Nineteenth
Century</u> (1974) and Cheryl Walker's <u>The Nightingale's
Burden</u> (1982). These works are not included. Nor are
sources that consider the authors' prose other than
fiction; Russell Lynes' <u>The Domesticated Americans</u>
(1963), for example, discusses Lydia Maria Child, Sarah
Josepha Hale, Eliza Leslie, and Catharine M. Sedgwick,
but is concerned only with their views on household
reform as expressed in their non-fiction writings. On
the other hand, histories of women's activities in the
nineteenth century that pay considerable attention to
fiction, such as Barbara Solomon's <u>In the Company of
Educated Women</u> (#315), are included here.

Only reluctantly did I adhere to a strong emphasis
on fiction and, indeed, restrict the authors included
to those who wrote it. I focused on fiction partly in
order to keep the book a manageable size and partly to
assist prospective writers of the histories of American
women's fiction and inclusive histories of American
fiction that we badly need. Fortunately, we have
adequate histories of American women's poetry--the
modern works just mentioned, plus Emily S. Watts's <u>The
Poetry of American Women from 1632 to 1945</u> (1977) and
Alicia Suskin Ostriker's <u>Stealing the Language</u> (1986)--
and numerous books about late nineteenth- and turn-of-

the-century women writers.

In defining exactly who would be included as
female writers of fiction in the period 1790-1870, I
decided that the author must have been born before 1841
and done a significant amount of publishing before
1870. My general principle was that she should have
published before 1870 either a third of her fiction or
her most important works. Thus, writers like Eliza
Frances Andrews and Constance Fenimore Woolson, who
were born in 1840 but did not start publishing until
the 1870's, are excluded; even some authors born in the
20's, such as Elizabeth Avery Meriwether and Mary
Elizabeth Wilson Sherwood, began writing after the
Civil War and are thereby thought to belong with late
nineteenth-century writers. On the other hand, Rose
Terry Cooke (1827-1892), who published significant work
before 1870 and, in fact, influenced later writers,
appears here. So do Louisa May Alcott (1832-1888) and
her friend Jane Goodwin Austin (1831-1894); while these
women wrote the bulk of their fiction in the 1870's and
80's, they produced their most important work in the
earlier period.

Several authors included are remembered primarily
as poets--for instance, Lydia Sigourney; I have not
omitted women known best for their poetry or writing in
some other genre if I know that they also wrote
fiction. I have included women who are treated by the
sources as fiction writers, even if recent findings may
contradict this classification. For example, Harriet
A. Jacobs appears on the author list because several
critics treat her Incidents in the Life of a Slave Girl
(1861) as fiction, even though recently discovered
letters prove it an authentic slave narrative. In the
case of African-American women, my rule that sources
included in the bibliography must discuss three or more
fiction writers proved too restrictive and I thus
relaxed it; in several cases works about African-
American fiction that discuss only two women writers
are included. I assume that when the results of the
Black Periodical Fiction Project are published, we will
have a greatly expanded list of African-American women
who wrote fiction in the period (see Angus Paul, "A
Wealth of Material in Black Literature Discovered by
Periodical Fiction Project," Chronicle of Higher
Education, pp. 1, 8-9).

ENTRIES IN PART 1

I have checked and annotated all entries. Entries
in Part 1 are arranged alphabetically by author or
editor or by Library of Congress main entry when known.
Except in the case of multi-volume works, the number of
pages in a book is indicated. My main concern has been
to describe the content of a work, rather than its
physical characteristics; thus collation statements are
not detailed. I sometimes list multiple appearances of
a work but have not attempted to register every single
appearance. The intent in both cases is to provide
enough information for easy access. I have not
preferred first editions, although I try to indicate
the date of the first edition in parentheses if I am
annotating a later edition. Often a revised edition of
a reference work will be more useful to the researcher
because it includes a larger number of authors.

Following the annotation appears an alphabetical
list of the individual authors discussed in the work.
(i.e. American women born before 1841 who published a
significant amount of their fiction before 1870). Last
names only are given, except when there is more than
one writer with the same last name, in which case full
names are used. As anyone who has worked with
nineteenth-century women's fiction knows, the authors
may have written under different names and may be
referred to variously in the criticism and reference
works. When a source spells an author's last name
differently or uses a different name than that
established in Part 2 of this bibliography, the author
is listed under the established name but in brackets,
with the name as given by the source following. Take,
for example, the following list:

> [Blake] Umsted
> [Bleecker] Bleeker
> Booth
> Cary, Alice (P)
> Cary, Phoebe

This means that the source refers to Lillie Devereux
Blake as Lillie Devereux Umsted, a name from an early
marriage. Ann Eliza Bleecker's name is spelled Bleeker
in this source, and two different Carys are discussed.
When a source provides a portrait of an author, this is
indicated with a P in parentheses after her name. So,
in the above source, one can find a portrait of Alice
Cary.

ENTRIES IN PART 2

The author list in Part 2 consists of the writers
discussed in the sources represented in Part 1 who
fulfill the criteria of being born before 1841 and
having published fiction by 1870. There are 328
authors included in Part 2, making it the most
comprehensive list in existence of early nineteenth-
century female authors. However, it is by no means a
complete list of women writing fiction in the period
because it excludes the following: 1) those who are not
discussed in secondary sources; and 2) those for whom
we have no birth date and who could have been born
after 1840.

As I noted in my discussion of entries in Part 1,
form of name poses problems in dealing with nineteenth-
century women writers. A Caroline Kirkland or Lucy
Larcom is less common than Mary Virginia Hawes Terhune,
who wrote under her pseudonym, "Marion Harland"; the
latter may be discussed in secondary sources under
Harland, Hawes, or Terhune. I chose the form of name
used by the majority of sources that discuss the
author. Additional known names are supplied in
brackets; a regularly used pseudonym by which an author
is commonly known appears in quotation marks following
the real name. Thus, Terhune appears as Terhune, Mary
Virginia [Hawes] "Marion Harland." The majority of
sources refer to her as Mary Virginia Terhune, and she
regularly used the pseudonym "Marion Harland." Other
pseudonyms may be noted under "Also wrote under"
following the author's dates. Thus, take the following
entry: Hale, Sarah Josepha [Buell] (1788-1879) Also
wrote under: Cornelia; A Lady of New Hampshire; Julia
Parley; S.J.H. Most sources refer to Hale as Sarah
Josepha Hale; her maiden name was Buell; she did not
regularly employ a pseudonym but at some point in her
career used "Cornelia," "A Lady of New Hampshire," etc.

Birth and death dates also appear as given by the
majority of sources (unless I happen to have good
evidence for an alternate date). The abbreviations I
use are "b." for born, "d." for died, "fl." for
flourished, and "ca." for approximately.

Following the author's names and dates in the
author list appears a list of numbers. These are the
numbers of the entries in Part 1 of this guide for
sources that discuss the author. A "P" in parentheses
after the number means that the source includes a
portrait of the author. Other information in
parentheses, such as an alternate name or date,

indicates that the information varies from the standard
as given in other sources. This is designed to alert
the researcher to significant variations in the name by
which an author is known and to uncertainties about her
dates.

INDEXES

There are three indexes. The first index is to
authors and editors of sources in Part 1. The second
provides a subject index to Part 1, allowing the
researcher to find sources on particular topics, such
as Southern literature, Ohio writing, children's
literature, Civil War novels, etc. In the first two
indexes numbers refer to entries rather than pages.
The third index is a pseudonym/alternative form of name
list for authors in Part 2.

ACKNOWLEDGMENTS

I appreciate the support of the Central University
Research Fund of the University of New Hampshire (UNH)
and the assistance of the UNH Library's Interlibrary
Loan and Special Collections staffs; I want to thank in
particular Theresa MacGregor and Susan Metcalf. I am
also grateful for the help of Susan Dumais, my student
assistant, and Mary M. Moynihan, who read the completed
manuscript.

AMERICAN WOMEN'S FICTION
1790–1870

PART 1. SOURCES

1.   Ackmann, Martha.   "Legacy Guide to American Women
     Writers' Homes." LEGACY 1 (Fall 1984): 10-12; 2
     (Spring 1985): 10-12.

     Gives information about the eight homes of nine-
teenth-century writers that have been preserved and are
open to the public.

     Alcott
     Cary, Alice
     Cary, Phoebe
     Stowe
     Warner, Anna B.
     Warner, Susan

2.   Adams, Bess Porter. ABOUT BOOKS AND CHILDREN:
     HISTORICAL SURVEY OF CHILDREN'S LITERATURE. New
     York: Henry Holt and Co., 1953. 573 pp.

     Chapter 3 on "American schools and books before
1900" contains brief descriptions of works by female
writers.

     Child
     Finley
     Stowe

3.   Adelman, Joseph. FAMOUS WOMEN. New York: Ellis
     M. Lonow Co., 1926. 328 pp.

     Contains one-to-two-paragraph biographical
sketches of 500 women throughout the ages. Arrangement
is by period, but there is an occupational index with
such categories as "Reformers and Philanthropists" and
"Authors." Includes portraits.

Alcott (P)
Blake
Botta
Cary, Alice
Cary, Phoebe
Child
Crosby
Davis, Rebecca Harding
Dodge, Mary Mapes
Farnham
Hale, Sarah Josepha
Larcom
Lewis
Livermore, Mary A.
Putnam
Sigourney
Stowe (P)
[Terhune] Harland
Warner, Anna B.
Warner, Susan

4.   Adickes, Sandra. "Mind among the Spindles: An
      Examination of Some of the Journals, Newspapers,
      and Memoirs of the Lowell Female Operatives."
      WOMEN'S STUDIES 1, no. 3 (1973): 279-87.

      Includes analysis of several short stories written
between 1840 and 1845 by mill women using pseudonyms.
Most of the short fiction is seen as presenting an
"idealized picture of factory life."

      Bagley
      Farley
      Larcom

5.   Agger, Lee. WOMEN OF MAINE. Portland, Me.: Guy
      Garnett Publishing Co., 1982. 237 pp.

      Survey by a journalist of accomplishments of
female authors from Maine. Includes portraits of all
the early writers.

      Clarke, Rebecca Sophia (P)
      [Fern] Parton (P)
      Prentiss (P)
      Smith, Elizabeth Oakes (P)
      Stowe (P)

Sweat (P)
Wood, Sally (P)

6.   Allen, Richard O. "If You Have Tears:
     Sentimentalism as Soft Romanticism." GENRE 8
     (June 1975): 119-45.

     Attempts to define "sentimentalism" as opposed to
"romanticism." "At the heart of the sentimental novel
is a disenchantment with middle-class life more drastic
than the disillusionment of the romantics." The sentimental novel is said to embody disillusionment with all
experience outside of home and "fear of daily life itself." Susan Warner's THE WIDE, WIDE WORLD is one of
the primary examples used.

     Rowson
     Warner, Susan
     [Wilson, Augusta Evans] Evans

7.   Allibone, S. Austin. A CRITICAL DICTIONARY OF
     ENGLISH LITERATURE AND BRITISH AND AMERICAN
     AUTHORS. 5 vols. Philadelphia: J.B. Lippincott
     Co., 1897. (First published 1858, 3 vols.; 2 sup-
     plements, 1891.)

     A dictionary of authors that is highly inclusive
but provides varying amounts of information, ranging
from a short list of the author's works with no biographical data to a substantial entry with excerpts from
reviews and biographies. Dates are frequently lacking
or, when given, prove inaccurate.

     Abbott
     Alcott
     Andrews
     Appleton, Anna E.
     Appleton, Elizabeth Haven
     Arey
     Austin
     Bache
     Bacon, Delia
     Bacon, Julia
     [Baker, Harriette Newell Woods] Leslie
     Baker, Sarah S.
     Barrow
     Beauchamp

Beecher
Bellamy
[Blake] Umsted
Bleecker
Bogart
Booth
[Botta] Lynch
Boyd
Bradley
Brewster
Bright
Brooks, Maria Gowen
Browne, Maria J.
Browne, Sara H.
Brownson
Bullard
Butt
Campbell, Jane C.
Campbell, Juliet H.
[Cary, Alice] Carey
[Cary, Phoebe] Carey
Cary, Virginia Randolph
Chaplin
Cheney
Chesebro'
Child
Church
Clack
[Clare] MacElhinney
Clarke, Mary Bayard
Clarke, Rebecca Sophia
Collins
Cook
[Cooke] Terry
Cooper, Susan Fenimore
[Crane] Seemuller
Cridge
Cruse
Coxe
[Cummins] Cummings
Cushing
[Cutler] Petit
Dall
Davis, Caroline E.
Davis, Minnie E.
Davis, Rebecca Harding
Denison
Diaz
Dinnies

Dodge, Mary Abigail
Dodge, Mary Mapes
Dorr
Dorsey, Anna Hanson
Dorsey, Sarah Anne
Doten
Downing
DuBose
Dumont
Duniway
Dunning
Dupuy
Eames
Eastman
Ellet
Embury
Farley
Farnham
Faugeres
[Fern] Parton
Finley
Fleming
Follen
Ford
Foster
Fowler
French
Gage
Gilman
[Goodwin, H.E.B.] Talcott
Goodwin, Lavinia S.
Graves, Adelia C.
Graves, Mrs. A.J.
Green
Greenough
Griffith, Mattie
Guernsey, Clara F.
Guernsey, Lucy Ellen
Gwyn
Hale, Lucretia P.
Hale, Sarah Josepha
Hall
Hanaford
Harlan
Harper
Harris
Haven
Hazlett
Hentz, Caroline Lee

Herndon
[Hildeburn] Reed
Holmes
Homes
Hooper
Hosmer
Hubbell, Martha
Janvrin
Jeffrey
Jerauld
[Jervey] Glover
Judson
Ketchum
King
Kinney
Kinzie
Kirkland
Larcom
Lasselle
[Latimer] Wormeley
Lawrence
Lee, Eliza Buckminster
Lee, Hannah Harnham
Lee, Mary Elizabeth
Leslie
Lewis
Lippincott
Little
Livermore, Mary A.
Locke
[Logan] Sikes
Longstreet
[McIntosh] MacIntosh
McKeever
[McLeod] Hulse
Manvill
Martin
Martyn
Mathews
Maxwell
Mayo
Moore, Clara Jessup
Moore, Mrs. H.J.
[Moragne] Morange
Morton
[Moulton] Chandler
[Mowatt] Ritchie
Murray
Myers

Nichols
O'Connor
Orne
Palfrey
Parker
Pearson
Peirson
Phelps, Almira H. Lincoln
Phelps, Elizabeth Stuart
Piatt
Pike
Pindar
Porter
Prentiss
Preston
Putnam
Read, Harriette Fanning
Remick
Rice
Roberts
Robinson
Rowson
Royall
Rush, Rebecca
Russell
[Sadlier] Madden
Savage
Sawyer
Schoolcraft
Sedgwick, Catharine M.
Sedgwick, E.
Sedgwick, Susan Ridley
Shindler
Sigourney
Smith, Elizabeth Oakes
Smith, Margaret Bayard
Snelling
Soule
Southworth, E.D.E.N.
Southworth, Mrs. S.A.
Spencer
[Spofford] Prescott
Stephens, Ann S.
Stephens, Harriet Marion
Stoddard
Stowe
Sweat
Tenney
Terhune

Thayer
Thomas
Thompson
Townsend, Mary Ashley
Townsend, Virginia Frances
Trowbridge
Turner
Tuthill, Cornelia
Tuthill, Louisa C.
Tyler
Vaughan
Victor, Frances Fuller
Victor, Metta Fuller
Warfield
Warner, Anna B.
Warner, Susan
[Warren] Thayer
Wells
Westmoreland
Whitcher
White
Whitney
Whittlesey
Williams, Catharine Read
Williams, Mary Bushnell
Wilson, Augusta Evans
Windle
Wood, Julia Amanda Sargent
Wood, Sally
Worthington
Yale

8. AMERICAN AUTHORS 1600-1900: A BIOGRAPHICAL
    DICTIONARY OF AMERICAN LITERATURE. Edited by
    Stanley J. Kunitz and Howard Haycraft. New York:
    H.W. Wilson Co., 1983. 846 pp.

    Includes numerous women. Consists of popularly
written biographical sketches, a page or less in
length, with brief bibliographies.

    Alcott (P)
    Austin (P)
    Bacon, Delia
    Bellamy
    Blake
    Bleecker
    Botta

Brooks, Maria Gowen (P)
Cary, Alice (P)
Cary, Phoebe (P)
[Chesebro'] Chesebrough
Child (P)
Clarke, Mary Bayard
Clarke, Rebecca Sophia
Cooke (P)
Cooper, Susan Fenimore
Crane
Cummins
Cutler
Davis, Rebecca Harding
Diaz
Dodge, Mary Abigail
Dodge, Mary Mapes (P)
Dorr
Dorsey, Anna Hanson
Dorsey, Sarah Anne
Duniway
Dupuy
Ellet
Embury
Farley (P)
Farnham
[Fern] Parton
Finley (P)
Follen
Foster
French
Gage
Green
Hale, Lucretia P.
Hale, Sarah Josepha (P)
Harris
Haven
Hentz, Caroline Lee
Holmes
Jeffrey
Judson
Kinney
Kirkland
Larcom (P)
Latimer
Lee, Eliza Buckminster
Lee, Hannah Farnham
Leslie
Lewis
Lippincott

Livermore, Mary A.
Logan
Martyn
Mayo
Moise
Morton (P)
Moulton
Mowatt (P)
Nichols
Parker
Phelps, Elizabeth Stuart
Pike
Preston
Rowson
Royall
Sedgwick, Catharine M. (P)
Sigourney (P)
Smith, Elizabeth Oakes
Southworth, E.D.E.N. (P)
Spofford (P)
Stoddard
Stowe (P)
Tenney
Terhune (P)
Townsend, Mary Ashley
Victor, Frances Fuller
Victor, Metta Fuller
Warner, Anna B.
Warner, Susan
[Warren] Thayer
Whitcher
Whitney
Williams, Catharine Read
[Wilson, Augusta Evans] Evans
Wood, Sally

9.   AMERICAN LITERATURE TO 1900. Introduction by Lewis
     Leary. Great Writers Students Library, no. 12.
     New York: St. Martin's Press, 1980. 331 pp.

     Follows the same format as NOVELISTS AND PROSE
WRITERS (#241). In fact, except for the entry on
Mowatt, which is newly added, the entries are
identical.

     Alcott
     Davis, Rebecca Harding
     Foster

Mowatt
Rowson
Sedgwick, Catharine M.
Stowe

10. AMERICAN NEWSPAPER JOURNALISTS, 1690-1872. Edited
    by Perry J. Ashley. Dictionary of Literary
    Biography, vol. 43. Detroit: Gale Research Co.,
    1985. 527 pp.

This contribution to the series of lavishly
illustrated biographical dictionaries includes some
female journalists who also wrote fiction. Their
fiction is discussed in as much detail as their newspaper work.

[Fern] Parton (P)
Lippincott (P)
Royall

11. AMERICAN NOVEL: BROWN TO JAMES. Edited by
    Frank N. Magill. Pasadena, Calif.: Salem
    Softbacks, 1980. 577 pp.

Masterplot format with a brief biographical sketch
of the novelist, plot summary, conventional critical
evaluation, and short bibliography.

Alcott
Rowson
Stowe

12. THE AMERICAN RENAISSANCE IN NEW ENGLAND. Edited
    by Joel Myerson. Dictionary of Literary
    Biography, vol. 1. Detroit: Gale Research Co.,
    1978. 224 pp.

Contains biographical/critical articles on
writers who lived in New England between 1830 and
1860. Sets the standard for both the strengths
(articles by scholars, attractive format) and
weaknesses (principles of selection--why are Orestes
Augustus Brownson and Theodore Parker "major" and
Louisa May Alcott, Lydia Maria Child, and Harriet
Beecher Stowe "minor"?) of the Dictionary of Literary
Biography series.

Alcott (P)
Bacon, Delia (P)
Child (P)
Dall (P)
Follen
Hale, Sarah Josepha (P)
Nichols
Sedgwick, Catharine M. (P)
Sigourney (P)
Smith, Elizabeth Oakes (P)
Stowe (P)

13. AMERICAN WOMEN WRITERS: A CRITICAL REFERENCE GUIDE
    FROM COLONIAL TIMES TO THE PRESENT. Edited by
    Lina Mainiero. 4 vols. New York: Frederick Ungar
    Publishing Co., 1979-82.

The most important source of information on early
nineteenth-century writers. Each entry provides
biography and criticism, a checklist of the author's
works, and a selected bibliography of secondary sources. As is the case with most pioneering multiple-
authored works, there are numerous errors and the
quality of the entries varies, ranging from poor to
excellent. There are some glaring omissions (e.g.
Susanna Rowson), but, in general, its inclusiveness
makes this guide invaluable.

Alcott
Andrews
Austin
Bacon, Delia
Bagley
Blake
Bleecker
Botta
Briggs
Brooks, Maria Gowen
Brownson
Campbell, Jane C.
Campbell, Juliet H.
Cary, Alice
Cary, Phoebe
Chaplin
[Chesebro'] Chesebrough
Child
Church
Clarke, Rebecca Sophia

Cooke
Cooper, Susan Fenimore
[Crosby] Van Alstyne
Cross
Cummins
Dall
Davis, Rebecca Harding
Denison
Diaz
Dinnies
Dodge, Mary Abigail
Dodge, Mary Mapes
Dorr
Dorsey, Anna Hanson
Dorsey, Sarah Anne
Duniway
Dupuy
Eastman
Ellet
Embury
Evans
Farley
Farnham
Faugeres
[Fern] Parton
Finley
Flanders
Follen
Ford
Foster
French
Gage
Gilman
Griffith, Mary
[Griffith, Mattie] Browne
Guernsey, Clara F.
Guernsey, Lucy Ellen
Hale, Lucretia P.
Hale, Sarah Josepha
Hall
Hanaford
Harper
Harris
Haven
Hazlett
Hentz, Caroline Lee
Holmes
Hooper
Jerauld

Jervey
Judson
[King] Bowen
Kinney
Kinzie
Kirkland
Larcom
Latimer
Lawrence
Lee, Eliza Buckminster
Lee, Hannah Farnham
Lee, Mary Elizabeth
Leslie
Lewis
Lippincott
Little
Livermore, Mary A.
Locke
Logan
Loughborough
McIntosh
Martyn
Mayo
Milward
Mitchell
Moise
[Moore, Clara Jessup] Bloomfield-Moore
Moore, Mrs. H.J.
Morton
Moulton
[Mowatt] Ritchie
Murray
O'Connor
Phelps, Almira H. Lincoln
Phelps, Elizabeth Stuart
Pike
Prentiss
Preston
Putnam
Read, Harriette Fanning
Read, Martha
Remick
Royall
Rush, Caroline E.
Rush, Rebecca
Schoolcraft
Sedgwick, Catharine M.
Sedgwick, Susan Ridley
Shindler

Sigourney
Smith, Elizabeth Oakes
Smith, Margaret Bayard
Smith, Sarah Pogson
Soule
Southworth, E.D.E.N.
Spofford
Stephens, Ann S.
Stoddard
Stowe
Tenney
[Terhune] Harland
Thompson
Townsend, Mary Ashley
Tuthill, Louisa C.
Tyler
[Vickery] Watson
Victor, Frances Fuller
Victor, Metta Fuller
Warfield
Warner, Anna B.
Warner, Susan
[Warren] Thayer
Whitcher
White
Whitney
Williams, Catharine Read
Windle
Wood, Sally

14. AMERICAN WOMEN WRITERS: A CRITICAL REFERENCE GUIDE
FROM COLONIAL TIMES TO THE PRESENT. Edited by
Langdon Lynne Faust. 2 vols. Abridged ed. New
York: Frederick Ungar Publishing Co., 1983.

Much less useful than the full edition. The
abridged edition is said to contain 400 of the "more
important writers" of the original 1,000, but no
principles of selection are given. The selection for
the nineteenth century is odd (for instance, Margaretta
Bleecker Faugeres is included and her pioneering
mother, Ann Eliza Bleecker, left out).

Alcott
Andrews
Blake
Brooks, Maria Gowen
Cary, Alice

Child
Cooke
[Crosby] Van Alstyne
Cummins
Dall
Davis, Rebecca Harding
Diaz
Dodge, Mary Abigail
Dodge, Mary Mapes
Dorr
Duniway
Farley
Farnham
Faugeres
[Fern] Parton
Finley
Follen
Foster
Gage
Gilman
Hale, Lucretia P.
Hale, Sarah Josepha
Harper
Harris
Hentz, Caroline Lee
Jerauld
Judson
Kirkland
Larcom
Latimer
Lewis
Lippincott
Locke
Logan
Morton
Moulton
[Mowatt] Ritchie
Phelps, Almira H. Lincoln
Phelps, Elizabeth Stuart
Putnam
Royall
Sedgwick, Catharine M.
Sigourney
Smith, Elizabeth Oakes
Smith, Margaret Bayard
Southworth, E.D.E.N.
Spofford
Stowe
Tenney

        Terhune
        Victor, Frances Fuller
        Victor, Metta Fuller
        Warner, Susan
        Whitcher
        White
        Williams, Catharine Read
        Wood, Sally

15. AMERICAN WRITERS BEFORE 1800: A BIOGRAPHICAL AND
    CRITICAL DICTIONARY. Edited by James A. Levernier
    and Douglas R. Wilmes. 3 vols. Westport, Conn.:
    Greenwood Press, 1983.

        Includes fewer women than Todd's similar
dictionary (#89) but more information in each entry.
The entries, written by scholars, consist of a list of
the author's works, biographical sketch, critical
appraisal, and secondary bibliography.

        Bleecker
        Faugeres
        Foster
        Morton
        Murray
        Rowson
        Wells

16. AMERICAN WRITERS FOR CHILDREN BEFORE 1900. Edited
    by Glenn E. Estes. Dictionary of Literary
    Biography, vol. 42. 441 pp.

        Essays focus on the author's work more than her
life. Length ranges from five to fifteen pages for the
more important writers for children, such as Louisa May
Alcott and Mary Mapes Dodge. Although several of the
authors are also represented in Volume 1 of the
Dictionary of Literary Biography series, the entries
here are new and by different scholars.

        Alcott (P)
        Clarke, Rebecca Sophia
        Cummins
        Dodge, Mary Mapes (P)
        Finley (P)
        Hale, Lucretia P. (P)
        Hale, Sarah Josepha (P)

Sigourney (P)
Stowe (P)
Warner, Susan (P)
Wilson, Augusta Evans (P)

17. AMERICAN WRITERS OF THE EARLY REPUBLIC. Edited by
     Emory Elliott. Dictionary of Literary Biography,
     vol. 37. Detroit: Gale Research Co., 1985.
     374 pp.

     Contains three-to-four-page entries, written by
scholars, on several women who were pioneers in fiction
writing. Essays emphasize works as well as life.

     Foster
     Morton (P)
     Murray
     Rowson (P)
     Tenney

18. Anderson, Della. 101 VIRGINIA WOMEN WRITERS: A
     SELECT BIBLIOGRAPHY. Richmond, Va.: Virginia
     Women's Cultural History Project, 1984. 151 pp.

     Actually a well-done bio-bibliography with
information on the authors' lives and relatively
complete lists of their works.

     Cary, Virginia Randolph
     Eastman
     French
     Preston
     Rives
     Southworth, E.D.E.N.
     [Terhune] Harland

19. ANTEBELLUM WRITERS IN NEW YORK AND THE SOUTH.
     Edited by Joel Myerson. Dictionary of Literary
     Biography, vol. 3. Detroit: Gale Research Co.,
     1979. 383 pp.

     Biographical dictionary which is well written and
illustrated but outdated in its (unstated) principles
of selection. One wonders why of sixty-seven authors,
only seven are female, why none of these women are
"major figures" with more space allotted them (Caroline

Kirkland and Susan Warner are not as "major" as Evert
Duyckinck and Henry William Herbert?), and why such
writers as Ann Eliza Bleecker, Elizabeth Drew Stoddard,
and Augusta Evans Wilson are omitted.

    Botta
    Gilman
    Hentz, Caroline Lee
    Kirkland
    [Mowatt] Ritchie
    Stephens, Ann S.
    Warner, Susan

20. Arbuthnot, May Hill. CHILDREN AND BOOKS.
     Chicago: Scott, Foresman and Co., 1947. 626 pp.

     History of literature for children. Includes one-
to-two-page descriptions of important works by
nineteenth-century American women.

    Alcott
    Dodge, Mary Mapes
    Finley
    Hale, Lucretia P.

21. Arrington, Leonard J., and Jon Haupt.
     "Intolerable Zion: The Image of Mormonism in
     Nineteenth Century American Literature."
     WESTERN HUMANITIES REVIEW 22, no. 3 (1968):
     243-60.

     Summary of the four earliest anti-Mormon novels,
which were published in 1855 or 1856 and written by
women. This "abominable" fiction is said to be
animated by "frustrated Victorian" women's resentment
of men.

    Belisle
    Bell
    Victor, Metta Fuller

22. Barnett, Louise K. THE IGNOBLE SAVAGE: AMERICAN
     LITERARY RACISM, 1790-1890. Westport, Conn.:
     Greenwood Press, 1975. 220 pp.

     Analysis of the "frontier romance," a body of

fiction "containing Indian characters and written
between 1790 and 1860." Emphasizes the white racist
philosophy characteristic of the genre. Several novels
by female authors are discussed, although women's work
in the genre is not distinguished, as it easily could
be, from men's.

        Bleecker
        Cheney
        Child
        Cushing
        Rowson
        Sedgwick, Catharine M.
        Snelling

23.   Barrows, Charles M. ACTS AND ANECDOTES OF AUTHORS.
      Boston: New England Publishing Co., 1887. 481 pp.

        Dictionary-style handbook with alphabetically
arranged entries on American and British authors,
titles, and publishers. Entries range in length from
one to two sentences to five to six pages. A large
number of women are mentioned very briefly; those
listed below receive more substantial treatment.

        Alcott
        Austin
        Bacon, Delia
        Brooks
        Cary, Alice
        Cary, Phoebe
        Child
        Dodge, Mary Abigail
        [Fern] Parton
        Haven
        Larcom
        Lippincott
        Stowe
        Terhune
        Warner, Susan
        Whitcher

24.   Baym, Nina. "Melodramas of Beset Manhood: How
      Theories of American Fiction Exclude Women
      Authors." AMERICAN QUARTERLY 33 (Summer 1981):
      123-39. Reprinted in THE NEW FEMINIST CRITICISM:
      ESSAYS ON WOMAN, LITERATURE, AND THEORY, edited by

Elaine Showalter, 63-80. New York: Pantheon
Books, 1985.

Excellent consideration of why works by women have
been omitted from the American literary canon; explains
clearly the virtual deification of nineteenth-century
male novelists and total exclusion of their female
contemporaries. Argues that male critics have
established "Americanness" as the criterion for
canonization and defined it as rebellion against an
entrammeling society, which women are made to
represent.

25. _____. NOVELS, READERS, AND REVIEWERS:
RESPONSES TO FICTION IN ANTEBELLUM AMERICA.
Ithaca: Cornell University Press, 1984.   287 pp.

Study of antebellum attitudes toward fiction,
based on reviews that appeared in major American
periodicals between 1840 and 1860. Contains much of
interest regarding women's fiction and includes many
quotations from reviews of novels by women (only
authors whose works are referred to several times are
listed below).

> [Cary, Alice] Carey
> [Chesebro'] Chesebrough
> Child
> Cummins
> [Haven] Neal
> Hentz, Caroline Lee
> Holmes
> Kirkland
> McIntosh
> Phelps, Elizabeth Stuart
> Sedgwick, Catharine M.
> Southworth, E.D.E.N.
> Stephens, Ann S.
> Stowe
> [Terhune] Harland
> Warner, Anna B.
> Warner, Susan

26. _____. "Portrayal of Women in American
Literature, 1790-1870." In WHAT MANNER OF WOMAN:
ESSAYS ON ENGLISH AND AMERICAN LIFE AND
LITERATURE, edited by Marlene Springer, 211-34.

New York: New York University Press, 1977.

There are separate discussions of the portrayal of women by "major" (primarily male) authors and by popular (female) authors. The three main female types in popular fiction are identified as the diabolic, angelic, and human, the human heroine being the orphan in search of autonomy described more fully in Baym's book, WOMAN'S FICTION (#28).

Alcott
[Wilson, Augusta Evans] Evans

27. _____. "Rewriting the Scribbling Women."
     LEGACY 2 (Fall 1985): 3-12.

Discusses the major project of LEGACY readers, "rewriting the scribbling women" or bringing to light and interpreting the work of nineteenth-century American women writers. Defines five critical approaches along a feminist continuum and warns against the tendency toward biological essentialism in recent studies of nineteenth-century women's writings, noting that "the certainty that women's writing is common to women and 'different' from men's writing produced at the same time may operate in part to construct the very difference that it claims to discover."

28. _____. WOMAN'S FICTION: A GUIDE TO
     NOVELS BY AND ABOUT WOMEN IN AMERICA, 1820-1870.
     Ithaca: Cornell University Press, 1978. 320 pp.

This book provided the first sustained analysis of early American women's fiction, focussing on the novels themselves rather than the authors' careers. Attention is limited to one type of fiction, the "trials and triumph" story of a girl who is deprived of the supports she had relied upon and "faced with the necessity of winning her own way in the world." Emphasizes plot summary and discussion of the works of Catharine M. Sedgwick, Maria McIntosh, E.D.E.N. Southworth, Caroline Lee Hentz, Susan Warner, Anna B. Warner, Maria Cummins, Ann S. Stephens, Mary Jane Holmes, Marion Harland, Caroline Chesebro', and Augusta Evans Wilson.

Alcott

Baker, Harriette Newell Woods
Briggs
Cary, Alice
Chesebro'
Child
Cooper, Susan Fenimore
Cummins
Denison
Dorr
Dupuy
Embury
Fern
Finley
Follen
Foster
Gilman
Graves, Mrs. A.J.
Hale, Sarah Josepha
Harris
[Haven] Neal
Hayden, Caroline A.
Hayden, Sarah Marshall
Hentz, Caroline Lee
Holmes
Hornblower
Lee, Hannah Farnham
Leslie
McIntosh
Moore, Mrs. H.J.
Moulton
Mowatt
Nichols
Phelps, Almira H. Lincoln
Phelps, Elizabeth Stuart
Pike
Preston
Robinson
Rose
Rowson
Sedgwick, Catharine M.
Smith, Elizabeth Oakes
Smith, Margaret Bayard
Southworth, E.D.E.N.
Stephens, Ann S.
Stephens, Harriet Marion
Stowe
[Terhune] Harland
Townsend, Virginia Frances
Tuthill, Louisa C.

Victor, Metta Fuller
Warner, Anna B.
Warner, Susan
[Wilson, Augusta Evans] Evans

29. Beach, Seth Curtis. DAUGHTERS OF THE PURITANS.
     Boston: American Unitarian Association, 1905.
     286 pp.

     Consists of biographical essays of about forty
pages each on major figures in early nineteenth-century
New England.

     Alcott (P)
     Child (P)
     Sedgwick, Catharine M. (P)
     Stowe (P)

30. Bell, Michael Davitt. HAWTHORNE AND THE
     HISTORICAL ROMANCE OF NEW ENGLAND. Princeton:
     Princeton University Press, 1971. 253 pp.

     Contains extensive discussion not only of
Hawthorne's views toward Puritans but of romances
written by other authors between 1820 and 1850 and
based on the history of seventeenth-century New
England. Some of the authors are female, and novels by
Catharine M. Sedgwick and Eliza Buckminster Lee are
treated in detail.

     Bacon, Delia
     Cheney
     Child
     Lee, Eliza Buckminster
     Sedgwick, Catharine M.

31. Benet, William Rose, ed. THE READER'S
     ENCYCLOPEDIA. 2nd ed. New York: Thomas Y.
     Crowell Co., 1965 (1st ed. 1948). 1118 pp.

     Comprehensive work containing paragraph-length
entries on writers of all types, countries, and eras.
Includes a surprising number of nineteenth-century
women, although the criteria for inclusion are unclear
(e.g. Maria Cummins is included but not Susan Warner).

        Alcott
        Cummins
        Davis, Rebecca Harding
        Dodge, Mary Mapes
        Foster
        Hale, Sarah Josepha
        Kirkland
        Morton
        Rowson
        Sedgwick, Catharine M.
        Southworth, E.D.E.N.
        Stowe

32. Benson, Mary Sumner. "Women in Early American
     Literature." Chap. 7 in WOMEN IN EIGHTEENTH-
     CENTURY AMERICA: A STUDY OF OPINION AND SOCIAL
     USAGE. New York: Columbia University Press, 1935.

     Provides information on conditions for women
writers in the eighteenth century and discusses some
early novels and contributions to women's periodicals.

        Bleecker
        Foster
        Murray
        Rowson
        Wood, Sally

33. Berzon, Judith R. NEITHER WHITE NOR BLACK: THE
     MULATTO CHARACTER IN AMERICAN FICTION. New York:
     New York University Press, 1978. 280 pp.

     Includes discussion of mulatto characters in
fiction by three nineteenth-century women.

        Davis, Rebecca Harding
        Harper
        Stowe

34. A BIBLIOGRAPHICAL GUIDE TO MIDWESTERN LITERATURE.
     Edited by Gerald Nemanic. Iowa City: University
     of Iowa Press, 1981. 380 pp.

     Contains author bibliographies that include short
summaries of authors' work and critical reputation, in
addition to lists of primary and secondary works.

Cary, Alice
Cary, Phoebe
Kirkland

35. THE BIBLIOPHILE DICTIONARY: A BIOGRAPHICAL RECORD
OF THE GREAT AUTHORS, WITH BIBLIOGRAPHICAL NOTICES
OF THEIR PRINCIPAL WORKS FROM THE BEGINNING OF
HISTORY. Detroit: Gale Research Co., 1966.
Unpaged. Originally published as vols. 29 and 30
of THE BIBLLIOPHILE LIBRARY OF LITERATURE, ART AND
RARE MANUSCRIPTS, ed. Nathan Haskell Dole, Forrest
Morgan, and Caroline Ticknor. New York: Inter-
national Bibliophile Society, 1904.

Contains, according to its preface, "a brief
biographical notice of every important author known in
literary history." The notices are not always accurate
but have the distinction of including pronunciation of
the author's name. Also included are paragraph-length
descriptions of some authors' major works. A
"masterpiece" is marked by an asterisk; the only early
nineteenth-century female author to be so honored is
A.D.T. Whitney.

Alcott
Austin
Baker, Harriette Newell Woods
Blake
Botta
Cary, Alice
Cary, Phoebe
Child
Church
Cooke
Cummins
Davis, Rebecca Harding
Diaz
Dodge, Mary Abigail
Dodge, Mary Elizabeth Mapes
Dorr
Ellet
Embury
Farley
Farnham
Fern
Hale, Sarah Josepha
Hanaford
Judson

Kirkland
Lee, Eliza Buckminster
Lippincott
Livermore, Mary A.
Moulton
[Mowatt] Ritchie
Preston
Putnam
Rowson
Sedgwick, Catharine M.
Southworth, E.D.E.N.
Spofford
Stoddard
Stowe
Terhune
Townsend, Mary Ashley
Townsend, Virginia Frances
Warner, Susan
Whitney
[Wilson, Augusta Evans] Evans
Yale

36. Blake, Fay M. THE STRIKE IN THE AMERICAN NOVEL.
     Metuchen, N.J.: Scarecrow Press, 1972. 292 pp.

     Traces chronologically American novelists'
treatment of the strike; the first chapter considers
fiction published before 1870. Several novels by women
are discussed, and plot summaries may be found in the
annotated bibliography, which is chronologically
arranged.

     Davis, Rebecca Harding
     [Goodwin, H.B.] Talcott
     Smith, Elizabeth Oakes
     Tyler

37. Bode, Carl. "The Scribbling Women: The Domestic
     Novel Rules the 'Fifties." Chap. 12 in THE
     ANATOMY OF AMERICAN POPULAR CULTURE, 1840-1861.
     Berkeley, Calif.: University of California Press,
     1959.

     Likens the fiction of the 1850's to the "soap
operas" of today and analyzes several of the most
popular novels by women in attempt to show that they
all contain five of the main Jungian archetypes: the

anima, the animus, the earth mother, the old wise man,
and the self as child.

> Cummins
> Fern
> Hentz, Caroline Lee
> Holmes
> Southworth, E.D.E.N.
> Stowe
> Warner, Susan

38. Bolger, Stephen Garrett. THE IRISH CHARACTER IN
     AMERICAN FICTION, 1830-1860. New York: Arno
     Press, 1976. 207 pp.

Finds no consistent image of the Irish in 277
novels of the period, although Irish characters always
play a minor role in the fiction in which they appear.
Does not consider gender, but many of the authors whose
works are briefly described are female.

> Botsford
> Child
> Church
> Curtis
> Dupuy
> Eastman
> [Fern] Parton
> Griffith, Mary
> Hale, Sarah Josepha
> Hall
> Hentz, Caroline Lee
> Jerauld
> Leslie
> Lippincott
> Mathews
> Otis
> Pearson
> Phelps, Elizabeth Stuart
> Russell
> Sedgwick, Catharine M.
> Southworth, E.D.E.N.
> Stephens, Ann S.
> Stowe
> Terhune
> Tuthill, Louisa C.
> Warner, Susan

39. Bolton, Sarah K. LIVES OF GIRLS WHO BECAME
FAMOUS. New York: Thomas Y. Crowell and Co.,
1886. 347 pp.

Contains biographical sketches about twenty pages
in length. An expanded edition, published in 1925,
does not include any additional nineteenth-century
authors.

Alcott (P)
Livermore, Mary A. (P)
Stowe (P)

40. Booth, Bradford A. "Taste in the Annuals."
AMERICAN LITERATURE 14 (Nov. 1942): 299-303.

Provides a list of American writers whose names
appear twenty-four or more times as contributors to
mid-century annuals and gift books. Of the ten names
occurring most frequently, eight are female. The
compiler thinks British writer Felicia Hemans "was
responsible for the spate of scribbling women. Her
influence was probably the most devitalizing in
American literature."

Botta
Child
Doten
Ellet
Embury
Hale, Sarah Josepha
Lee, Mary Elizabeth
Leslie
Livermore, Mary A.
Mayo
Sawyer
Sedgwick, Catharine M.
Sigourney
Smith, Elizabeth Oakes

41. Branch, E. Douglas. THE SENTIMENTAL YEARS, 1836-
1860. New York: D. Appleton-Century Co., 1934.
432 pp.

Social history of the era with some attention to
literature and women writers, particularly in Chapters
4 and 5. Individual authors are not discussed in

depth, but background is provided on such topics as gift books, children's literature, and literary salons.

Child
Fern
Hale, Sarah Josepha
McIntosh
Mowatt
Sigourney
Smith, Elizabeth Oakes
Stephens, Ann S.
Stowe
Warner, Susan

42. Broderick, Dorothy M. IMAGE OF THE BLACK IN
     CHILDREN'S FICTION. New York: R.R. Bowker Co.,
     1973. 219 pp.

     Works by several early nineteenth-century white
women are briefly discussed in this analysis of the
images of black people presented in children's books
published in the U.S. between 1827 and 1967. The fact
that black authors are not included in this study
reveals a problem in selection criteria.

Alcott
Andrews
Clarke, Rebecca Sophia
Finley
Warner, Susan

43. Brooks, Van Wyck. THE FLOWERING OF NEW ENGLAND,
     1815-1865. New and revised edition. New York:
     E.P. Dutton & Co., 1940. 550 pp.

     Only Harriet Beecher Stowe is considered at length
in this literary history that focuses on "the New
England Mind"; however, other female authors are
discussed briefly in passing.

Bacon, Delia
Child
Cummins
Sedgwick, Catharine M.
Stowe
Warner, Susan

44. Brown, Herbert Ross. THE SENTIMENTAL NOVEL IN
AMERICA, 1789-1860. Durham, N.C.: Duke
University Press, 1940. 407 pp.

Much of the book concerns female novelists and the
chapters "Sex and Sensibility" and "Home Sweet Home"
are exclusively about women. Contains detailed
descriptions of novels; emphasizes their "limited
scope" and "intense concern with marriage."

Bleecker
Botsford
Bradley
Buckley
Chesebro'
Child
Cooper, Susan Fenimore
Cummins
Eastman
Evans
Faugeres
[Fern] Parton
Flanders
Foster
Gilman
Griffith, Mary
[Griffith, Mattie] Griffiths
Hale, Sarah Josepha
Haven
Hentz, Caroline Lee
Holmes
Kirkland
Lee, Hannah Farnham
Leslie
McIntosh
Mayfield
Morton
Mowatt
Pearson
Read, Martha
Rowson
Rush, Caroline E.
Rush, Rebecca
Schoolcraft
Sedgwick, Catharine M.
Sigourney
Smith, Elizabeth Oakes
Southworth, E.D.E.N.
Southworth, Mrs. S.A.

Stephens, Ann S.
Stowe
Tenney
Thayer
[Victor, Metta Fuller] Fuller
Warner, Susan
Warren
Wells
Weston
[Wilson, Augusta Evans] Evans
Wood, Sally

45. Brown, Ruth Elizabeth. "A French Interpreter of
New England's Literature, 1846-1865." NEW ENGLAND
QUARTERLY 13 (June 1940): 305-21.

Discussion of the views of French critic Emile
Montegut, including his comments on female authors,
whom he saw as realists writing the "novel of custom."

Cummins
[Fern] Parton
Stowe

46. Brown, Sterling. THE NEGRO IN AMERICAN FICTION.
Washington, D.C.: Associates in Negro Folk
Education, 1937. Reprint. New York: Arno Press,
1969. 209 pp.

Several novels by white female authors are
discussed, both in Chapter 2, "The Plantation
Tradition: Proslavery Fiction," and Chapter 3,
"Antislavery Fiction."

Davis, Rebecca Harding
Eastman
Harper
Hentz, Caroline Lee
McIntosh
[Pearson] Pierson
Rush, Caroline E.
Schoolcraft
Stowe
Victor, Metta Fuller

47. Bryan, William Alfred. GEORGE WASHINGTON IN

AMERICAN LITERATURE, 1775-1865. New York:
Columbia University Press, 1952. 280 pp.

Chapter 7, "Fiction," includes discussion of
novels by female authors in which Washington is
portrayed.

Kilbourn
[Collins] Lorraine
Sedgwick, Catharine M.

48. Butler, Joyce. "Maine Women Writers Collection."
MAINE LIFE (October 1980): 19-24.

Discussion of Maine authors represented in the
Maine Women Writers Collection at Westbrook College in
Portland.

Bullard
Clarke, Rebecca Sophia
[Fern] Parton
Prentiss
Smith, Elizabeth Oakes (P)
Stephens, Ann S. (P)
Sweat (P)
Wood, Sally

49. Cadogan, Mary, and Patricia Craig. "Pilgrims and
Pioneers." Chap. 2 in YOU'RE A BRICK, ANGELA! A
NEW LOOK AT GIRLS' FICTION FROM 1839 TO 1975.
London: Victor Gollancz, 1976.

Chapter on early American authors of girls'
fiction who influenced British writers (the focus of
the book). Emphasis is on the conservatism and racism
of the nineteenth-century American fiction.

Alcott
Dodge, Mary Mapes
Finley
Stowe

50. Cairns, William B. A HISTORY OF AMERICAN
LITERATURE. New York: Oxford University Press,
1912. 502 pp.

Contains brief references to various women as

"minor authors."

    Alcott
    Cary, Alice
    Child
    Cooke
    Dodge, Mary Mapes
    Foster
    Hale, Sarah Josepha
    Kirkland
    Larcom
    Leslie
    Preston
    Rowson
    Sedgwick, Catharine M.
    Sigourney
    Stowe
    Townsend, Mary Ashley
    Whitcher

51. THE CAMBRIDGE HISTORY OF AMERICAN LITERATURE.
Edited by William Peterfield Trent, John Erskine,
Stuart P. Sherman, and Carl Van Doren. 3 vols.
New York: Macmillan Co., 1972 (1st ed, 1917-21).

Standard literary history consisting of chapters
by scholars on various genres, chronologically
arranged. One of the least useful histories for study
of nineteenth-century female writers. Except for Rose
Terry Cooke and Harriet Beecher Stowe, no woman is
accorded more than a brief mention. Women are lumped
together for discussion in Chapter 7 of Volume 2,
"Books for Children," whether or not they wrote
primarily for children; UNCLE TOM'S CABIN is called a
"juvenile."

    Cooke
    Stowe

52. THE CAROLYN SHERWIN BAILEY HISTORICAL COLLECTION
OF CHILDREN'S BOOKS: A CATALOGUE. Edited by
Dorothy R. Davis. Hamden, Conn.: Southern
Connecticut State College, 1967. 232 pp.

Description of English and American children's
books, 1657-1930, in the Bailey Collection at Southern
Connecticut State College. Catalogue is arranged

alphabetically by author and provides short but informative biographies of numerous authors (only those women for whom biographical information is given are listed below). There is no index.

Alcott
Austin
Baker, Harriette Newell Woods
Baker, Sarah S.
Barrow
Cary, Alice
Child
Clarke, Rebecca Sophia
Diaz
Dodge, Mary Mapes
Farley
Finley
Hale, Lucretia P.
Lippincott
Moulton
Sigourney
Stowe
Warner, Anna B.
Warner, Susan

53. Carpenter, Humphrey, and Mari Prichard. THE OXFORD COMPANION TO CHILDREN'S LITERATURE. New York: Oxford University Press, 1984. 587 pp.

Dictionary-style guide that emphasizes England but includes many nineteenth-century American women. It is necessary to look under the title of a novel, as well as the author's name, and to consult various non-obvious topical headings, such as "Evangelical Writings," "Girls' Stories," and "United States."

Alcott
Andrews
Child
[Clarke, Rebecca Sophia] May
Cummins
Diaz
Dodge, Mary Mapes
Finley
Follen
Hale, Lucretia P.
Hale, Sarah Josepha
Prentiss

Stowe
Warner, Susan
Whitney

54. Carrier, Esther Jane. FICTION IN PUBLIC
     LIBRARIES, 1876-1900. New York: Scarecrow Press,
     1965. 458 pp.

     Detailed treatment of controversies over the value
of fiction in public libraries, with extensive
quotations from library leaders on different sides of
the question. Most of the librarians simply mention
authors and titles with no description, but Chapter 4,
"Controversial Literature and Authors," includes
quotations from reviews of the works of several
authors, including Martha Finley, Mary Jane Holmes,
E.D.E.N. Southworth, and Augusta Evans Wilson. These
and other early nineteenth-century women appear on the
lists included of authors whose works were excluded
from many public libraries.

     Alcott
     Finley
     Hentz, Caroline Lee
     Holmes
     [Judson] Forrester
     Southworth, E.D.E.N.
     Stephens, Ann S.
     Wilson, Augusta Evans

55. CASSELL'S ENCYCLOPAEDIA OF WORLD LITERATURE.
     Edited by S.H. Steinberg in 2 vols. (1953).
     Revised and enlarged in 3 vols. by J. Buchanan-
     Brown. New York: William Morrow and Co., 1973.

     The first volume consists of essays on literary
topics, such as "German Literature" or "Novel," while
the second and third volumes contain very short
biographies of authors, including a few early
nineteenth-century American women.

     Alcott
     Child
     Mowatt
     [Robinson] Talvj
     Sigourney
     Stowe

56. Cawelti, John G. ADVENTURE, MYSTERY, AND ROMANCE:
     FORMULA STORIES AS ART AND POPULAR CULTURE.
     Chicago: University of Chicago Press, 1976.
     336 pp.

     In a discussion in Chapter 2 of the typology of
melodrama and in Chapter 9, "The Best-Selling Social
Melodrama," works by E.D.E.N. Southworth, Harriet
Beecher Stowe, and Augusta Evans Wilson are briefly
discussed.

          Southworth, E.D.E.N.
          Stowe
          [Wilson, Augusta Evans] Evans

57. CHAMBERS'S CYCLOPAEDIA OF ENGLISH LITERATURE.
     Edited by David Patrick and J. Liddell Geddie.
     Vol. 3. Philadelphia: J.B. Lippincott Co., 1904.
     858 pp.

     The last 100 pages of this voluminous literary
encyclopedia are devoted to nineteenth-century American
authors. A few women receive paragraph-length entries.

          Alcott
          Cary, Alice
          Cary, Phoebe
          Child
          Cummins
          Sigourney
          Stowe
          Warner, Susan

58. Chambers-Schiller, Lee Virginia. LIBERTY, A
     BETTER HUSBAND: SINGLE WOMEN IN AMERICA: THE
     GENERATION OF 1780-1840. New Haven: Yale
     University Press, 1984. 285 pp.

     A number of writers are represented in the sample
used in this study of northeastern spinsters who sought
personal autonomy through single status. There is
extensive consideration of the attitudes toward
marriage and toward authorship of Louisa May Alcott,
Alice Cary, Mary Abigail Dodge, Lucy Larcom, and
Catharine M. Sedgwick. Chapters 1-3 include discussion
of fiction (and poetry) about the single state.

Alcott
Cary, Alice
Cary, Phoebe
Dodge, Mary Abigail
Hanaford
Harper
[Haven] Neal
Hentz, Caroline Lee
Larcom
Mayo
Sedgwick, Catharine M.
Stowe
Tuthill, Louisa C.

59. THE CHARLESTON BOOK: A MISCELLANY IN PROSE AND
    VERSE. Edited by William Gilmore Simms, with a
    new introduction and notes by David Moltke-Hansen.
    Spartanburg, S.C.: Reprint Co., 1983 (1st ed.
    1845). 455 pp.

    Reprint of the 1845 edition; contains page-length
biographical sketches of the authors included in the
original anthology.

    Dinnies
    Gilman
    Lee, Mary Elizabeth
    Moise
    [Shindler] Dana

60. Cheesborough, E.B. "The Female Writers of the
    South." THE LAND WE LOVE 2 (March 1867): 331-2.

    Brief laudatory notice of Southern women writers,
claiming that Southern women excel as authors and
should receive more attention.

    King
    Terhune
    Warfield
    [Wilson, Augusta Evans] Evans

61. Clark, Edward. BLACK WRITERS IN NEW ENGLAND.
    Boston: National Park Service, 1985. 76 pp.

    Bibliography, with substantial biographical notes,

of books by and about African-American writers
associated with New England. Bibliography is based on
the Collection of Afro-American Literature developed by
Suffolk University, Museum of Afro-American History,
and Boston African American National Historic Site.

[Griffith Mattie] Browne
Harper
Jacobs
Wilson, Harriet E.

62. Cleveland, Charles D. A COMPENDIUM OF AMERICAN
    LITERATURE. Philadelphia: E.C. & J. Biddle,
    1858. 740 pp.

    Early anthology of American literature. Includes
biographical sketches of the authors, ranging from a
paragraph to two pages in length, and selections
ranging from two to five pages. Preface defines
American literature and argues that it originated with
the Revolution. About twenty percent of the authors
included are female.

Child
Dinnies
Embury
Hale, Sarah Joseph
Kirkland
Lippincott
Sedgwick, Catharine M.
[Shindler] Dana
Sigourney
Smith, Elizabeth Oakes
Stowe

63. Cogan, Frances B. "Weak Fathers and Other Beasts:
    An Examination of the American Male in Domestic
    Novels, 1850-1870." AMERICAN STUDIES 25 (Fall
    1984): 5-20.

    Contends that the domestic novelists presented
male characters as weak and incompetent. The purpose
of the protrayal was to provide a rationale for
allowing the heroines to be strong, capable, and self-
sufficient while still "feminine."

Hentz, Caroline Lee

Holmes
[Wilson, Augusta Evans] Evans

64.   Cohn, Jan. "The Civil War in Magazine Fiction of
       the 1860's." JOURNAL OF POPULAR CULTURE 4 (Fall
       1970): 355-82.

       Thorough study that includes summaries of many
short stories by women. Author's thesis that the Civil
War story became less sentimental and more realistic as
the decade advanced is weakened by conventional
assumptions about men's and women's writing, for
instance, that "men's writing is both more realistic
and more serious than women's," and that battle stories
("actual portrayal of war") are more important than
"narratives of the effect of war on the domestic and
personal loves of women."

       Alcott
       Appleton, Elizabeth Haven
       Chesebro'
       Cooke
       Davis, Rebecca Harding
       Dodge, Mary Mapes
       Haven
       Moulton
       Palmer
       Spencer
       Spofford
       Stoddard
       Walker

65.   _____. "The Negro Character in Northern
       Magazine Fiction of the 1860's." NEW ENGLAND
       QUARTERLY 43 (December 1970): 572-92.

       Sees the 1860's as the one decade in the
nineteenth century in which white authors tried to
create non-stereotyped black characters. Does not
distinguish between male and female authors, but many
of the authors are women.

       Alcott
       Davis, Rebecca Harding
       Dodge, Mary Abigail
       Palmer
       [Spofford] Prescott

Walker

66. CONCISE DICTIONARY OF AMERICAN LITERATURE.   Edited
     by Robert Fulton Richards.   New York:
     Philosophical Library, 1955.   253 pp.

     Dictionary with paragraph-length entries that
attempt to characterize the author's work.

     Alcott (P)
     Bacon, Delia
     Brooks, Maria Gowen
     Cooke
     Finley
     Foster
     Hale, Sarah Josepha
     Holmes
     Lewis
     Morton
     Rowson
     Sedgwick, Catharine M.
     Sigourney
     Smith, Elizabeth Oakes
     Southworth, E.D.E.N.
     Spofford
     Stowe
     Tenney
     Terhune

67. Cone, Helen Gray.   "Woman in American Literature."
     CENTURY MAGAZINE 40 (Oct. 1890): 921-30.   Also
     appears as "Women in Literature" in WOMAN'S WORK
     IN AMERICA, edited by Annie Nathan Meyer, 107-127.
     New York: Henry Holt and Co., 1891.

     Historical survey of women's contributions to
American literature; mentions many authors.   Argues
that women were at a disadvantage in creating
literature because of poor education, feelings of
inferiority, and unfair treatment by critics.   However,
women have "steadily gained in art," especially in
fiction, the field in which they excel.

     Child
     Sedgwick, Catharine M.
     [Spofford] Prescott
     Stoddard

Stowe

68. CONJURING: BLACK WOMEN, FICTION, AND LITERARY
     TRADITION. Edited by Marjorie Pryse and Hortense
     J. Spillers. Bloomington: Indiana University
     Press, 1985. 266 pp.

     Most of the essays in this collection concern
     twentieth-century African-American women; however,
     Pryse's introduction discusses Frances E.W. Harper and
     Harriet E. Wilson, and the first two essays, Frances
     Smith Foster's "Adding Color and Contour to Early
     American Self-Portraitures: Autobiographical Writings
     of Afro-American Women" and Minrose C. Gwin's "Green-
     eyed Monsters of the Slavocracy: Jealous Mistresses in
     Two Slave Narratives," include Wilson and Harriet
     Jacobs, respectively.

          Harper
          Jacobs
          Wilson, Harriet E.

69. Conrad, Susan Phinney. PERISH THE THOUGHT:
     INTELLECTUAL WOMEN IN ROMANTIC AMERICA, 1830-1860.
     New York: Oxford University Press, 1976. 292 pp.

     A significant study in 1976 but now outdated in
     terms of its separation of intellectual women from
     "female scribblers." Contains an interesting account
     of female intellectuals' reaction to Fanny Fern's RUTH
     HALL and discusses briefly some fiction by the
     intellectuals.

          Booth
          Child (P)
          Dall
          Ellet
          [Fern] Willis, Sarah
          Hale, Sarah Josepha (P)
          Smith, Elizabeth Oakes (P)

70. Conway, Jill K., Linda Kealey, and Janet E.
     Schultz. THE FEMALE EXPERIENCE IN EIGHTEENTH AND
     NINETEENTH-CENTURY AMERICA: A GUIDE TO THE HISTORY
     OF AMERICAN WOMEN. New York: Garland Publishing,
     1982. 290 pp.

One section of this bibliography and guide to sources concerns women writers and journalists (pp. 115-160). There are short, sketchy essays discussing secondary works on women's fiction and journalism of the period and a list of primary works by selected writers.

        Child
        Hale, Sarah Josepha
        Mowatt
        Sedgwick, Catharine M.
        Sigourney
        Smith, Elizabeth Oakes
        Southworth, E.D.E.N.
        Stephens, Ann S.
        Stowe
        Warner, Susan

71.   Coultrap-McQuin, Susan M. "Why Their Success?
      Some Observations on Publishing by Popular
      Nineteenth-Century Women Writers." LEGACY 1 (Fall
      1984): 1, 8-9.

      Describes characteristics of the publishing industry that enabled women to succeed in the literary marketplace; includes brief discussion of the author-publisher relationship and business practices of female writers as reflected in their correspondence with the publisher.

        Cooke
        Dodge, Mary Abigail
        Stowe

72.   Cowie, Alexander. "The Domestic Sentimentalists
      and Other Popular Writers (1850-1870)." Chap. 10
      in THE RISE OF THE AMERICAN NOVEL. New York:
      American Book Co., 1948.

      Includes amusing "recipe for a domestic novel," which illuminates its typical plot pattern, and summarizes the lives and works of ten popular writers: Maria Cummins, Fanny Fern, H.B. Goodwin, Caroline Lee Hentz, Mary Jane Holmes, E.D.E.N. Southworth, Ann S. Stephens, Mary Virginia Terhune, Susan Warner, and Augusta Evans Wilson. Other women who wrote in the nineteenth century are discussed individually in other parts of the book.

Alcott
Bleecker
Child
Cummins
[Fern] Parton
Foster
Goodwin, H.B.
Hentz, Caroline Lee
Holmes
Kirkland
Morton
Rowson
Sedgwick, Catharine M.
Smith, Elizabeth Oakes
Southworth, E.D.E.N.
Stephens, Ann. S.
Stowe
Tenney
Terhune
Warner, Susan
Warren
Wells
Wilson, Augusta Evans
Wood, Sally

73. _____. "The Vogue of the Domestic Novel,
     1850-1870." SOUTH ATLANTIC QUARTERLY 41 (Oct.
     1942): 416-24.

     Early version of "The Domestic Sentimentalists and
Other Popular Writers (1850-1870)." Treats the
"domestic novel" generally, without going into detail
about the individual novelists. Emphasizes the
conservatism of the writers, claiming that they were
against reform movements. They argued against women's
rights and, although they believed slavery was wrong,
portrayed abolitionists unfavorably.

     Cummins
     Hentz, Caroline Lee
     Holmes
     Sedgwick, Catharine M.
     Southworth, E.D.E.N.
     Warner, Susan
     Wilson, Augusta Evans

74. Coyle, William, ed. OHIO AUTHORS AND THEIR BOOKS. Cleveland and New York: World Publishing Co., 1962. 741 pp.

Comprehensive biographical dictionary, alphabetically arranged, of Ohio residents who published between 1796 and 1950. Entries range from a short paragraph to several pages.

>Appleton, Elizabeth Haven
>Arey
>Bacon, Delia
>Boyd
>Cary, Alice
>Cary, Phoebe
>Corwin
>Coxe
>Dumont
>Finley
>Gage
>Graves, Adelia C.
>Hentz, Caroline Lee
>Hoyt
>Livermore, Elizabeth D.
>Logan
>Piatt
>Preston
>Rice
>Stowe
>Thomas
>Victor, Frances Fuller
>Victor, Metta Fuller

75. Cruse, Amy. "Books from America." In THE VICTORIANS AND THEIR READING, 236-59. Boston: Houghton Mifflin, 1935.

Discussion of books from America read by Victorians during the first fifty years of the Queen's reign. Emphasis is on readers' reaction to Harriet Beecher Stowe and the "successful invasion of England by American children's stories."

>Alcott
>Stowe
>[Warner, Susan] Wetherell

76. Cushman, Alice B. "A Nineteenth Century Plan for
     Reading: The American Sunday School Movement." In
     THE HEWINS LECTURES, 1947-1962, edited by Siri
     Andrews, 205-33. Boston: Horn Book, 1963.

     Contains brief discussion of authors known to have
contributed to Sunday school literature.

     Guernsey, Lucy Ellen
     Haven
     Tuthill, Louisa C.

77. CYCLOPAEDIA OF AMERICAN LITERATURE. Edited by
     Evert A. Duyckinck and George L. Duyckinck. 2
     vols. Philadelphia: William Rutter and Co.,
     1875. 990 pp., 1054 pp.

     Contains, as the title page notes, "personal and
critical notices of authors, and selections from their
writings, from the earliest period to the present day,
with portraits, autographs, and other illustrations."
Organization is chronological by author's date of
birth; there is an index at the end of the second
volume. Entries on female authors tend to be brief and
to emphasize the subject's gender. For instance,
Susanna Rowson is presented as an imitator of Laurence
Sterne, "though the sharp wit and knowledge of the
world of the original are not feminine qualities, and
are not to be looked for from a female pen."

     Alcott (P)
     Bleecker (P)
     Booth
     Botta (P)
     Brooks, Maria Gowen (P)
     Cary, Alice
     Cary, Phoebe
     Chesebro'
     Child
     Comstock
     Dorr (P)
     Ellet
     Embury
     Farley
     Farnham
     Faugeres
     Fern
     Follen

Gilman (P)
Hale, Sarah Josepha
Hall
Haven (P)
Hentz, Caroline Lee
Hooper
Janvrin
[Jervey] Glover
Judson (P)
Kirkland (P)
Lee, Hannah Farnham
Leslie (P)
Lewis (P)
Lippincott (P)
Locke
McIntosh (P)
Morton
Moulton
[Mowatt] Ritchie (P)
Palfrey
Preston
Robinson
Rowson
Sawyer
Sedgwick, Catharine M. (P)
Sigourney (P)
Smith, Elizabeth Oakes (P)
Southworth, E.D.E.N. (P)
Spofford
Stephens, Ann S.
Stowe
Tenney
Terhune
Tuthill, Louisa C.
Warfield
Warner, Anna B.
Warner, Susan
Whitney
Worthington

78.   CYCLOPAEDIA OF FEMALE BIOGRAPHY.   Edited by H.G.
      Adams.   Glasgow: Robert Forrester, 1866.   788 pp.

     Universal female biography that draws heavily from
Sarah Josepha Hale's WOMAN'S RECORD (#145).   Arranged
alphabetically, entries range in length from a
paragraph to several pages.

Bleecker
[Botta] Lynch
Brooks, Maria Gowen
[Cary, Alice] Carey
[Cary, Phoebe] Carey
Cheney
Child
Cooper, Susan Fenimore
Coxe
Dinnies
Ellet
Embury
Farley
Faugeres
Follen
Gilman
Green
Hall
[Haven] Neal
Hentz, Caroline Lee
Hooper
Judson
Kirkland
Lee, Hannah Farnham
Lee, Mary Elizabeth
Leslie
Lewis
[Lippincott] Clarke
Mayo
McIntosh
Mowatt
Nichols
Peirson
Phelps, Almira H. Lincoln
Robinson
Rowson
Sawyer
Sedgwick, Catharine M.
Shindler
Sigourney
Smith, Elizabeth Oakes
Smith, Margaret Bayard
Southworth, E.D.E.N.
Stephens, Ann S.
Stowe

79.   DARING TO DREAM: UTOPIAN STORIES BY UNITED STATES
      WOMEN: 1836-1919. Edited by Carol Farley Kessler.

Boston: Pandora Press, 1984.   266 pp.

In the editor's introduction, Utopian fiction by
Louisa May Alcott, Rebecca Harding Davis, and Sarah
Josepha Hale is briefly discussed as revealing "the
hegemony of patriarchal ideology, particularly in the
control of women's labor." The selections include
excerpts from visions of positive societies by Mary
Griffith and Jane Sophia Appleton.

Alcott
Appleton, Jane Sophia
Cridge
Davis, Rebecca Harding
Griffith, Mary
Hale, Sarah Josepha

80. Davenport, Walter, and James C. Derieux.   LADIES,
GENTLEMEN AND EDITORS.   Garden City, N.Y.:
Doubleday and Co., 1960.   386 pp.

Glib account of nineteenth-century American
editors, written for a popular audience.   Includes
discussion of Sarah Josepha Hale and of Robert Bonner,
whose business relationships with several female
authors are detailed.

Fern
Hale, Sarah Josepha
Sigourney
Southworth, E.D.E.N.

81. Davidson, Cathy N.   "Flirting with Destiny:
Ambivalence and Form in the Early American
Sentimental Novel."   STUDIES IN AMERICAN FICTION
10 (1982): 17-39.

Argues that the late eighteenth-century
sentimental novels, many of which were written by
women, deserve more attention than they have received.
In them the art of the American novel began and they
should be credited for their occasional complexities,
particularly the "disjunctions between the conventional
meanings and the covert ones."

Foster
Murray

    Rowson
    Sansay
    Tenney
    Wells
    Wood, Sally

82.   . "Mothers and Daughters in the
    Fiction of the New Republic." In THE LOST
    TRADITION: MOTHERS AND DAUGHTERS IN LITERATURE,
    edited by Cathy N. Davidson and E.M. Broner,
    115-127. New York: Frederick Ungar Publishing
    Co., 1980.

    Focuses on the novel of seduction in the late
    1700's in attempt to show "how a pervasive rhetoric of
    motherhood was conjoined with a submerged language of
    feminism."

        Foster
        Rowson
        Sansay

83. Davidson, James Wood. THE LIVING WRITERS OF THE
    SOUTH. New York: Carleton, Publisher, 1869.
    635 pp.

    About one third of the writers are female. Gives
    scant biographical information and few dates but does
    discuss the authors' works, with comments ranging from
    one paragraph to five pages in length. Includes some
    excerpts, usually poetry.

        Bacon, Julia
        Ball, Caroline A.
        Blount
        [Butt] Bennett
        Clack
        Clarke, Mary Bayard
        Creswell
        Cross
        Cruse
        Cutler
        Dinnies
        Dorsey, Sarah Anne
        Downing
        DuBose
        Dupuy

[Elemjay] Elenjay
Ford
French
Gilman
Gwyn
Jeffrey
Jervey
Ketchum
King
McIntosh
McLeod
Martin
[Mowatt] Ritchie
Phelps, Almira H. Lincoln
Preston
Shindler
Southworth, E.D.E.N.
Terhune
[Towles] Barber
Townsend, Mary Ashley
Upshur
Walsingham
Warfield
Whitaker
[Whittlesey] Whittlesley
Williams, Mary Bushnell
Wilson, Augusta Evans
Windle

84. Dearborn, Mary V. POCAHONTAS'S DAUGHTERS: GENDER
     AND ETHNICITY IN AMERICAN CULTURE. New York:
     Oxford University Press, 1985. 266 pp.

     Fiction by nineteenth-century black women is
considered as part of an "ethnic" women's literary
tradition. Emphasis is on its "mediating" nature.

          Harper
          Wilson, Harriet E.

85. DeMenil, Alexander Nicolas. THE LITERATURE OF THE
     LOUISIANA TERRITORY. St. Louis: St. Louis News
     Co., 1904. 354 pp.

     Anthology that includes short selections and two-
to-three-page biographical sketches of authors.

Dinnies
Dorsey, Sarah Anne
Townsend, Mary Ashley
Wood, Julia Amanda Sargent

86. Derby, J.C.   FIFTY YEARS AMONG AUTHORS, BOOKS AND
     PUBLISHERS.   New York: G.W. Carleton & Co., 1884.
     739 pp.

     Recollections of a publisher, arranged as a series
of chapters about authors with whom he was acquainted.
Packed with useful information, such as personal
reminiscences, letters, and quotations from reviews.

     Campbell, Jane C.
     Cary, Alice
     Cary, Phoebe
     Fern
     Harris
     Holmes
     Kinney
     Kirkland
     Preston
     Smith, Elizabeth Oakes
     Stephens, Ann S.
     Stowe
     [Terhune] Harland
     Townsend, Mary Ashley
     Victor, Metta Fuller
     Whitcher
     Wilson, Augusta Evans

87. Dexter, Elisabeth Anthony.   "The Inky-Fingered
     Sisterhood."   Chap. 5 in CAREER WOMEN OF AMERICA,
     1776-1840.   Boston: Houghton Mifflin Co., 1950.

     Notes that early career women found a kinder
reception in the realm of letters than in most fields
and provides a brief and selective survey of their
accomplishments.

     Brooks, Maria Gowen
     Child
     Foster
     Morton
     Rowson
     Royall

Sedgwick, Catharine M.
Sigourney

88. DICTIONARY OF AMERICAN BIOGRAPHY. Edited by Allen
Johnson et al. 20 vols. with index and 7
supplements. New York: Charles Scribner's Sons,
1928-81. CONCISE DICTIONARY OF AMERICAN
BIOGRAPHY. 3rd ed. (1980).

Scholarly collection of biographies of over 14,000
Americans. Entries contain bibliographies and note the
location of manuscripts. Includes a larger number of
early women who wrote fiction than NOTABLE AMERICAN
WOMEN (#239) but still lives up (or down?) to its
reputation as a chronicle of the lives of white,
socially prominent citizens; one looks in vain for even
the best known black or working-class women, such as
Frances E.W. Harper and Sarah Bagley. The CONCISE
DICTIONARY contains sharply abridged entries.

Alcott
Austin
Bacon, Delia
Bellamy
Blake
Bleecker
Booth, Maria Gowen
Botta
Brooks
Brown
Cary, Alice
Cary, Phoebe
[Chesebro'] Chesebrough
Child
Clarke, Mary Bayard
Clarke, Rebecca Sophia
Cook
Cooke
Cooper, Sarah Brown Ingersoll
Cooper, Susan Fenimore
Crane
Crosby
Cummins
Cutler
Dall
Davis, Rebecca Harding
Diaz
Dodge, Mary Abigail

Dodge, Mary Mapes
Dorr
Dorsey, Anna Hanson
Dorsey, Sarah Anne
Duniway
Dupuy
Ellet
Embury
Farley
Farnham
[Fern] Parton
Finley
Follen
Foster
French
Gage
Gilman
Green
Hale, Lucretia P.
Hale, Sarah Josepha
Hanaford
Harris
[Haven] Neal
Hentz, Caroline Lee
Holmes
Jeffrey
Judson
Kinney
Kirkland
Ladd
Larcom
Latimer
Lee, Eliza Buckminster
Lee, Hannah Farnham
Leslie
Lewis
Lippincott
Livermore, Mary A.
Logan
Martyn
Mayo
Moise
Morton
Moulton
Mowatt
Murray
Nichols
Parker
Phelps, Almira H. Lincoln

Phelps, Elizabeth Stuart
Pike
Prentiss
Preston
Robinson
Rowson
Royall
Sadlier
Sedgwick, Catharine M.
Sigourney
Smith, Elizabeth Oakes
Smith, Margaret Bayard
Southworth, E.D.E.N.
Spofford
Stephens, Ann S.
Stoddard
Stowe
Tenney
Terhune
Townsend, Mary Ashley
Townsend, Virginia Frances
Victor, Frances Fuller
Warfield
Warner, Anna B.
Warner, Susan
Whitcher
Whitney
Williams, Catharine Read
[Wilson, Augusta Evans] Evans
Wood, Sally

89. A DICTIONARY OF BRITISH AND AMERICAN WOMEN
     WRITERS, 1660-1800. Edited by Janet Todd.
     Totowa, N.J.: Rowman & Allanheld, 1985. 344 pp.

     Emphasis is on the British, with non-British
writers being identified only by the designation
"American" given before the genre specialization.
Entries average about two pages in length and are
written by scholars.

Bleecker
Faugeres
Foster
Murray
Rowson
Tenney
Wells

Wood, Sally

90. Dobson, Joanne, and Judith Fetterley.
    "Nineteenth-Century American Novel: A Revised
    Syllabus." LEGACY 1 (Spring 1984): 6.

    Presents and discusses a list of twelve novels
equally divided between female and male authors.

    Sedgwick, Catharine M.
    Stoddard
    Stowe
    Warner, Susan

91. Dondore, Dorothy Anne. THE PRAIRIE AND THE MAKING
    OF MIDDLE AMERICA: FOUR CENTURIES OF DESCRIPTION.
    Cedar Rapids, Iowa: Torch Press, 1926. 472 pp.

    Scholarly, detailed study of literary treatments
of the Middle West. Early fiction is discussed
primarily in Chapter 5, "Early Romantic Treatments,"
and Chapter 6, "The Realism of the Mississippi Valley."
Of female authors, only Caroline Kirkland is dealt with
at length.

    Cary, Alice
    Cary, Phoebe
    Dumont
    Hentz, Caroline Lee
    Holmes
    Kirkland
    Royall
    Sigourney
    Snelling
    Soule

92. Donovan, Josephine. "Toward the Local Colorists:
    Early American Women's Traditions." Chap. 2 in
    NEW ENGLAND LOCAL COLOR LITERATURE: A WOMEN'S
    TRADITION. New York: Frederick Ungar Publishing
    Co., 1983.

    Discusses the "Cinderella script" of "senti-
mentalist" fiction, which is seen as the dominant
women's tradition of the nineteenth century, and then
contrasts tendencies toward realism that form a "minor

tradition that existed side by side with the much more visible and popular sentimentalist tradition." The book also includes chapters on Rose Terry Cooke and Harriet Beecher Stowe.

> Cary, Alice
> Child
> Cooke
> Hale, Sarah Josepha
> [Haven] Neal
> Jerauld
> [Judson] Chubbuck
> Kirkland
> Lee, Hannah Farnham
> Rowson
> Sedgwick, Catharine M.
> Stowe
> Tenney
> Warner, Susan
> Whitcher
> [Wilson, Augusta Evans] Evans

93. Dorland, W.A. Newman. THE SUM OF FEMININE ACHIEVEMENT. Boston: Stratford Co., 1917. 237 pp.

Odd book, which tries to prove that women can be geniuses by listing women of achievement (Chapter 8, "Woman in Literature," lists a large number of female writers) and charts their mental accomplishments. Woman reaches the "acme of her mental ability at about the age of 45," which is five years earlier than man's acme. Although no writer is discussed in detail, those noted below are represented in the charts giving dates of "initial mental activity," acme of ability, and duration of mental activity.

> Alcott
> Andrews
> Austin
> Baker, Harriette Newell Woods
> Barrow
> Botta
> Cary, Alice
> Cary, Phoebe
> Child
> Clarke, Rebecca Sophia
> Cooke

Crosby
Cummins
Dodge, Mary Abigail
Dodge, Mary Mapes
Dorr
[Fern] Parton
Finley
Fleming
Hale, Lucretia P.
Hale, Sarah Josepha
Holmes
Larcom
Lee, Hannah Farnham
Leslie
Lewis
Lippincott
Livermore, Mary A.
[Mowatt] Ritchie
Prentiss
Putnam
Robinson
Sedgwick, Catharine M.
Sigourney
Southworth, E.D.E.N.
Stephens, Ann S.
Stowe
Townsend, Virginia Frances
Warner, Anna B.
Warner, Susan
Whitney
Wilson, Augusta Evans

94. Douglas, Ann. THE FEMINIZATION OF AMERICAN
     CULTURE. New York: Alfred A. Knopf, 1977.
     403 pp.

     Claims that the disestablishment of the clergy and
of women in the early nineteenth century led
northeastern ministers and middle-class literary women
to join together in producing a sentimental popular
literature that marks the beginning of modern mass
culture. Although marred by victim blaming and by the
author's unqualified admiration for Calvinism and scorn
for "sentimentalism," the book contains numerous
insights and interesting interpretations of women's
fiction.

     Alcott

Bacon, Delia
Cary, Alice
Child
Cummins
Farley
Farnham
[Fern] Willis
Finley
Follen
Hale, Sarah Josepha
Holmes
[Jerauld] Fillebrown
Judson
Larcom
Lee, Eliza Buckminster
Lippincott
Mayo
Prentiss
Sedgwick, Catharine M.
Sigourney
Smith, Elizabeth Oakes
Spencer
Stephens, Ann S.
Stowe
Warner, Susan
Whitney

95.   _____. "Heaven Our Home: Consolation
Literature in the Northern United States,
1830-1880." AMERICAN QUARTERLY 26 (December
1974): 496-515.

Argues that in compensation for their low status,
liberal clergymen and women "were intent on claiming
death as their peculiar property" and wrote a large
amount of consolation literature. They exalted
domesticity and portrayed Heaven as a continuation of
the domestic sphere.

Prentiss
Sigourney

96.   _____ [Ann Douglas Wood]. "The Literature
of Impoverishment: The Women Local Colorists in
America 1865-1914." WOMEN'S STUDIES 1, no. 1
(1972): 3-40.

Compares ten sentimental "authoresses" and ten
female local colorists in arguing that the later
writers regressed when they rejected the literary
tradition established by the sentimentalists. While
the sentimentalist sensibility was aggressive and
covertly feminist, the local colorists despaired and
retreated from life. Argument relies on several shaky
premises, such as that covert power struggles are
revolutionary and that single women have cause for
despair as they "cling to their ugliness and age" and
"grow poisonous in their wasted feminity [sic]."

    Cooke
    Cummins
    Fern
    Hale, Sarah Josepha
    Hentz, Caroline Lee
    Sigourney
    Smith, Elizabeth Oakes
    Southworth, E.D.E.N.
    [Stephens, Ann S.] Stephens, Ann M.
    Stowe
    [Terhune] Harland
    Warner, Susan

97. _____ [Ann Douglas Wood]. "The 'Scribbling
Women' and Fanny Fern: Why Women Wrote." AMERICAN
QUARTERLY 23 (Spring 1971): 3-24.

Discusses the ambivalence of mid-nineteenth-
century American women writers. Most women felt guilty
about "taking over a man's field and enjoying the
conquest" and thus, with the support of male reviewers,
tried to justify their work as morally elevating and
downplayed their economic motives. Fanny Fern was an
exception, exposing in her writings the ambition,
economic motives, anger, and bitterness against men her
peers were striving to conceal. Article overstates the
differences between Fern and her colleagues and terms
Fern "hysterical," but in 1971 it stimulated interest
in the subject.

    Cary, Alice
    Fern
    Hale, Sarah Josepha
    Hentz, Caroline Lee
    [Judson] Forester
    [Lippincott] Greenwood

Sedgwick, Catharine M.
Sigourney
Warner, Susan
Whitney

98. Dowty, Alan. "Urban Slavery in Pro-Southern
Fiction of the 1850's." JOURNAL OF SOUTHERN
HISTORY 32 (Feb. 1966): 25-41.

Discussion of the portrayal of urban slavery in
responses to UNCLE TOM'S CABIN. Distinguishes between
the "'subliterary' literature, written almost entirely
by women" and the "more serious literature," written by
luminaries such as Joseph Holt Ingraham and Joseph B.
Cobb.

[Butt] Bennett
Eastman
Hentz, Caroline Lee
Holmes
McIntosh
Rush, Caroline E.
Schoolcraft
Southworth, E.D.E.N.

99. Doyle, Brian, ed. THE WHO'S WHO OF CHILDREN'S
LITERATURE. New York: Schocken Books, 1968.
380 pp.

Dictionary of "the most notable" authors and
illustrators of children's books from the early
nineteenth century to the present; heavily British in
emphasis, but includes the best known American women.
Sometimes inaccurate.

Alcott (P)
Cummins
Dodge, Mary Mapes
Finley
Hale, Lucretia P.
Stowe
[Warner, Susan] Wetherell

100. DuBreuil, Alice Jouveau. THE NOVEL OF DEMOCRACY
IN AMERICA. Baltimore: J.H. Furst Co., 1923.
114 pp.

Attempt at establishing the "novel of democracy" as a genre, vaguely defining it as "a novel in which is expressed the spirit that has made possible our gradual development toward religious freedom and political, economic, and social equality of opportunity." Includes descriptions of historical novels by nineteenth-century women.

    Austin
    Child
    Sedgwick, Catharine M.

101. Dunlap, George Arthur. THE CITY IN THE AMERICAN
     NOVEL, 1789-1900. New York: Russell & Russell,
     1965 (1st ed. 1934). 187 pp.

Discussion of fiction set in New York, Philadelphia, or Boston. Emphasizes plot summary, analysis, and evaluation of novels, including several by women.

    Cummins
    Davis, Rebecca Harding
    Mowatt
    Otis
    Sedgwick, Catharine M.
    Stowe

102. Earle, Alice Morse. "Early Prose." In EARLY
     PROSE AND VERSE, edited by Alice Morse Earle and
     Emily Ellsworth Ford, 3-103. New York: Harper &
     Brothers, 1893.

Introduction to selections from the writings of New York women. Briefly reviews their careers and discusses the lack of educational facilities for women in New York State in the eighteenth century and the variety of prejudices against female writers.

    Bleecker
    Embury
    Faugeres
    Smith, Elizabeth Oakes
    Stoddard

103. Earnest, Ernest. THE AMERICAN EVE IN FACT AND

FICTION, 1775-1914. Urbana: University of
Illinois Press, 1974. 280 pp.

Account of "the American girl" between the
Revolution and World War I. Contends that real women
were "vastly more lively, able, full blooded, and
interesting" than novelists portrayed them. Female
novelists are discussed only briefly and often
dismissed as too sentimental or prudish.

Alcott
[Cummins] Cummings
[Fern] Parton
Foster
Hale, Sarah Josepha
Holmes
Larcom
Rowson
Sigourney
Smith, Margaret Bayard
Stowe

104. Eaton, Anne. "Widening Horizons 1840-1890." In A
CRITICAL HISTORY OF CHILDREN'S LITERATURE, edited
by Cornelia Meigs, 167-295. New York: Macmillan
Co., 1953. Revised ed., 1969, pp. 155-272.

American women who wrote literature for children
during this time period are discussed primarily in
Chapter 6, "The American Family." They are accorded
more respect than in general literary histories, with
their positive as well as negative qualities being
pointed out.

Alcott
Clarke, Rebecca Sophia
Diaz
Dodge, Mary Mapes
Finley
Follen
Larcom
Lippincott
Stowe
Warner, Susan
Whitney

105. Ellison, Rhoda Coleman. EARLY ALABAMA

PUBLICATIONS: A STUDY IN LITERARY INTERESTS.
University: University of Alabama Press, 1947.
213 pp.

Includes extensive discussion of early fiction,
with focus on themes of slavery, secession, and
religion. Sees Caroline Lee Hentz's heroines as more
typical of early Alabama fiction than Augusta Evans
Wilson's.

[Cowden] Cowdin
Cruse
Hentz, Caroline Lee
[Towles] Towle
Wilson, Augusta Evans

106. _____. "Propaganda in Early Alabama
Fiction." ALABAMA HISTORICAL QUARTERLY, 7 (Fall
1945): 425-33.

Classifies antebellum novels defending slavery
into two types. The first type, which portrays the
joys of plantation life, is represented by the fiction
of Caroline Lee Hentz, and the second, attacking
corruption in the North, by Mrs. V.G. Cowdin.

[Cowden] Cowdin
Hentz, Caroline Lee
Wilson, Augusta Evans

107. Emch, Lucille B. "Ohio in Short Stories,
1824-1839." OHIO STATE ARCHAEOLOGICAL AND
HISTORICAL SOCIETY QUARTERLY 53 (July-September
1944): 209-50.

Discusses portrayal of Ohio by several early
writers, including Julia L. Dumont, Pamilla W. Ball,
and Mrs. H.W. Haynes.

Ball, Pamilla W.
Dumont
Haynes

108. EMINENT WOMEN OF THE AGE; BEING NARRATIVES OF THE
LIVES AND DEEDS OF THE MOST PROMINENT WOMEN OF THE
PRESENT GENERATION. Edited by James Parton.

Hartford, Conn.: S.M. Betts and Co., 1868.
628 pp.

Biographical source that includes some authors.
Sketches range from twenty to thirty pages and contain
anecdotes and discussion of the subject's works. In a
few cases the writer of the sketch is an author and
subject herself; for instance, "Grace Greenwood" (Sara
J. Lippincott) wrote the article on "Fanny Fern" (Sara
Parton), who wrote the article on "Gail Hamilton" (Mary
Abigail Dodge).

Cary, Alice
Cary, Phoebe
Child
Dall
[Dodge, Mary Abigail] Hamilton
Fern
[Lippincott] Greenwood
Sigourney (P)
Stowe

109. Ernest, Joseph M., Jr. "Whittier and the
     'Feminine Fifties.'" AMERICAN LITERATURE 28
     (March 1956 - January 1957): 184-96.

Discusses John Greenleaf Whittier's encouragement
of struggling women writers in the 1850's and his
influence on the careers of such women as Lucy Larcom
and E.D.E.N. Southworth.

Cary, Alice
Cary, Phoebe
Dodge, Mary Abigail
Hooper
Larcom
[Lippincott] Greenwood
Southworth, E.D.E.N.

110. EVERYMAN'S DICTIONARY OF LITERARY BIOGRAPHY.
     Revised ed. compiled after John W. Cousin by D.C.
     Browning. New York: E.P. Dutton and Co., 1969.
     812 pp.

Biographical dictionary with paragraph-length
entries on the best known British and American authors;
contains a few nineteenth-century women.

Alcott
Brooks, Maria Gowen
Cary, Alice
Cary, Phoebe
Child
Cummins
Hale, Sarah Josepha
Sigourney
Stowe
Warner, Susan

111. Exman, Eugene. THE BROTHERS HARPER: A UNIQUE
    PUBLISHING PARTNERSHIP AND ITS IMPACT UPON THE
    CULTURAL LIFE OF AMERICA FROM 1817 TO 1853. New
    York: Harper & Row, 1965. 415 pp.

    Includes discussion of book publishers Harper &
Brothers' relations with Sarah Josepha Hale, Catharine
M. Sedgwick, and Lydia Sigourney. There are also brief
references to other female writers of the time.

    Hale, Sarah Josepha
    Sedgwick, Catharine M.
    Sigourney

112. THE FACTORY GIRLS. Edited by Philip S. Foner.
    Urbana: University of Illinois Press, 1977.
    360 pp.

    Collection of writings, including fiction, by
young women who worked in New England factories in the
early nineteenth century. Editor notes that militant
leaders are represented, as well as the more "genteel"
contributors to the LOWELL OFFERING.

    Bagley
    Curtis
    Farley
    [Green] Whipple
    Larcom

113. Fatout, Paul. "Yarning in the Eighteen Fifties."
    AMERICAN SCHOLAR 3 (Summer 1934): 281-93.

    Pretentiously written attack on women writers.
The fifties are seen as a "low tide in American

letters. The ebb left rank malarial flats breathing a
miasma poisonous with affectation and sentimentality
... The now dusty landscape was submerged then in a
deluge of feminine fiction that flowed to low tide in
rivers of sticky complacency and floods of enervating
tears." Does include sales figures and quotations
from contemporary reviews.

    [Fern] Parton
    Stowe

114. Fetterley, Judith, and Joan Schulz. "The Status
     of Women Authors in American Literature
     Anthologies." MELUS 9 (Winter 1982): 3-17.

Dialogue at the 1981 Modern Language Association
convention, in which the paucity of women represented
in eight anthologies is attributed to the
incompatibility of women and current concepts of an
American writer. Includes discussion of the
nineteenth century.

    Leslie
    Sedgwick, Catharine M.
    Stowe

115. "Fiction." In LIST OF BOOKS FOR GIRLS AND WOMEN
     AND THEIR CLUBS, edited by Augusta H. Leypoldt and
     George Iles, 1-40. Boston: Library Bureau, 1895.

The list includes a paragraph or two about each
author and a list of his or her "best" books; many
female authors are represented.

    Alcott
    Austin
    Cooke
    Cummins
    Holmes
    Southworth, E.D.E.N.
    Spofford
    Stowe
    Terhune
    Townsend, Virginia Frances
    Warner, Susan
    Whitney
    Wilson, Augusta Evans

116. Fidler, William Perry. "Recipe for an Old-
     Fashioned Best Seller." GEORGIA REVIEW 8 (Spring
     1954): 5-16.

     Attempts to identify the main characteristics of
the American "novel of domestic sentimentalism" and to
account for its popularity. Concludes that the
nineteenth-century readers appreciated didacticism,
pathetic situations, love interest, and reflections of
the past.

     Wilson, Augusta Evans

117. Fiedler, Leslie A. LOVE AND DEATH IN THE AMERICAN
     NOVEL. Rev. ed. New York: Stein and Day, 1966
     (1st ed. 1959). 512 pp.

     Although "the American novelist" discussed in this
provocative book is usually male, female writers
occasionally seem to be included in the author's thesis
that American novelists have failed to treat mature
love and have been obsessed with death. The writings
of nineteenth-century women are presented as
preoccupied with images of men as "seducers and
blackguards" and of women as "sexless saviors."

     Cummins
     Foster
     Rowson
     Stowe
     Warner, Susan
     Wilson, Augusta Evans
     Wood, Sally

118. Fishburn, Katherine. WOMEN IN POPULAR CULTURE: A
     REFERENCE GUIDE. Westport, Ct.: Greenwood Press,
     1982. 267 pp.

     The introduction contains a very brief discussion
of popular nineteenth-century women's fiction, and
Chapter 2, "Women in Popular Literature," pp. 86-124,
provides a survey of scholarship on female writers of
popular fiction. The survey is selective rather than
inclusive but gives detailed summaries of a few works
on nineteenth-century writers, including Papashvily
(#257) and Baym (#28).

Alcott
Cummins
Fern
Hentz, Caroline Lee
Holmes
Manvill
Rowson
Southworth, E.D.E.N.
Stowe
Terhune
Warner, Susan
[Wilson, Augusta Evans] Evans

119. Flanagan, John T. "Native Themes in Early
Nineteenth-Century American Fiction." In POPULAR
LITERATURE IN AMERICA: A SYMPOSIUM IN HONOR OF
LYON N. RICHARDSON, edited by James C. Austin and
Donald A. Koch, 53-69. Bowling Green: Bowling
Green University Popular Press, 1972.

A few female novelists are mentioned in this
sketchy and sometimes inaccurate survey (Caroline
Kirkland is said to be "primarily interested in
domestic life").

Kirkland
Rowson
Sedgwick, Catharine M.
Stowe

120. Flory, Claude Reherd. ECONOMIC CRITICISM IN
AMERICAN FICTION, 1792-1900. New York: Russell
and Russell, 1937. 261 pp.

Discusses American fiction treating economic
themes and argues that although economic criticism was
not a central purpose in novels before the Civil War,
the first seeds of realism in American fiction can be
discovered in the elements of economic criticism in
early novels, such as works by Rebecca Harding Davis.

Child
Cummins
Davis, Rebecca Harding
Haven
Sedgwick, Catharine M.
Stowe

121. Forrest, Mary [Julia Deane Freeman]. WOMEN OF THE
     SOUTH DISTINGUISHED IN LITERATURE. New York:
     Derby and Jackson, 1861. 511 pp.

     Biographical sketches and selections from the work
of thirty-five writers. Often includes quotations
from contemporary reviews.

     Blount
     Cross
     [Cutler] Petit
     Dinnies
     DuBose
     Dupuy
     Ford
     French
     Gilman
     Hentz, Caroline Lee
     Jacobus
     [Jeffrey] Johnson
     [Jervey] Howard
     Lee, Mary Elizabeth
     McIntosh
     McLeod
     [Mowatt] Ritchie
     Phelps, Almira H. Lincoln
     Shindler
     Southworth, E.D.E.N.
     Terhune
     Warfield
     [Wilson, Augusta Evans] Evans
     Windle
     Worthington

122. Foster, Edward Halsey. THE CIVILIZED WILDERNESS:
     BACKGROUNDS TO AMERICAN ROMANTIC LITERATURE,
     1817-1860. New York: The Free Press, 1975.
     220 pp.

     In a book about the ways Romantic literature "was
shaped by and therefore reflected certain extraliterary
interests," several female writers are briefly
discussed. In Chapter 5, "Idealized Domesticity,"
women are simplistically seen as expressing a cultural
concept of idealized domesticity and concluding in
their novels that "families and domestic life
provide the best of all possible worlds."

Cummins
Davis, Rebecca Harding
Holmes
Jacobs
Sedgwick, Catharine M.
Southworth, E.D.E.N.
Stowe
Warner, Susan
[Wilson, Augusta Evans] Evans

123. Foster, Richard Allen. THE SCHOOL IN AMERICAN
LITERATURE. Baltimore: Warwick and York, 1930.
199 pp.

Works by a few nineteenth-century women are
included in this discussion of the portrayal of schools
and teachers in American literature.

[Clarke, Rebecca Sophia] Clark
Foster
Kirkland

124. Frederick, John T. "Hawthorne's 'Scribbling
Women.'" NEW ENGLAND QUARTERLY 48 (June 1975):
231-40.

Summarizes five best-selling novels by American
women published from 1850-1855, the period just
preceding Hawthorne's famous letter decrying the
"damned mob of scribbling women." Takes Hawthorne's
comment as having "dismaying accuracy." Also discusses
women's contributions to and editorship of magazines
during the period and surmises that Hawthorne resented
female journalists as much as female novelists.

Cummins
[Fern] Willis
Holmes
Kirkland
[Lippincott] Greenwood
Smith, Elizabeth Oakes
Southworth, E.D.E.N.
Warner, Susan

125. Fredrickson, George M. "Uncle Tom and the
Anglo-Saxons: Romantic Racialism in the North."

Chap. 4 in THE BLACK IMAGE IN THE WHITE MIND,
97-129. New York: Harper and Row, 1971.

Includes discussion of three novels--Mary Lowell
Putnam's RECORD OF AN OBSCURE MAN, Harriet Beecher
Stowe's UNCLE TOM'S CABIN, and Metta Victor's MAUM
GUINEA, AND HER PLANTATION "CHILDREN"--as evidence of a
romantic conception of racial differences based on
stereotyping African-Americans as docile and emotional.

Putnam
Stowe
Victor, Metta Fuller

126. Fullerton, B.M. SELECTIVE BIBLIOGRAPHY OF
AMERICAN LITERATURE 1775-1900: A BRIEF ESTIMATE
OF THE MORE IMPORTANT AMERICAN AUTHORS AND A
DESCRIPTION OF THEIR REPRESENTATIVE WORKS. New
York: William Farquhar Payson, 1932. 327 pp.

More useful today as collective biography than as
bibliography. Includes basic biographical information
on the authors and (direct and often funny) evaluative
comments on their works. Women are unusually fairly
represented and evaluated.

Alcott
Andrews
Bleecker
Brooks, Maria Gowen
Cary, Alice
Cary, Phoebe
Chesebro'
Child
Clarke, Rebecca Sophia
Cooke
Cummins
Dodge, Mary Mapes
Embury
[Fern] Parton
Finley
Foster
Hale, Lucretia P.
Hale, Sarah Josepha
Holmes
Judson
Kirkland
Larcom

Leslie
Morton
Moulton
Phelps, Elizabeth Stuart
Preston
Rowson
Rush, Rebecca
Sedgwick, Catharine M.
Sedgwick, Susan Ridley
Sigourney
Southworth, E.D.E.N.
Spofford
Stoddard
Stowe
[Tenney] Tenny
Terhune
[Warner, Susan] Wetherell
Warren
Whitcher
Whitney
Wilson, Augusta Evans
Wood, Sally

127. Furness, Clifton Joseph, ed. THE GENTEEL FEMALE:
     AN ANTHOLOGY. New York: Alfred A. Knopf, 1931.
     306 pp.

     Contains excerpts from nineteenth-century American
works for or about women. There are selections by
female authors and references to writers throughout but
especially in the section entitled "The Literary Lady"
(pp. 256-66). Furness discusses prejudice against
women's writing, which "began in a colonial narrowness
of mind" and lingered through the nineteenth century,
as in the case of Harriet Beecher Stowe, who was
accused of neglecting her family.

     Stowe

128. Gaines, Francis Pendleton. THE SOUTHERN
     PLANTATION: A STUDY IN THE DEVELOPMENT AND THE
     ACCURACY OF A TRADITION. New York: Columbia
     University Press, 1925. 243 pp.

     Study of the concept of the plantation in
literature. Refers to many novels by women, especially
in the section, "The Plantation in Domestic Romance."

The section that follows this one, "The Plantation in
Serious Art," covers such well-known male novelists as
P.H. Strother, George W. Bagby, and Edward A. Pollard.
Has no index.

    Bradley
    [Cutler] Petit
    Dorsey, Sarah Anne
    Dupuy
    Eastman
    Flanders
    Gilman
    [Griffith, Mattie] Griffin
    Hale, Sarah Josepha
    Hentz, Caroline Lee
    Holmes
    Jeffrey
    Latimer
    McIntosh
    [Pearson] Pierson
    [Pike] Langdon
    [Royall] Royal
    Rush, Caroline E.
    Schoolcraft
    Southworth, E.D.E.N.
    Stowe
    [Terhune] Harland
    Victor, Metta Fuller
    Warfield
    Wilson, Harriet E.

129. Gardiner, Jane. "The Assault upon Uncle Tom:
     Attempts of Pro-Slavery Novelists to Answer UNCLE
     TOM'S CABIN, 1852-1860." SOUTHERN HUMANITIES
     REVIEW 12 (Fall 1978): 313-24.

     Attempt at categorizing pro-slavery arguments
and distinguishing between southern and northern
fictional responses to UNCLE TOM'S CABIN. There is
little emphasis on individual authors or works.

    Hentz, Caroline Lee
    Rush, Caroline E.
    Schoolcraft
    Stowe

130. _____. "Pro-slavery Propaganda in Fiction

Written in Answer To UNCLE TOM'S CABIN, 1852-1861:
An Annotated Checklist." RESOURCES FOR AMERICAN
LITERARY STUDY 7 (Autumn 1977): 201-9.

The annotations include plot summaries and
evaluations of the novels; a good deal of this fiction
was written by women.

Butt
[Cowden] Cowdin
Eastman
Hentz, Caroline Lee
McIntosh
Rush, Caroline E.
Schoolcraft
Townsend, Mary Ashley

131. Garrison, Dee. "Immoral Fiction in the Late
Victorian Library." AMERICAN QUARTERLY 28 (Spring
1976): 71-89.

Discusses major themes in the British and American
best-selling fiction most often declared "immoral" and
excluded from American public libraries around 1880.
Traces the popularity of this "low quality" fiction to
its "covert anti-masculinity" and considers its
dominant theme to be "how strong woman decisively
conquers and slyly manipulates weak man."

Hentz, Caroline Lee
Holmes
Southworth, E.D.E.N.
Stephens, Ann S.
Wilson, Augusta Evans

132. Geary, Susan. "The Domestic Novel as a Commercial
Commodity: Making a Commercial Best Seller in the
1850's." PAPERS OF THE BIBLIOGRAPHICAL SOCIETY OF
AMERICA 70 (July-September 1976): 365-95.

Argues that women's "domestic novels" were
commercial successes less because of an increasingly
female reading audience than because public demand was
"artificially perpetuated and even heightened by the
techniques publishers used to market them," most
particularly, new and aggressive advertising
strategies. Includes lengthy discussion of the

Mason Brothers' advertising of Fanny Fern's RUTH HALL.

     Cummins
     Fern
     Hentz, Caroline Lee
     Phelps, Almira H. Lincoln
     Southworth, E.D.E.N.
     Stowe
     Terhune
     Warner, Susan
     [Wilson, Augusta Evans] Evans

133. Gilman, Amy. "'Cogs to the Wheels': The Ideology
     of Women's Work in Mid-Nineteeth-Century Fiction."
     SCIENCE AND SOCIETY 47 (Summer 1983): 178-204.

     Discusses the topic of women's work and portrayal
of poor working women in nineteenth-century American
fiction; although "sentimental" literature by women is
described, emphasis is on male authors such as Charles
Burdett. Concludes that sentimental novelists could
not deal effectively with the issues of class.

     Alcott
     [Fern] Parton
     Maxwell

134. Goodrich, J.E. "Vermont Literature." VERMONTER 9
     (Oct. 1903): 69-83.

     A rather disorganized survey of the contributions
of Vermonters to various kinds of literature.

     Allen
     Botta
     Dorr (P)
     Marsh
     Phelps, Almira H. Lincoln

135. Gordon, Jean, and Jan McArthur. "Living Patterns
     in Antebellum Rural America as Depicted by
     Nineteenth-Century Women Writers." WINTERTHUR
     PORTFOLIO 19 (Summer/Autumn 1984): 177-92.

     Presents descriptions of household interiors by
popular novelists as evidence of living patterns in

rural New England and the upper South in the nineteenth century.

    [Fern] Parton
    Hale, Sarah Josepha
    Stowe
    Terhune
    Warner, Susan

136. Gossett, Thomas F. UNCLE TOM'S CABIN AND AMERICAN CULTURE. Dallas: Southern Methodist University Press, 1985. 484 pp.

    Thorough study of the writing of and reactions to Harriet Beecher Stowe's UNCLE TOM'S CABIN. Includes discussion of her female contemporaries' fiction about slavery, particularly in Chapter 12, "Anti-Uncle Tom Literature."

    Cowdin
    Eastman
    Flanders
    Hale, Sarah Josepha
    Hentz, Caroline Lee
    McIntosh
    Rush, Caroline E.
    Schoolcraft
    Stowe

137. Gostwick, Joseph. HAND-BOOK OF AMERICAN LITERATURE: HISTORICAL, BIOGRAPHICAL AND CRITICAL. Port Washington, N.Y.: Kennikat Press, 1971 (1st pub. 1856). 319 pp.

    Survey of American literature from 1620 to 1855. Emphasis is on the historical and critical; includes evaluation of writers' work and some brief selections. Typically, the only women discussed are the author's contemporaries; he does not mention pioneers like Susanna Rowson and Catharine M. Sedgwick.

    Brooks, Maria Gowen
    Child
    Fern
    Kirkland
    Leslie
    Sigourney

Stowe

138. Grade, Arnold E. THE MERRILL GUIDE TO EARLY
     JUVENILE LITERATURE. Columbus, Ohio: Charles E.
     Merrill Publishing Co., 1970. 43 pp.

     Brief survey of nineteenth-century American
fiction for children. Treats juvenile literature
sympathetically, noting its impact on American thought
and its place in the vanguard of the nineteenth-century
"shift from romanticism to realism."

     Alcott
     Child
     Dodge, Mary Mapes
     Finley
     Whitney

139. Gray, Virginia Gearhart. "Activities of Southern
     Women: 1840-1860." SOUTH ATLANTIC QUARTERLY 27
     (July 1928): 265-79.

     Accomplishments of some writers of the period are
briefly discussed.

     Gilman
     Hentz, Caroline Lee
     McIntosh
     Phelps, Almira H. Lincoln
     Southworth, E.D.E.N.

140. Griswold, Rufus Wilmot. THE PROSE WRITERS OF
     AMERICA. Philadelphia: Carey and Hart, 1847.
     552 pp.

     Women are given short shrift in this nineteenth-
century source. Only four female writers receive
entries (an entry being a biographical sketch and
selections from the author's work). Other women are
mentioned very briefly on the one page devoted to
female authors in a fifty-page introduction discussing
American literature.

     Child
     Kirkland
     Leslie

Sedgwick, Catharine M.

141. Griswold, W.M.   A DESCRIPTIVE LIST OF NOVELS AND
     TALES DEALING WITH THE HISTORY OF NORTH AMERICA.
     Cambridge, Mass.: W.M. Griswold, Publisher, 1895.
     183 pp.

     List arranged chronologically by the year in which
the fiction is set. Contains no information on the
authors but for each novel or story gives plot summary
and comments from contemporary reviews.

     Bacon, Delia
     Cheney
     Child
     Denison
     Dupuy
     Foster
     Lee, Eliza Buckminster
     [Lippincott] Greenwood
     Rowson
     Sedgwick, Catharine M.
     Sigourney
     Southworth, E.D.E.N.
     [Stephens, Ann S.] Winterbotham
     Stowe
     Terhune

142. Gwin, Minrose C.   BLACK AND WHITE WOMEN OF THE OLD
     SOUTH: THE PECULIAR SISTERHOOD IN AMERICAN
     LITERATURE.   Knoxville: University of Tennessee
     Press, 1985.   238 pp.

     Examines relationships between black and white
women in several novels and autobiographies from the
nineteenth and twentieth centuries.   Harriet Beecher
Stowe's UNCLE TOM'S CABIN and Mary H. Eastman's AUNT
PHILLIS'S CABIN, although opposite in polemic intent
since Eastman's novel was proslavery, are shown to be
similar in their creation of a cross-racial female
world of nurturance.   Harriet A. Jacobs and Harriet E.
Wilson, by their portrayal of cruel and jealous white
mistresses, reject this vision of female bonding.

     Eastman
     Jacobs
     Stowe

Wilson, Harriet E.

143. Habegger, Alfred. GENDER, FANTASY, AND REALISM IN
     AMERICAN LITERATURE. New York: Columbia
     University Press, 1982. 378 pp.

     Discusses nineteenth-century women's fiction in an
attempt to "seize the center" for W.D. Howells and
Henry James. Howells and James are seen as becoming
great realistic novelists by reacting both against the
"rough masculine world" and popular women's fiction.
Men are (incorrectly) viewed as having created the
realistic novel.

     Alcott
     Cummins
     Davis, Rebecca Harding
     [Fern] Willis
     Hentz, Caroline Lee
     Holmes
     Phelps, Elizabeth Stuart
     Southworth, E.D.E.N.
     Stephens, Ann
     Stowe
     Warner, Susan
     Whitcher
     Whitney
     [Wilson, Augusta Evans] Evans

144. _____. "Nineteenth-Century American
     Humor: Easygoing Males, Anxious Ladies, and
     Penelope Latham." PMLA 91 (Oct. 1976): 884-99.

     Confused attempt to compare male and female
humorists, using a small and select sample of female
humor. Views women as civilizers and concludes that
women's humor "rested on an assumption of superiority
--the superiority of the cultured mandarin or that of
women's innate spirituality." Thus, women's humor has
been justly forgotten and the more relaxed male writers
"produced American humor."

     Alcott
     Whitcher

145. Hale, Sarah Josepha. WOMAN'S RECORD. 3rd ed.,

revised, with additions. New York: Harper and
Brothers, 1873. (1st ed. 1851, 2nd 1855.)
918 pp.

Many American authors are included in this
monumental source by the editor of GODEY'S LADY'S BOOK;
it contains over 1,500 biographical sketches and
selections from the writings of women. The sketches
are informed (often amusingly) by Hale's personal
prejudices, so that a woman may be admonished for her
political activism, like Lydia Maria Child, or even
described as "a lady of more wit than taste."

Bleecker
Bogart
Brooks, Maria Gowen
Campbell, Juliet H.
[Cary, Alice] Carey (P)
[Cary, Phoebe] Carey
Cheney
Child
Cooper, Susan Fenimore
Coxe
Dinnies
[Dodge, Mary Abigail] Hamilton
Eames
Ellet
Embury (P)
Farley (P)
Faugeres
Follen
Gilman (P)
Green
Hale, Sarah Josepha
Hall
[Haven] Neal (P)
Hentz, Caroline Lee (P)
Hooper
Hosmer
Judson (P)
Kirkland
Larcom
Lee, Hannah Farnham
Lee, Mary Elizabeth (P)
Leslie (P)
Lewis
[Lippincott] Clarke (P)
Little
Locke

McIntosh
Mayo
Mowatt (P)
Peirson
Phelps, Almira H. Lincoln (P)
Phelps, Elizabeth Stuart
Pindar
Robinson
Rowson
Sawyer
Sedgwick, Catharine M. (P)
Shindler
Sigourney (P)
Smith, Elizabeth Oakes (P)
Southworth, E.D.E.N. (P)
Stephens, Ann S. (P)
Stowe
Terhune
Tuthill, Louisa C.
[Victor, Frances Fuller] Fuller
[Victor, Metta Fuller] Fuller
Warfield
Warner, Anna B.
[Warner, Susan] Wetherell
Whitney

146. HALF-HOURS WITH THE BEST AMERICAN AUTHORS. Edited
by Charles Morris. 4 vols. Philadelphia: J.B.
Lippincott Co., 1887.

Women are well represented in this nineteenth-
century anthology. Before each selection there is a
short biographical sketch of the author.

Alcott
Cary, Alice
Cary, Phoebe
Child
[Cooke] Terry
Dodge, Mary Abigail
Dorr
[Fern] Parton
Kirkland
Larcom
Leslie
Lippincott
Preston
Sedgwick, Catharine M.

Sigourney
Spofford
Stowe
Whitcher
Whitney

147. Hall, Ernest Jackson. THE SATIRICAL ELEMENT IN
     THE AMERICAN NOVEL. New York: Haskell House, 1969
     (first published 1922). 89 pp.

Discussion of satire in novels published in the
U.S. that deal with American traits or institutions.
Covers a rather limited number of novelists but
includes women as well as men.

Morton
Rowson
Sedgwick, Catharine M.
Stowe

148. Halsey, Rosalie V. FORGOTTEN BOOKS OF THE
     AMERICAN NURSERY. Boston: Charles E. Goodspeed
     and Co., 1911. Reprint. Detroit: Book Tower,
     Singing Tree Press, 1969. 245 pp.

Several works by nineteenth-century women are
briefly but intelligently discussed and evaluated. The
author performs the rare feat of distinguishing one
female author from another and pointing out their
differences.

Embury
Hale, Sarah Josepha
Leslie
Sedgwick, Catharine M.
Sigourney
Stowe

149. Hanaford, Phebe A. WOMEN OF THE CENTURY. Boston:
     B. B. Russell, 1877. 648 pp. Rev. ed. under
     title DAUGHTERS OF AMERICA; OR, WOMEN OF THE
     CENTURY. 1883. 730 pp.

Record of women's accomplishments in the first
century of existence of the U.S. After preliminary
chapters on women in earlier times, the book is

organized by occupation--scientists, educators,
physicians, etc. Most fiction writers can be found in
Chapter 7, "Literary Women," but they are also
discussed under other headings, such as "women
lecturers," "women reformers," and "women journalists";
occasionally a name appears in several different
chapters, so the index is helpful (though it is not
complete). Many women are simply mentioned in passing;
those listed receive more than a brief mention. The
revised edition adds only late nineteenth-century
subjects.

Alcott
Appleton, Anna E.
Blake
Booth
Botta
Cary, Alice (P, rev. ed.)
Cary, Phoebe (P, rev. ed.)
Cheney
Child
Cooper, Susan Fenimore
Coxe
Dall
Davis, Minnie S.
Dinnies
Dodge, Mary Mapes
Ellet
Embury
Farley
Follen
Gage
Gilman
Hale, Sarah Josepha
Hall
Hanaford (P)
Harper
[Haven] Neal
Hentz, Caroline Lee
Hooper
Judson
Kirkland
Larcom
Lee, Hannah Farnham
Leslie
Lippincott
Livermore, Mary A. (P)
Mayo
McIntosh

Moulton
[Mowatt] Ritchie
Phelps, Elizabeth Stuart
Sawyer
Sedgwick, Catharine M.
[Shindler] Spindler
Sigourney
Smith, Elizabeth Oakes
Smith, Margaret Bayard
Soule
Southworth, E.D.E.N.
Spofford
Stephens, Ann S.
Stowe
Tuthill, Cornelia
Tuthill, Louisa C.
[Warner, Susan] Warner, Elizabeth

150. HANDBOOK OF AMERICAN POPULAR CULTURE. Edited by M.
Thomas Inge. 3 vols. Westport, Conn.: Greenwood
Press, 1978. 399 pp., 423 pp., 558 pp.

CONCISE HISTORIES OF AMERICAN POPULAR CULTURE.
Edited by M. Thomas Inge. Westport, Conn.:
Greenwood Press, 1982. 504 pp.

HANDBOOK contains short superficial histories of
"major areas" in American popular culture. Female
authors of the nineteenth century are mentioned but
seldom discussed in any depth in such essays as "Best
Sellers," "Children's Literature," "Gothic Novels," and
"Women." In "Romantic Fiction," Kay J. Mussell
characterizes the "domestic sentimentalists" as having
written primarily about "relationships between men and
women." CONCISE HISTORIES includes the short histories
with few changes but omits the longer bibliographic
sections and literature reviews of the HANDBOOK.

Cummins
Hale, Sarah Josepha
Rowson
Southworth, E.D.E.N.
Stowe
Wood, Sally

151. Hanson, Mrs. E.R. OUR WOMEN WORKERS: BIOGRAPHICAL
SKETCHES OF WOMEN EMINENT IN THE UNIVERSALIST

CHURCH FOR LITERARY, PHILANTHROPIC AND CHRISTIAN
WORK. Chicago: Star and Covenant Office, 1882.
500 pp.

As suggested in the subtitle, emphasis is on the
writers' Christian virtues. Sketches range from one to
five pages. Includes some portraits.

Cary, Alice
Cary, Phoebe
Gage
Hanaford (P)
Jerauld (P)
Livermore, Mary A. (P)
Mayo (P)
Remick (P)
Sawyer (P)
Smith, Elizabeth Oakes
Soule (P)

152. Harap, Louis. THE IMAGE OF THE JEW IN AMERICAN
LITERATURE. Philadelphia: Jewish Publication
Society of America, 1974. 586 pp.

Comprehensive literary history of the image of the
Jew and works by American Jewish writers from the end
of the eighteenth century through the early twentieth
century. Fiction by women is mentioned throughout,
though it is sometimes dismissed as "unreadable";
literary treatment of Jews by non-Jewish women
seems to range from sympathetic portrayal to
condescension, as in "conversion novels," where whole
Jewish families are converted to Christianity.

Baker, Harriette Newell Woods
Baker, Sarah S.
Child
Hanaford
Lee, Eliza Buckminster
Richards
Rowson
Smith, Sarah Pogson
Southworth, E.D.E.N.
Warner, Susan

153. Hart, James D. THE POPULAR BOOK: A HISTORY OF
AMERICA'S LITERARY TASTE. New York: Oxford

University Press, 1950.   351 pp.

Chapter 6, "Home Influence," pp. 85-105, gives an
account of popular fiction in the 1850's, emphasizing
domestic themes and settings.   There is brief
discussion of etiquette books and gift books, as well
as works by Maria Cummins, Fanny Fern, E.D.E.N.
Southworth, and other women of the time.   Chapter 4, on
the American novel at the end of the eighteenth
century, and Chapter 7, on mid-nineteenth-century
reform novels, also mention female writers.

> Alcott
> Bleecker
> Cary, Alice
> Cummins
> [Fern] Willis
> Foster
> Hale, Sarah Josepha
> Hentz, Caroline Lee
> Holmes
> [Judson] Forrester
> Moulton
> Phelps, Elizabeth Stuart
> Rowson
> Sedgwick, Catharine M.
> Sigourney
> Smith, Elizabeth Oakes
> Southworth, E.D.E.N.
> Stephens, Ann S.
> Stowe
> Victor, Metta Fuller
> Warner, Anna B.
> Warner, Susan
> Whitcher
> [Wilson, Augusta Evans] Evans
> Wood, Sally

154. Hart, John S.   THE FEMALE PROSE WRITERS OF
     AMERICA.   WITH PORTRAITS, BIOGRAPHICAL NOTICES,
     AND SPECIMENS OF THEIR WRITINGS.   Rev. ed.
     Philadelphia: E.H. Butler & Co., 1855 (1st ed.
     1852).   536 pp.

Biographical sketches, with characterizations of
the authors' works and substantial excerpts (usually
running to several pages).   The rationale for the book,
given in the preface, is that "women, far more than

men, write from the heart. Their own likes and
dislikes, their feelings, opinions, tastes, and
sympathies are so mixed up with those of their subject,
that the interest of the reader is often enlisted quite
as much for the writer, as for the hero, of a tale."

        Bogart
        Browne, Maria J.B.
        Browne, Sara H.
        [Cary, Alice] Carey
        Chesebro'
        Child
        Cooper, Susan Fenimore
        Dorr
        Eastman
        Ellet
        Embury
        Farley
        Fern
        Gilman
        Hale, Sarah Josepha
        [Haven] Neal (P)
        Hentz, Caroline Lee (P)
        Judson (P)
        Kinney
        Kirkland (P)
        Lee, Hannah Farnham
        Lee, Mary Elizabeth
        Leslie
        Lewis
        [Lippincott] Clarke
        McIntosh (P)
        Moore, Clara Jessup
        Moragne
        [Moulton] Chandler
        Orne
        Phelps, Almira H. Lincoln
        Porter
        Robinson
        Sedgwick, Catharine M. (P)
        Shindler
        Sigourney (P)
        Smith, Elizabeth Oakes
        Southworth, E.D.E.N.
        Stephens, Ann S. (P)
        Stowe
        [Turner] Sproat
        Tuthill, Louisa C.
        [Warner, Anna B.] Lothrop

[Warner, Susan] Wetherell
[Whitcher] Berry
Windle

155. _____. A MANUAL OF AMERICAN LITERATURE.
     Philadelphia: Eldredge & Brother, 1873.   641 pp.

     Considered a textbook in the nineteenth century,
this is closer to what we would call a biographical
dictionary; it consists of biographical sketches
arranged chronologically and within eras by type of
writing. Excerpts from authors' works are occasionally
included. Has the advantage of being very inclusive
and the disadvantage of frequently being inaccurate
about dates.

     Alcott
     Bache
     Bacon, Delia
     Baker, Harriette Newell Woods
     Ball, Caroline A.
     Bellamy
     Blount
     Bogart
     Botta
     Brooks, Maria Gowen
     Browne, Maria J.B.
     Browne, Sara H.
     Cary, Alice
     Cary, Phoebe
     Chaplin
     Cheney
     Chesebro'
     Child
     Clark
     Clarke, Mary Bayard
     Cooper, Susan Fenimore
     [Crane] Seemuller
     Creswell
     Cross
     Cruse
     [Cummins] Cummings
     Cutler
     Dall
     Davis, Caroline E.
     Denison
     Dinnies
     Dodge, Mary Abigail

Dorr
Dorsey, Sarah Anne
Downing
DuBose
Dumont
Dunning
Dupuy
Eastman
[Elemjay] Elenjay
Ellet
Embury
Farley
Farnham
[Fern] Parton, Sarah Payson
Finley
Follen
Ford
French
Gage
Gilman
Green
Guernsey, Clara F.
Guernsey, Lucy Ellen
Hale, Sarah Josepha
Haven
Hall
Hentz, Caroline Lee
Hildeburn
Holmes
Homes
Hooper
Hosmer
Jeffrey
Jervey
Judson
Ketchum
King
Kinney
Kirkland
Larcom
Lee, Eliza Buckminster
Lee, Hannah Farnham
Lee, Mary Elizabeth
Leslie
Lewis
Lippincott
Little
Logan
McIntosh

McKeever
McLeod
Martyn
Mayo
Moulton
[Mowatt] Ritchie
Myers
Orne
Palfrey
Parker
Peirson
Phelps, Almira H. Lincoln
Pike
Pindar
Preston
Putnam
Robinson
Rowson
Royall
Sadlier
Sedgwick, Catharine M.
Shindler
Sigourney
Smith, Elizabeth Oakes
Southworth, E.D.E.N.
Spofford
Stephens, Ann S.
Stowe
Tenney
Terhune
Thomas
[Towles] Barber
Trowbridge
Tuthill, Louisa C.
Upshur
Victor, Metta Victoria
Warfield
Warner, Anna B.
Warner, Susan
Whitaker
[Whitcher] Whitaker
Whitney
Whittlesey
Wilson, Augusta Evans

156. Haviland, Virginia, and Margaret N. Coughlan, eds.
YANKEE DOODLE'S LITERARY SAMPLER OF PROSE, POETRY,
AND PICTURES. New York: Thomas Y. Crowell Co.,

1974.   466 pp.

Chronologically arranged anthology of works
published for children in America from the 1770's. to
1900.   The lavishly illustrated collection contains
facsimile pages, complete short works, selections from
longer works, and brief comments by the editors on the
authors and their writings.

    Alcott
    Andrews
    Child
    Clarke, Rebecca Sophia
    Dodge, Mary Mapes
    Finley
    Hale, Lucretia P.
    Hale, Sarah Josepha
    Stowe
    Warner, Susan

157. Hedin, Raymond. "Strategies of Form in the
     American Slave Narrative." In THE ART OF SLAVE
     NARRATIVE, edited by John Sekora and Darwin T.
     Turner, 25-35. Macomb, Ill.: Western Illinois
     University, 1982.

     Views Mattie Griffith and Harriet Jacobs as
using the form of the sentimental novel in order to
assert the full humanity of their female narrators.
The narrators "show themselves truly women by embodying
and intensifying the sentimental heroine's plight."

     Griffith, Mattie
     Jacobs

158. Helbig, Alethea K., and Agnes Regan Perkins.
     DICTIONARY OF AMERICAN CHILDREN'S FICTION,
     1859-1959. Westport, Conn.: Greenwood Press,
     1985. 666 pp.

     Since it does not cover children's books published
before 1859, this dictionary-style reference work
includes only a few early nineteenth-century women.
Entries are well written; there are title, as well as
author, entries to be consulted.

     Alcott

Dodge, Mary Mapes
Hale, Lucretia P.

159. Helsinger, Elizabeth K., Robin Lauterbach Sheets,
     and William Veeder. THE WOMAN QUESTION: LITERARY
     ISSUES, 1837-1883. Vol. 3 of THE WOMAN QUESTION:
     SOCIETY AND LITERATURE IN BRITAIN AND AMERICA,
     1837-1883. New York: Garland Publishing, 1983.
     237 pp.

Tries to present "the Victorian debate" over women
as poets and novelists and as heroines of fiction in
the nineteenth century. Mixes historical and critical
commentary with extensive quotations from the
Victorians themselves. Emphasis is on British writers,
although some Americans are discussed.

Alcott
Fern
Kirkland
Stowe
Warner, Anna B.
Warner, Susan

160. Hemstreet, Charles. LITERARY NEW YORK. New York:
     G.P. Putnam's Sons, 1903. 271 pp.

Chatty account of literary people who lived in New
York City in the nineteenth century; emphasizes men,
but some female authors are briefly discussed.

Bleecker
Botta
Cary, Alice
Cary, Phoebe
Child
Haven
Kirkland
Smith, Elizabeth Oakes
Stephens, Ann S.

161. HER WAY: BIOGRAPHIES OF WOMEN FOR YOUNG PEOPLE.
     Edited by Mary-Ellen Kulkin. Chicago: American
     Library Association, 1976. 449 pp. 2nd ed.
     Edited by Mary-Ellen Siegel. Chicago: American
     Library Association, 1984. 415 pp.

Excellent guide to biographies intended for preschool through high school youth; contains a two-to-three-paragraph profile of each woman, followed by an annotated list of biographies. Of course, only the best known nineteenth-century authors have been the subjects of biographies. Unfortunately, the second edition drops Mary Mapes Dodge and Anna Cora Mowatt.

        Alcott
        Child
        Dodge, Mary Mapes
        Hale, Sarah Josepha
        Mowatt
        Stowe

162. Herron, Ima Honaker. THE SMALL TOWN IN AMERICAN LITERATURE. New York: Pageant Books, 1959. 477 pp.

History of literature about the small town. Emphasis is on "major" figures and late nineteenth-century and twentieth-century literature; however, a few earlier women are discussed as "pioneers of realism."

        Cooke
        Kirkland
        Sedgwick, Catharine M.
        Stowe

163. Hersh, Blanch Glassman. THE SLAVERY OF SEX: FEMINIST-ABOLITIONISTS IN AMERICA. Urbana: University of Illinois Press, 1978. 280 pp.

Several of the fifty-one women included in this study of the antebellum feminist-abolitionist movement wrote fiction. The emphasis here is on their lives as activists rather than their writings; however, the group profile of feminist-abolitionists in Chapter 4 may be of interest to literary scholars constructing a similar profile for authors.

        Child
        Dall
        Gage
        Livermore, Mary A.
        Smith, Elizabeth Oakes

164. Hewins, Caroline M. A MID-CENTURY CHILD AND HER
     BOOKS. New York: Macmillan Co., 1926. 136 pp.

     Recollections of her childhood reading in the
1850's and 1860's by the pioneering children's
librarian.

     Bache
     Child
     Cummins
     Leslie
     Lippincott
     Stowe
     Warner, Anna B.
     Warner, Susan

165. THE HEWINS LECTURES, 1947-1962. Edited by Siri
     Andrews. Boston: Horn Book, 1963. 375 pp.

     A series of annual papers on the writing and
publishing of children's books in nineteenth-century
New England. Contains essays on A.D.T. Whitney,
Lucretia P. Hale, and contributors to ST. NICHOLAS
magazine, as well as Alice M. Jordan's "From Rollo to
Tom Sawyer" (#183) and Alice B. Cushman's "A Nineteenth
Century Plan for Reading" (#76).

     Alcott
     Dodge, Mary Mapes
     Hale, Lucretia P.
     Whitney

166. HIDDEN HANDS: AN ANTHOLOGY OF AMERICAN WOMEN
     WRITERS, 1790-1870. Edited by Lucy M. Freibert
     and Barbara A. White. New Brunswick, N.J.:
     Rutgers University Press, 1985. 409 pp.

     First modern collection of women's popular
writings from this time period. Consists of selections
from novels, arranged according to genre, and includes
representative selections from literary criticism on
nineteenth-century women's fiction. Introduction
relates the fiction "chronologically and thematically
to the standard (male) American literary canon";
discussion emphasizes the women's criticism of rampant
individualism, violence, and industrial capitalism,
which they associated with men, and their promotion of

opposite values.

        Bleecker (P)
        Chesebro' (P)
        Child (P)
        Cummins (P)
        [Fern] Parton (P)
        Finley (P)
        Foster
        Hale, Sarah Josepha (P)
        Hentz, Caroline Lee (P)
        Jacobs
        Kirkland (P)
        Rowson (P)
        Sedgwick, Catharine M. (P)
        Southworth, E.D.E.N. (P)
        Tenney
        Victor, Metta Fuller (P)
        Warner, Susan (P)
        Whitcher
        Wilson, Augusta Evans (P)
        Wood, Sally (P)

167. Hilldrup, Robert LeRoy. "Cold War against the
     Yankees in the Antebellum Literature of Southern
     Women." NORTH CAROLINA HISTORICAL REVIEW 31 (July
     1954): 370-84.

     Summary of southern women's criticisms of the
North in antebellum literature, mainly fiction. The
women attacked northern Puritanism and commercialism
and used as one of their main themes the hard lot of
laborers and free blacks in the North.

        Butt
        Eastman
        Flanders
        Hentz, Caroline Lee
        Homes
        [King] Bowen
        McIntosh
        Royall
        Rush, Caroline E.
        Schoolcraft
        Southworth, E.D.E.N.
        Terhune
        Warfield
        Wilson, Augusta Evans

Wilson, Harriet E.
Windle

168. THE HISTORY OF SOUTHERN LITERATURE. Edited by
Louis D. Rubin, Jr., et al. Baton Rouge:
Louisiana State University Press, 1985. 626 pp.

Collective work by numerous scholars; includes
brief discussions of fiction by nineteenth-century
women.

Gilman
Hentz, Caroline Lee
Preston
Southworth, E.D.E.N.
Stowe
Wilson, Augusta Evans

169. Hofstader, Beatrice. "Popular Culture and the
Romantic Heroine." AMERICAN SCHOLAR 30 (Winter
1960-1961): 98-116.

Discusses the theme of romantic love in several
best-selling novels published from 1850-1920. Includes
discussion of Warner's THE WIDE, WIDE WORLD and
Wilson's ST. ELMO, emphasizing the "underground
rebellion" of the heroines.

Warner, Susan
[Wilson, Augusta Evans] Evans

170. Holliday, Carl. A HISTORY OF SOUTHERN LITERATURE.
New York: Neale Publishing Co., 1906. 406 pp.

Early survey of Southern literature that treats
only a few women (three to four pages each) but
distinguishes between them in evaluating their work.
For instance, E.D.E.N. Southworth is dismissed but
Marion Harland seen as holding "a permanently high
place among American writers."

Dorsey, Sarah Anne
Preston
Southworth, E.D.E.N.
[Terhune] Harland
Wilson, Augusta Evans

171. Holloway, Laura C. THE WOMAN'S STORY. New York:
     John B. Alden, Publisher, 1889. 541 pp.

     Collection of short fiction by twenty American
women, supposedly forming "a composite picture of the
representative fiction work of the female writers of
the republic." According to the editor, each story
included was selected by its author as her best. The
selections are introduced by a portrait of the author
and a two-to-three-page biographical sketch.

     Alcott (P)
     Cooke (P)
     Davis, Rebecca Harding
     Dorr (P)
     Holmes (P)
     Lippincott (P)
     Moulton (P)
     Spofford (P)
     Stowe (P)
     [Terhune] Harland (P)
     Wilson, Augusta Evans (P)

172. Hubbell, Jay B. THE SOUTH IN AMERICAN LITERATURE,
     1607-1900. Durham, N.C.: Duke University Press,
     1954. 987 pp.

     The only early nineteenth-century women treated in
any detail are Harriet Beecher Stowe, Margaret Junkin
Preston, and Augusta Evans Wilson. The latter two are
seen as representative of "Women Writers, 1830-1865,"
who produced "subliterary" writings. The author does
discuss (nineteenth-century) "condescension toward
women writers," including the difficulties women
encountered with "timid and skeptical" critics and
publishers.

     Holmes
     Gilman
     Preston
     Southworth, E.D.E.N.
     Stowe
     [Terhune] Harland
     Wilson, Augusta Evans

173. _____. WHO ARE THE MAJOR AMERICAN
     WRITERS?: A STUDY OF THE CHANGING LITERARY CANON.

Durham, N.C.: Duke University Press, 1972.
344 pp.

Documents changes in literary fashion, though
without much consideration of why and how standards are
formed. Hardly mentions any women other than Emily
Dickinson but describes and gives the results of
several nineteenth-century popularity polls; women
appear prominently in the polls of readers and
not at all in the polls of critics, a fact the author
attributes to the readers' "confused literary taste."

Alcott
Cary, Alice
Cary, Phoebe
Davis, Rebecca Harding
Embury
Fleming
Hale, Sarah Josepha
Holmes
Mayo
Sigourney
Smith, Elizabeth Oakes
Southworth, E.D.E.N.
Stowe
[Terhune] Harland
Whitney
[Wilson, Augusta Evans] Evans

174. Huf, Linda. A PORTRAIT OF THE ARTIST AS A YOUNG
WOMAN: THE WRITER AS HEROINE IN AMERICAN
LITERATURE. New York: Frederick Ungar Publishing
Co., 1983. 196 pp.

This study of the kunstlerroman, or portrait-of-
the-artist novel, by American women includes a chapter
on Fanny Fern's RUTH HALL and discussion of artist
novels by Caroline Chesebro' and Augusta Evans Wilson.

Chesebro'
Fern
[Wilson, Augusta Evans] Evans

175. Hull, Raymona E. "'Scribbling' Females and
Serious Males: Hawthorne's Comments from Abroad on
Some American Authors." THE NATHANIEL HAWTHORNE
JOURNAL 1975, ed. C.E. Frazer Clark, Jr., 35-58.

Englewood, Colorado: Microcard Editions Books, 1975.

Discussion of Nathaniel Hawthorne's comments on American authors in letters written in the 1850's when he was U.S. Consul in Liverpool. Hawthorne scorned female writers as a class; he believed that women should be homemakers and should not reveal themselves in public.

Bacon, Delia (P)
Cummins
Fern
[Lippincott] Greenwood (P)
Mowatt (P)
Stowe (P)

176. INDIANA AUTHORS AND THEIR BOOKS, 1816-1916.
Edited by R.E. Banta. Crawfordsville, Ind.:
Wabash College, 1945. 352 pp.

Short biographical sketches (about half a page) of Indiana writers including some obscure female authors.

Brooks, M. Sears
Boyd
Collins
Dumont
Finley
Rose

177. THE INTERNATIONAL DICTIONARY OF WOMEN'S BIOGRAPHY.
Edited by Jennifer S. Uglow. New York: Continuum,
1982. 534 pp.

Biographical source covering prominent women from all periods; includes the best known early nineteenth-century American authors. Entries are brief (one or two paragraphs).

Alcott
Child
Davis, Rebecca Harding
Hale, Sarah Josepha
Stowe

178. Jackson, Joseph. LITERARY LANDMARKS OF
PHILADELPHIA. Philadelphia: David McKay Co.,
1939. 344 pp.

   Contains two-to-three-page biographical sketches
of authors associated with Philadelphia, along with
photographs of their homes.

   Davis, Rebecca Harding
   Hale, Sarah Josepha
   Leslie
   Rowson

179. Jehlen, Myra. "Archimedes and the Paradox of
Feminist Criticism." SIGNS 6 (Summer 1981):
575-601.

   Discusses women's "sentimental" best sellers from
1820 to 1870 in attempt to illustrate a critical
method. Suggests that instead of struggling with the
contradiction between the sentimentalists' acceptable
ideology (their insistence on strong, successful and
autonomous heroines) and the "low quality" of their
writing, feminist critics should consider whether the
ideological success is tied to artistic failure.
Perhaps the novel is intrinsically patriarchal, one of
its structuring assumptions being that female
characters must be weak and victimized. Interesting
thesis, but knowledge of the authors is sketchy.

   Rowson
   Southworth, E.D.E.N.
   Warner, Susan

180. Johannsen, Albert. THE HOUSE OF BEADLE AND ADAMS
AND ITS DIME AND NICKEL NOVELS: THE STORY OF A
VANISHED LITERATURE. 2 vols. Norman: University
of Oklahoma Press, 1950. 476 pp., 443 pp.

   Comprehensive account of the "dime novels"
published by Beadle and Adams from 1860 to 1897.
Volume 1 contains a history of the Beadle firm and
bibliography of the various series of novels. Volume 2
consists of biographical sketches of Beadle authors,
several of whom were women.

   Arey (P)

Blake
Denison (P)
Ellet
Fleming (P)
Logan (P)
[Longstreet] Gildersleeve
Porter
Rowson (P)
Smith, Elizabeth Oakes (P)
Stephens, Ann S. (P)
[Victor] Barritt (P)
Victor, Metta Fuller (P)
Warfield
Whittlesey (P)

181. Joint Committee on North Carolina Literature and
     Bibliography. NORTH CAROLINA FICTION 1734-1957:
     AN ANNOTATED BIBLIOGRAPHY. Edited by William S.
     Powell. Chapel Hill: University of North Carolina
     Library, 1958. 189 pp.

Annotations include plot summaries of fiction by
early nineteenth-century women.

Harper
Hentz
Mason
Stowe
Talbot
Whittlesey

182. Jones, W.A.   "Female Novelists."   DEMOCRATIC
     REVIEW 14 (May 1844): 484-89.

Claims that women excel in writing the novel of
manners and the novel of sentiment. Focuses on English
women but selects Lydia Maria Child, Caroline Kirkland,
and Catharine M. Sedgwick as the best American writers.

[Child] Childs
Kirkland
Sedgwick, Catharine M.

183. Jordan, Alice M.   FROM ROLLO TO TOM SAWYER AND
     OTHER PAPERS. Boston: Horn Book, 1948. 160 pp.

Many female authors are discussed in these essays on nineteenth-century American children's books and periodicals.

Alcott
Child
[Clarke, Rebecca Sophia] May
Cummins
Dodge, Mary Abigail
Dodge, Mary Mapes
Finley
Hale, Sarah Josepha
Larcom
Leslie
Sedgwick, Catharine M.
Sigourney
Stowe
Warner, Anna B.
Warner, Susan
Whitney

184. Josephson, Hannah. "Fame: The Literary Mill Girls." Chap. 9 in THE GOLDEN THREADS: NEW ENGLAND'S MILL GIRLS AND MAGNATES, 178-203. New York: Duell, Sloan and Pearce, 1949.

Discusses THE LOWELL OFFERING and other literary magazines of the New England "mill girls" in the 1840's. Includes information on the backgrounds of several editors and contributors.

Bagley
Cate
Curtis
Farley
Larcom

185. THE JUNIOR BOOK OF AUTHORS. Edited by Stanley J. Kunitz and Howard Haycraft. New York: H.W. Wilson Co., 1934. 400 pp.

Contains one-to-two-page biographical sketches, along with portraits, of writers for children. The second edition (1951), which repeats 160 of the original 268 entries, drops all five of the early nineteenth-century women included in the first edition.

Alcott (P)
Austin (P)
Dodge, Mary Mapes (P)
Hale, Lucretia P. (P)
Stowe (P)

186. Kelley, Mary. "The Literary Domestics: Private
     Women on a Public Stage." In IDEAS IN AMERICA'S
     CULTURES: FROM REPUBLIC TO MASS SOCIETY, edited by
     Hamilton Cravens, 83-102. Ames: Iowa State
     University Press, 1982.

Introduces the infelicitous term "literary
domestics" to replace "sentimentalists" as a
designation for the popular mid-nineteenth-century
women writers. Argues that because they were "branded
by their society with a sense of intellectual
inferiority and guilt that as writers they might be
abandoning their prescribed female domestic role," the
writers were ambivalent about achieving fame.

Cummins
[Fern] Parton
Gilman
Hentz, Caroline Lee
Holmes
McIntosh
Sedgwick, Catharine M.
Southworth, E.D.E.N.
Stowe
Terhune
Warner, Susan
Wilson, Augusta Evans

187. _____. PRIVATE WOMAN, PUBLIC STAGE:
     LITERARY DOMESTICITY IN NINETEENTH-CENTURY
     AMERICA. New York: Oxford University Press, 1984.
     409 pp.

Book-length consideration of the twelve authors
discussed in Kelley's articles; develops the thesis
(see #186) that the writers were ambivalent about
public achievement and insisted on a primary identity
as private domestic beings. Main strength of the book
is the use of primary sources (diaries, letters,
journals) in investigating the authors' motives for
writing and reactions to their literary success.

Weaknesses include dullness and lack of attention
to the authors' works.

Cummins
[Fern] Parton
Gilman
Hentz, Caroline Lee
Holmes
McIntosh
Sedgwick, Catharine M.
Southworth, E.D.E.N.
Stowe
Terhune
Warner, Susan
Wilson, Augusta Evans

188. _____. "The Sentimentalists: Promise and
Betrayal in the Home." SIGNS 4 (Spring 1979):
434-46. Reprinted in FICTION BY AMERICAN WOMEN:
RECENT VIEWS, ed. Winifred Farrant Bevilacqua,
11-19. Port Washington, N.Y.: Associated Faculty
Press, 1983.

Begins with a useful summary of previous criticism
on the "sentimentalists." Goes on to argue, based on
the works of twelve authors, that the sentimentalists
imparted a contradictory message; although they
prescribed an idyll of domesticity, they described a
darker reality in which materialism and rampant
individualism, symbolized by men, made the idealized
home and family impossible to achieve.

Cummins
[Fern] Parton
Gilman
Hentz, Caroline Lee
Holmes
McIntosh
Sedgwick, Catharine M.
Southworth, E.D.E.N.
Stowe
Terhune
Warner, Susan
Wilson, Augusta Evans

189. Kerber, Linda K. WOMEN OF THE REPUBLIC: INTELLECT
AND IDEOLOGY IN REVOLUTIONARY AMERICA. Chapel

Hill: University of North Carolina Press, 1980.
304 pp.

Includes considerable discussion of fiction in the
Revolutionary era, especially in Chapter 8 on women's
reading in the early republic and Chapter 9 on the
republican mother.

    Cushing
    Foster
    Murray
    Sedgwick, Susan Ridley
    Tenney

190. Keysor, Jennie Ellis. SKETCHES OF AMERICAN
     AUTHORS. Vol. 2. New York: Educational
     Publishing Co., 1895. 194 pp.

Consists of separate essays, fifteen to twenty
pages in length, with appended questions and study
outline. Emphasis is biographical rather than
critical.

    Alcott
    Cary, Alice
    Cary, Phoebe

191. Kinney, James. AMALGAMATION! RACE, SEX, AND
     RHETORIC IN THE NINETEENTH-CENTURY AMERICAN NOVEL.
     Westport, Ct.: Greenwood Press, 1985. 259 pp.

Study of miscegenation as portrayed in American
fiction from 1792 to 1914. Chapter 2, "Origins,
1792-1849" and 3, "Abolition and Civil War, 1850-64"
contain substantial discussion of novels by women.
Chapter 3 also considers the "tragic octaroon"
character in relation to the characteristic sentimental
heroine of the time.

    Davis, Rebecca Harding
    Flanders
    [Green] McDougall
    Harper
    Pearson
    Southworth, E.D.E.N.
    Stephens, Harriet Marion
    Stoddard

Stowe
Victor, Metta Fuller
Wilson, Harriet E.

192. Kirkland, Caroline. "Novels and Novelists."
     NORTH AMERICAN REVIEW 76 (January 1853):
     104-123.

     Survey by a novelist of the novel in English,
focusing on fiction by women. Considers American
fiction to be in the "picturesque" or descriptive and
realistic tradition, rather than the romantic or
didactic. Ends with a review of novels by the
Warner sisters.

     Sedgwick, Catharine M.
     Stowe
     Warner, Anna B.
     Warner, Susan

193. Knapp, Samuel L. FEMALE BIOGRAPHY, CONTAINING
     NOTICES OF DISTINGUISHED WOMEN IN DIFFERENT
     NATIONS AND AGES. New York: J. Carpenter, 1834.
     502 pp.

     Approximately one third of the subjects are
American, and several writers are included. Entries
average about five pages, including excerpts from the
writer's works.

     Bleecker
     Faugeres
     Murray
     Rowson

194. Koch, Donald A. Introduction to TEMPEST AND
     SUNSHINE, by Mary Jane Holmes, and THE
     LAMPLIGHTER, by Maria Cummins. New York: Odyssey
     Press, 1968.

     Valuable as a summary of received opinion about
nineteenth-century domestic novels: they were "second-
or third-rate, inferior, and imitative" but succeeded
because they were religious, "thoroughly feminine," and
imparted a sense of security in troubled times.
Includes discussion of the English originals of

American characters ("the domestic novels owed more to
foreign genius than to native originality") and an
interesting and telling comparison of Holmes's TEMPEST
AND SUNSHINE and PEYTON PLACE.

    Cummins
    Holmes
    Warner, Susan

195. Kolba, Ellen D. "Stories for Sale." ENGLISH
     JOURNAL 69 (October 1980): 37-40.

    Brief, popular treatment based on secondary
sources. Summarizes some plots of domestic novels (THE
WIDE, WIDE WORLD, THE LAMPLIGHTER, ST. ELMO) and
discusses their appeal.

    Cummins
    Fern
    Fleming
    Hale, Sarah Josepha
    Southworth, E.D.E.N.
    Warner, Susan
    [Wilson, Augusta Evans] Evans

196. Kolodny, Annette. THE LAND BEFORE HER: FANTASY
     AND EXPERIENCE OF THE AMERICAN FRONTIERS,
     1630-1860. Chapel Hill: University of North
     Carolina Press, 1984. 293 pp.

    Discusses several novelists in exploring women's
private and public responses to the American frontiers.
Three chapters concern the domestic novels with western
settings that became popular in the 1850's. It is
argued that the authors sought to avoid the ills of
industrial North and slave South by looking to the West
for a new locale for domestic fantasies; they projected
on to western landscapes idealized notions of home and
community and the centrality of women's domestic work.

    Bleecker
    Cary, Alice
    Child
    Cummins
    Farnham
    Kirkland
    Pike

Sedgwick, Catharine M.
Sigourney
Soule
Southworth, E.D.E.N.
Stephens, Ann S.

197. "Ladies' Laughter." Chap. 1 in LAUGHING THEIR
     WAY: WOMEN'S HUMOR IN AMERICA, edited by Martha
     Bensley Bruere and Mary Ritter Beard, 1-26. New
     York: Macmillan Co., 1934.

     The first chapter of this anthology contains
humorous passages from fiction by early nineteenth-
century women. The selections are preceded by
editorial comments and brief summary of the life and
work of the author.

     Cooke
     Dodge, Mary Abigail
     Dodge, Mary Mapes
     [Fern] Parton
     Kirkland
     Leslie
     Stephens, Ann S.
     Stowe
     Whitcher

198. Levy, David W. "Racial Stereotypes in Antislavery
     Fiction." PHYLON 26 (Summer 1970): 265-79.

     Contends that the authors of antislavery fiction
employed the same stereotypes of blacks as childish and
stupid that the proslavery writers used. Quotes
extensively from antebellum novels to prove the point.

     Child
     Dall
     Hale, Sarah Josepha
     Pike
     Southworth, E.D.E.N.
     Stowe
     Victor, Metta Fuller

199. LIBERTY'S WOMEN. Edited by Robert McHenry. 1980.
     Reprinted as FAMOUS AMERICAN WOMEN: A
     BIOGRAPHICAL DICTIONARY FROM COLONIAL TIMES TO THE

PRESENT. New York: Dover Publications, 1983.
482 pp.

Contains biographical sketches averaging 400 words
in length; includes many writers. Arranged alphabetically and indexed by field.

Alcott
Bacon, Delia
Bagley
Blake
Booth
Briggs
Brooks, Maria Gowen
Cary, Alice
Cary, Phoebe
Child
Clare
Clarke, Rebecca Sophia
Cooke
Cooper, Sarah Brown Ingersoll
Cooper, Susan Fenimore
Crosby
Cummins
Dall
Davis, Rebecca Harding
Diaz
Dodge, Mary Abigail
Dodge, Mary Mapes
Dorr
Duniway
Eastman
Ellet
Farley
Farnham
[Fern] Parton
Finley
Foster
Fowler
Gilman
Hale, Lucretia P.
Hale, Sarah Josepha
Harper
Haven
Hentz, Caroline Lee
Holmes
Kinzie
Kirkland
Larcom

Latimer
Lippincott
Livermore, Mary A.
Morton
Moulton
Mowatt
Murray
Phelps, Almira H. Lincoln
Pike
Prentiss
Robinson
Rowson
Royall
Sadlier
Sedgwick, Catharine M.
Sigourney
Southworth, E.D.E.N.
Spofford
Stephens, Ann S.
Stowe
Terhune
Victor, Frances Fuller
Victor, Metta Fuller
Warner, Anna B.
Warner, Susan
Whitcher
Whitney
Wilson, Augusta Evans

200. THE LIBRARY OF LITERARY CRITICISM OF ENGLISH AND
     AMERICAN AUTHORS. Edited by Charles Wells Moulton.
     8 vols. Buffalo, N.Y.: Moulton Publishing Co.,
     1901-04.

   Each entry consists of a one-paragraph
biographical notice and two to three pages of excerpts
from the criticism, chronologically arranged. The
volumes are also in chronological order.

Alcott
Bacon, Delia
Cary, Alice
Cary, Phoebe
Child
Dodge, Mary Abigail
Sedgwick, Catharine M.
Sigourney
Stowe

201. LIBRARY OF SOUTHERN LITERATURE. Edited by Edwin
     A. Alderman et al. 17 vols. Atlanta: Martin and
     Hoyt Co., 1909-23. Vol. 15, BIOGRAPHICAL
     DICTIONARY OF AUTHORS, edited by Lucian Lamar
     Knight, reprinted as BIOGRAPHICAL DICTIONARY OF
     SOUTHERN AUTHORS. Detroit: Gale Research Co.,
     1978. 478 pp.

     Anthology of selections from southern authors,
     including biographical sketches and arranged
     alphabetically by author; only five women from the
     early period appear in the first fourteen volumes:
     Mary Bayard Clarke, Caroline Gilman, Mary Ashley
     Townsend, Catharine A. Warfield, and Augusta Evans
     Wilson. Other women are included in the fifteenth
     volume, a compilation of short (usually one-paragraph)
     biographies of "less significant" writers. Dates and
     other information often prove inaccurate.

          Ball, Caroline A.
          Barrow
          Bellamy
          Blake
          Blount
          Bradley
          Bright
          [Butt] Bennett
          Clack
          Clarke, Mary Bayard
          [Cowden] Cowdin
          Crane
          Creswell
          Cross
          Cruse
          Cutler
          Davis, Minnie S.
          Dinnies
          Dorr
          Dorsey, Anna Hanson
          Dorsey, Sarah Anne
          Downing
          DuBose
          Dupuy
          Eastman
          [Elemjay] Ellemjay
          Finley
          Ford
          French
          Gilman

Graves, Adelia C.
Griffith, Mattie
Gwyn
Hentz, Caroline Lee
Hentz, Caroline Therese
Herndon
Holmes
Homes
Jeffrey
Jervey
Ketchum
King
Ladd
[Latimer] Wormeley
Lee, Mary Elizabeth
Lewis
Loughborough
McAdoo
McIntosh
[McLeod] Hulse
Martin
Phelps, Almira H. Lincoln
Preston
Rives
Royall
Schoolcraft
[Shindler] Palmer
Southworth, E.D.E.N.
Terhune
Thomas
Townsend, Mary Ashley
[Upshur] Upshaw
[Walsingham] Walsington
Warfield
Westmoreland
Whitaker
Whittlesey
Williams, Mary Bushnell
Wilson, Augusta Evans
Worthington

202. LIBRARY OF THE WORLD'S BEST LITERATURE. Edited by
    Charles Dudley Warner. 46 vols. New York: J.A.
    Hill & Co., 1896-97.

    Selections "of the best literature and of all
literatures," including works by a few nineteenth-
century American women. Vols. 42 and 43 are a

biographical dictionary that not only covers the
writers represented by selections but is more
comprehensive, providing very basic data (birth dates
and brief list of works) for many other authors.

    Alcott (P)
    Cooke
    Dodge, Mary Mapes (P)
    Spofford (P)
    Stoddard
    Stowe (P)

203. LITERARY HISTORY OF THE UNITED STATES. Edited by
     Robert E. Spiller, Willard Thorp, Thomas H.
     Johnson, Henry Seidel Canby, and Richard M.
     Ludwig. 2 vols. New York: Macmillan Co., 1974
     (1st ed. 1948).

     Standard survey in a format similar to CAMBRIDGE
HISTORY (#51) but including more female authors;
there are paragraph-length discussions of the work of
several early nineteenth-century women. Second volume
contains bibliographies only.

    Alcott
    Child
    Davis, Rebecca Harding
    Foster
    Kirkland
    Rowson
    Sedgwick, Catharine M.
    Sigourney
    Stoddard
    Stowe

204. "Literature." In A GUIDE TO THE STUDY OF THE
     UNITED STATES OF AMERICA: REPRESENTATIVE BOOKS
     REFLECTING THE DEVELOPMENT OF AMERICAN LIFE AND
     THOUGHT, edited by Roy P. Basler, Donald H.
     Mugridge, and Blanche P. McCrum, 1-175.
     Washington, D.C.: Library of Congress, 1960.

     Chapter 1, "Literature," includes brief
descriptions of female authors. Evaluations of their
work are conventional.

    Alcott

Child
Kirkland
Rowson
Stowe

205. THE LITERATURE OF THE AMERICAN PEOPLE. Edited by
Arthur Hobson Quinn. New York: Appleton-Century-
Crofts, 1951. 1172 pp.

Essays by scholars on various genres, arranged
chronologically. Includes paragraph-length references
to nineteenth-century women writers.

Child
Davis, Rebecca Harding
Hale, Sarah Josepha
Kirkland
Mowatt
Rowson
Sedgwick, Catharine M.
Stowe

206. "Literature of the Nineteenth Century." In THE
NORTON ANTHOLOGY OF LITERATURE BY WOMEN: THE
TRADITION IN ENGLISH, edited by Sandra M. Gilbert
and Susan Gubar, 161-947. New York: W.W. Norton
and Co., 1985.

Some American women who wrote in the early part of
the century are included in this first comprehensive
collection of women's writings, but emphasis is on
British authors. Thus, the introduction to the section
on the nineteenth century highlights women's creation
of "a new kind of character, a Byronic heroine" and in
a brief mention of American writers mistakenly refers
to Maria Cummins as the author of THE WIDE, WIDE WORLD.
The biographical sketches and selected bibliographies
of the authors included are accurate.

Alcott
Davis, Rebecca Harding
Harper
[Jacobs] Brent
Stoddard
Stowe
Wilson, Harriet E.

207. LITTLE CLASSICS. Vol. 16, BIOGRAPHICAL SKETCHES
     OF THE AUTHORS REPRESENTED IN THE SERIES. Edited
     by Rossiter Johnson. Boston: James R. Osgood and
     Co., 1875. 262 pp.

     Consists of biographical notices one to two pages
in length; includes only authors whose works are
represented in the series.

     Davis, Rebecca Harding
     Judson
     Spofford
     Walker

208. Lively, Robert A. FICTION FIGHTS THE CIVIL WAR.
     Chapel Hill: University of North Carolina Press,
     1957. 230 pp.

     Female writers are grouped as "the lady
sentimentalists" and said to exhibit in their Civil War
novels "admiration for Christian sacrifice" and
uncritical sectional pride; Louisa May Alcott's WORK
and Lydia Maria Child's A ROMANCE OF THE REPUBLIC
receive the greatest share of ridicule. The author
notes that more than half the pro-South novels of the
war era (in the Wilmer Collection) were written by
women, while only a quarter of the pro-North novels had
female authors.

     Alcott
     Child
     Cruse
     Ford
     Martyn
     Terhune
     Whittlesey
     Wilson, Augusta Evans

209. LIVES OF MISSISSIPPI AUTHORS, 1817-1967. Edited
     by James B. Lloyd. Jackson: University Press of
     Mississippi, 1981. 489 pp.

     Contains a mixture of biographical sketches as
short as one paragraph and longer critical studies of
Mississippi authors who published between 1817 and
1967. Sarah Anne Dorsey, Eliza A. Dupuy, and Catharine
A. Warfield receive the most extensive treatment, with

consideration of their fiction and its relation to that of other women of the nineteenth century.

Dorsey, Sarah Anne
Dupuy
Jeffrey
Warfield

210. Logan, Mrs. John A. [Mary S.]. THE PART TAKEN BY WOMEN IN AMERICAN HISTORY. Wilmington, Del.: Perry-Noble Publishing Co., 1912. 927 pp.

Writers receive short biographical sketches and are included mainly in the section entitled "Women in Professions," pp. 736-882. Sketches can be difficult to locate because there is no logic to their order, and the index is not always reliable.

Alcott (P)
Blake
Cary, Alice (P)
Cary, Phoebe (P)
Child
Dodge, Mary Mapes
Dorsey, Sarah Anne
[Hale, Sarah Josepha] Buell
Larcom (P)
Latimer
Lippincott
Livermore, Mary A.
Moore, Clara Jessup
Moulton (P)
Palmer
Phelps, Almira H. Lincoln
Preston
Sedgwick, Catharine M.
Sigourney (P)
Southworth, E.D.E.N.
Spofford
Stowe
Terhune
Wilson, Augusta Evans

211. Loggins, Vernon. THE NEGRO AUTHOR: HIS DEVELOPMENT IN AMERICA. New York: Columbia University Press, 1931. 480 pp.

In this standard survey, African-American
literature before 1900 is presented as an all-male
affair. Frances E.W. Harper becomes a "puerile" writer
of "poor stories and fair verse," and Harriet A. Jacobs
is dismissed in one sentence--"Linda Brent's story,
INCIDENTS IN THE LIFE OF A SLAVE GIRL (1861), is fairly
readable, probably because of the 'editing' of Lydia
Maria Child." The author identifies Mattie Griffith's
THE AUTOBIOGRAPHY OF A FEMALE SLAVE (1857) as fiction.

      [Griffith, Mattie] Griffiths
      Harper
      [Jacobs] Brent

212. Loshe, Lillie Deming. THE EARLY AMERICAN NOVEL.
     New York: Columbia University Press, 1907. 131
     pp.

      Study of the American novel between 1789 and 1830.
Important source of information on female writers of
the time. Emphasizes "tales of the time-worn didactic
and sentimental types, the brief reign of the
marvellous, [and] the first experimenting with
historical and Indian materials."

      Bleecker
      Cheney
      Child
      Foster
      Morton
      Rowson
      Royall
      Rush, Rebecca
      Sedgwick, Catharine M.
      Tenney
      Warren
      Wells
      Wood, Sally

213. THE LOWELL OFFERING: WRITINGS BY NEW ENGLAND MILL
     WOMEN (1840-1845). Edited by Benita Eisler.
     Philadelphia: J.B. Lippincott Co., 1977. 223 pp.

      Selections from the famous LOWELL OFFERING, a
magazine edited and written by female factory
operatives. Contains fictionalized sketches by several
mill women, along with commentary by the editor.

Bagley
Cate
Farley
Larcom

214. McDowell, Tremaine. "Sensibility in the
     Eighteenth-Century American Novel." STUDIES IN
     PHILOLOGY 24 (July 1927): 383-402.

     Discussion of the importance of sensibility, or
readiness in perceiving and responding to emotional
stimuli, in eighteenth-century American fiction.
Demonstrates the influence of Laurence Sterne on the
early novelists, several of whom were women.

     [Bleecker] Bleeker
     Foster
     Murray
     Rowson

215. Macksey, Joan, and Kenneth Macksey. THE BOOK OF
     WOMEN'S ACHIEVEMENTS. New York: Stein & Day,
     1976. 288 pp.

     Purports to cover all countries and time periods
and includes many writers. Entries are paragraph
length.

     Alcott
     Bagley
     Child
     Crosby
     Hale, Sarah Josepha
     Larcom
     Stephens, Ann S.
     Stowe

216. MacLeod, Anne Scott. A MORAL TALE: CHILDREN'S
     FICTION AND AMERICAN CULTURE, 1820-1860. Hamden,
     Conn.: Archon Books, 1975. 196 pp.

     The most comprehensive and scholarly, if not the
liveliest, account of early nineteenth-century fiction
for children. Focus is on how the fiction reflects the
hopes and fears of the time, the children's literature
being seen as "a testimonial both to the optimism of

the period and to its anxieties." The careers and
works of Lydia Maria Child and Eliza Follen are
discussed in detail.

Abbott
Baker, Harriette Newell Woods
[Baker, Sarah S.] Aunt Friendly
Child
Fern
Follen
Hale, Sarah Josepha
Leslie
McIntosh
[Mayo] Edgarton
Sedgwick, Catharine M.
Sedgwick, E.
Sedgwick, Susan Ridley
Sigourney
Tuthill, Louisa C.

217. McNall, Sally Allen. WHO IS IN THE HOUSE?: A
PSYCHOLOGICAL STUDY OF TWO CENTURIES OF WOMEN'S
FICTION IN AMERICA, 1795 TO THE PRESENT. New
York: Elsevier North-Holland, 1981. 153 pp.

Examination of popular fiction by women based on
psychoanalytic object-relations theory of Melanie
Klein. Views the heroines as ambivalent about
dependency and unable to accomplish the basic
developmental tasks. Emphasis is on the mother-child
relationship and on the ubiquitous house image as a
metaphor for the female body. In the fiction of the
mid-nineteenth century, treated in Chapter 3, heroines
were allowed to achieve greater differentiation and
autonomy than in the fiction of the early national
period (Chapter 2).

Briggs
Chesebro'
Child
Cummins
Downing
[Fern] Parton
Foster
Gilman
Hentz, Caroline Lee
Holmes
Lee, Hannah Farnham

McIntosh
Moore, Mrs. H.J.
Rowson
Sedgwick, Catharine M.
Sigourney
Southworth, E.D.E.N.
Stephens, Ann S.
Tenney
Terhune
Warner, Susan
Warren
[Wilson, Augusta Evans] Evans

218. Manly, Louise. SOUTHERN LITERATURE FROM 1579-
     1895. Richmond, Va.: B.F. Johnson Publishing Co.,
     1895. 514 pp.

     Textbook with brief biographical sketches and
selections; includes a few women.

     Dorsey, Sarah Anne
     Preston
     Terhune
     Wilson, Augusta Evans

219. Manthorne, Jane. "The Lachrymose Ladies." HORN
     BOOK 43 (June 1967): 375-84; (Aug. 1967): 501-13;
     (Oct. 1967): 622-30.

     Patronizing account of mid-nineteenth-century
bestsellers. Focuses on the attitudes and fictional
heroines of Susan Warner, Maria Cummins, and Martha
Finley.

     Cummins
     Finley
     Warner, Susan

220. Marshall, Alice Kahler. PEN NAMES OF WOMEN
     WRITERS FROM 1600 TO THE PRESENT. Camp Hill, Pa.:
     Alice Marshall, 1985. 181 pp.

     This compendium of pseudonyms of female authors
also contains portraits and miscellaneous information
useful in the study of nineteenth-century American
writers. There are cartoons, quotations from

contemporary periodicals about women writing, and
quotations from the authors themselves.

Alcott (P)
Dodge, Mary Abigail
Dorr (P)
Fern (P)
Gage (P)
Haven (P)
Kirkland (P)
Leslie (P)
Lippincott (P)
Sedgwick, Catharine M. (P)
Sigourney (P)
Southworth, E.D.E.N. (P)
Stowe (P)

221. Martin, Terence. THE INSTRUCTED VISION: SCOTTISH
     COMMON SENSE PHILOSOPHY AND THE ORIGINS OF
     AMERICAN FICTION. Bloomington: Indiana University
     Press, 1961. 197 pp.

     Includes some women in a brief discussion of early
novelists and their attitudes toward fiction as
expressed in the prefaces to their novels.

     Bleecker
     Foster
     Manvill
     Read, Martha
     Rowson
     Tenney
     Vickery

222. _____. "Social Institutions in the Early
     American Novel." AMERICAN QUARTERLY 9 (Spring
     1957): 72-84.

     Discussion of the institutions of nation and
family as presented in American fiction before 1820.
Refers only briefly to individual novels but includes a
constructed plot summary of a "typical though
nonexistent early American novel" by "an American
Lady."

     Foster
     Rowson

Rush, Rebecca
[Warren] Vickery

223. MASTERPIECES OF THE WORLD'S LITERATURE. Edited by
     Harry Thurston Peck. 20 vols. New York: American
     Literary Society, 1899.

     Selections are arranged alphabetically by author;
each is prefaced by a short biographical sketch.
Several nineteenth-century American women are included.

     Alcott
     Cummins
     Davis, Rebecca Harding
     Hale, Sarah Josephine
     Moulton
     Spofford
     Stowe
     Warner, Susan
     Whitney

224. Meserole, Harrison T. "The 'Famous BOSTON POST
     List': Mid-Nineteenth Century American
     Bestsellers." PAPERS OF THE BIBLIOGRAPHICAL
     SOCIETY OF AMERICA 52 (1958): 93-110.

     Compilation in chart form of sales figures
provided by a correspondent of the BOSTON POST in 1859.
Includes several novels published by women in the
1850's.

     Cummins
     [Fern] Parton
     Ford
     Hentz, Caroline Lee
     Holmes
     Hubbell, Martha
     Stowe
     Terhune
     Warner, Susan
     Whitcher

225. Mitchell, Donald G. AMERICAN LANDS AND LETTERS.
     New York: Charles Scribner's Sons, 1897. 402 pp.

     Early literary history restricted in coverage to

writers born before 1800. Catharine M. Sedgwick and
Lydia Sigourney are given serious treatment.

    Brooks, Maria Gowen
    Gilman
    Sedgwick, Catharine M.
    Sigourney

226. Moses, Montrose J. "Concerning Now and Then."
    Chap. 4 in CHILDREN'S BOOKS AND READING. New
    York: Mitchell Kennerley, 1907.

    Contains an "English Table" and an "American
Table" consisting of one-paragraph summaries of
information about nineteenth-century authors of
children's books; arrangement is chronological by
author's birth date. Includes more women than is
usually the case, but dates are often inaccurate.

    Andrews
    Baker, Harriette Newell Woods
    Browne, Maria J.B.
    Browne, Sara H.
    Cheney
    Child
    Clark
    Davis, Caroline E.
    Gilman
    Hale, Sarah Josepha
    Haven
    Lee, Mary Elizabeth
    Leslie
    McIntosh
    Martyn
    [Porter] Emerson
    Sedgwick, Catharine M.
    Sedgwick, Susan Ridley
    Shindler
    Sigourney
    Smith, Elizabeth Oakes
    Stowe
    Trowbridge
    [Tuthill, Cornelia] Pierson
    Tuthill, Louisa C.
    Warner, Susan

227. Mott, Frank Luther. GOLDEN MULTITUDES: THE STORY

OF BEST SELLERS IN THE UNITED STATES.   New York:
Macmillan Co., 1947. 357 pp.

Standard source on best sellers, defining them as
books that had a sale equal to one percent of the U.S.
population during the decade published. Provides lists
of the best sellers and runners up and discussion of
numerous nineteenth-century women and their novels.

    Alcott
    Cummins
    Dodge, Mary Mapes
    Foster
    Harris
    Holmes
    Lee, Hannah Farham
    Rowson
    Sigourney
    Southworth, E.D.E.N.
    Stephens, Ann S.
    Stowe
    Warner, Susan
    Whitney
    [Wilson, Augusta Evans] Evans

228. Musgrave, Marian E.   "Patterns of Violence and
     Non-Violence in Pro-Slavery and Anti-Slavery
     Fiction."   COLLEGE LANGUAGE ASSOCIATION JOURNAL 16
     (June 1973): 426-37.

Finds racist attitudes, especially "a deep-seated
horror of black violence and revenge, and a fascinated
willingness to see horror and violence visited upon
Blacks," in both pro- and anti-slavery fiction by men
and women before the Civil War.

    Pike
    Rowson
    Schoolcraft
    Stowe

229. Mussell, Kay. WOMEN'S GOTHIC AND ROMANTIC
     FICTION: A REFERENCE GUIDE. Westport, Ct.:
     Greenwood Press, 1981.

Wide-ranging guide to research on women's gothic
and romantic fiction with the two forms broadly

defined.   Refers often to nineteenth-century American
writers, especially in the interpretive Chapter 1,
"History of Women's Gothic and Romantic Fiction," but
also in the bibliographic essays that follow.
Individual authors are discussed in Chapter 2 and
literary criticism surveyed in Chapter 4.

> Child
> Cummins
> Foster
> Hale, Sarah Josepha
> Hentz, Caroline Lee
> Holmes
> Rowson
> Sedgwick, Catharine M.
> Sigourney
> Smith, Elizabeth Oakes
> Southworth, E.D.E.N.
> Spofford
> Stephens, Ann S.
> Terhune
> Warner, Anna B.
> Warner, Susan
> Wilson, Augusta Evans
> Wood, Sally

230. THE NATIONAL EXPOSITION SOUVENIR: WHAT AMERICA
     OWES TO WOMEN.   Edited by Lydia Hoyt Farmer.
     Buffalo: Charles Wells Moulton, 1893.   505 pp.

Compilation of women's achievements, similar in
many ways to A WOMAN OF THE CENTURY (#376), and
intended as a souvenir of the Columbian Exposition.
The section "Women in Literature" contains three
essays: "Women in Literature and Poetry" by the editor,
"Women Fiction Writers of America" by Ellen Olney Kirk,
and "Women Journalists in America" by Susan E.
Dickinson; these are surveys that mention many names
but devote no more than a sentence or two to any one
author.

> Austin (P)
> Dodge, Mary Mapes (P)
> Larcom (P)

231. Nelson, John Herbert.   THE NEGRO CHARACTER IN
     AMERICAN LITERATURE.   College Park, Md.: McGrath

Publishing Co., 1926. 146 pp.

Scholarly but outdated treatment. Considers UNCLE
TOM'S CABIN "artistically poor" and many other women's
novels "feeble imitations" of Stowe's work.
Apparently, the creators of "American literature" are
white, as Nelson claims that "few American negroes have
been true makers of literature"; he gives an inadequate
list and calls Frances E.W. Harper's work "crude."

Child
Eastman
Flanders
Gilman
Griffith
Holmes
[Jacobs] Brent
Little
[Pearson] Pierson
Pike
Southworth, E.D.E.N.
Stowe
Victor, Metta Fuller

232. Neuberg, Victor. THE POPULAR PRESS COMPANION TO
     POPULAR LITERATURE. Bowling Green, Ohio: Bowling
     Green State University Popular Press, 1983.
     207 pp.

Dictionary-style guide to popular literature, with
emphasis on British authors. Principles of selection
are questionable--for instance, Maria Cummins is
included and Susan Warner omitted.

Cummins
Southworth, E.D.E.N.
Stowe
Victor, Metta Fuller

233. New York Public Library. INDEPENDENCE: A LITERARY
     PANORAMA, 1770-1850, edited by Lola L. Szladits.
     New York: New York Public Library and Readex
     Books, 1975. 72 pp.

Catalog of exhibit using materials from the Berg
Collection of American literature. Includes specific
mention of contributions of female writers in the

foreword, plus description of works by several
nineteenth-century women.

> Child
> Hale, Sarah Josepha
> Sedgwick, Catharine M.
> Sigourney

234. NINETEENTH-CENTURY LITERATURE CRITICISM: EXCERPTS
FROM CRITICISM OF THE WORKS OF NOVELISTS, POETS,
PLAYWRIGHTS, SHORT STORY WRITERS, AND OTHER
CREATIVE WRITERS WHO DIED BETWEEN 1800 AND 1900,
FROM THE FIRST PUBLISHED CRITICAL APPRAISALS TO
CURRENT EVALUATIONS. Edited by Laurie Lanzen
Harris et al. 8 vols. Detroit: Gale Research,
1981-85.

Entries provide a short biographical sketch, list
of major works, selections from the criticism, and
selected bibliography of secondary sources.

> Alcott (P)
> Child (P)
> Rowson (P)
> Stowe (P)

235. Nirenberg, Morton. THE RECEPTION OF AMERICAN
LITERATURE IN GERMAN PERIODICALS, 1820-1850.
Heidelberg: Carl Winter, 1970. 130 pp.

In Chapter 5, the reception in Germany of works by
Catharine M. Sedgwick, Sarah Josepha Hale, and Lydia
Maria Child is discussed. Sedgwick was by far "the
most popular authoress" in Germany in the first half of
the nineteenth century.

> Child
> Hale, Sarah Josepha
> Sedgwick, Catharine M.

236. Noel, Mary. VILLAINS GALORE: THE HEYDAY OF THE
POPULAR STORY WEEKLY. New York: Macmillan Co.,
1954. 320 pp.

Detailed account of the "story paper," or literary
newspaper, from its rise in the 1830's to its decline

in the 1880's. Many of the contributors were women.
Fiction of E.D.E.N. Southworth and Ann S. Stephens is
discussed at length. The study is based on original
research but lacks documentation.

> Alcott
> Cary, Alice
> Dall
> Dupuy
> Fern
> Fleming
> [Haven] Neal
> Holmes
> Leslie
> Moise
> Sigourney
> Southworth, E.D.E.N.
> Stephens, Ann S.
> Vaughan
> Victor, Metta Fuller

237. NORTH CAROLINA AUTHORS: A SELECTIVE HANDBOOK.
Chapel Hill: University of North Carolina Library,
1952. 136 pp.

A few nineteenth-century women are included in
this handbook containing one-page biographical sketches
of authors considered by a joint committee of the North
Carolina Library Association and the North Carolina
English Teachers Association to be the "most
significant in the North Carolina literary scene."

> Clarke, Mary Bayard
> Gales
> Hentz, Caroline Lee
> Mason

238. THE NORTON ANTHOLOGY OF AMERICAN LITERATURE.
Edited by Nina Baym et al. 2nd ed. Vol. 1. New
York: W.W. Norton and Co., 1985. 2535 pp.

The second edition of this standard anthology
breaks new ground in including fiction by early
nineteenth-century women other than Harriet Beecher
Stowe. "Two newly rediscovered works," a short story
by Elizabeth Drew Stoddard and LIFE IN THE IRON-MILLS
by Rebecca Harding Davis have been added. The

introductions to the selections are two to three pages
in length.

Davis, Rebecca Harding
Stoddard
Stowe

239. NOTABLE AMERICAN WOMEN, 1607-1950. Edited by
Edward T. James. 3 vols. Cambridge, Mass.:
Belknap Press of Harvard University Press, 1971.

The major biographical source covering American
women in all fields. Includes numerous early
nineteenth-century writers, though not as many as the
DICTIONARY OF AMERICAN BIOGRAPHY (#88), after which it
is patterned. Each entry contains a short
bibliography.

Alcott
Andrews
Bacon, Delia
Bagley
Blake
Bleecker
Booth
Botta
Briggs
Brooks, Maria Gowen
Cary, Alice
Cary, Phoebe
Child
Clare
Clarke, Mary Bayard
Clarke, Rebecca Sophia
Cooke
Cooper, Sarah Brown Ingersoll
Cooper, Susan Fenimore
Crosby
Cummins
Davis, Rebecca Harding
Denison
Diaz
Dodge, Mary Abigail
Dodge, Mary Mapes
Dorsey, Sarah Anne
Duniway
Dupuy
Eastman

Ellet
Farley
Farnham
[Fern] Parton
Finley
Follen
Foster
Fowler
Gage
Gilman
Hale, Lucretia P.
Hale, Sarah Josepha
Hanaford
Harper
Haven
Hentz, Caroline Lee
Holmes
Judson
Kinzie
Kirkland
Larcom
Leslie
Lippincott
Livermore, Mary A.
Logan
McIntosh
Moore, Clara Jessup
Morton
Moulton
Mowatt
Murray
Nichols
Phelps, Almira H. Lincoln
Phelps, Elizabeth Stuart
Pike
Prentiss
Preston
Rowson
Royall
Sadlier
Sawyer
Sedgwick, Catharine M.
Sigourney
Smith, Elizabeth Oakes
Smith, Margaret Bayard
Soule
Southworth, E.D.E.N.
Spofford
Stephens, Ann S.

Stowe
Tenney
Terhune
Turner
Tuthill, Louisa C.
Victor, Frances Fuller
Victor, Metta Fuller
Warner, Anna B.
Warner, Susan
Whitcher
Whitney
Wilson, Augusta Evans
Wood, Julia Amanda Sargent
Wood, Sally

240. NOTABLE WOMEN OF PENNSYLVANIA. Edited by Gertrude
     Bosler Biddle and Sarah Dickinson Lowrie.
     Philadelphia: University of Pennsylvania Press,
     1942. 307 pp.

     Consists of biographical essays, one to three
pages in length, prepared by the Committee of 1926,
Philadelphia Sesquicentennial Celebration; each essay
is signed. Arrangement is chronological by birth date.

     Davis, Rebecca Harding
     Hale, Sarah Josepha
     Leslie
     [Lippincott] Greenwood
     Preston

241. NOVELISTS AND PROSE WRITERS. Vol. 2 of GREAT
     WRITERS OF THE ENGLISH LANGUAGE, edited by James
     Vinson. New York: St. Martin's Press, 1979.
     1367 pp.

     Follows the same format as other titles in the
series: a few biographical facts about the author, a
list of primary and secondary works, and a brief
assessment (about two pages) by a scholar of the
author's contribution to literature. Principles of
selection are unclear (for instance, N.P. Willis is
included but not his sister Fanny Fern, T.S. Arthur but
not Susan Warner); however, for the nineteenth-century
female writers included, the source may provide one of
the few thoughtful assessments available.

Alcott
Davis, Rebecca Harding
Foster
Rowson
Sedgwick, Catharine M.
Stowe

242. Nye, Russel B. "The Novel as Dream and Weapon:
Women's Popular Novels in the 19th Century."
HISTORICAL SOCIETY OF MICHIGAN CHRONICLE 11 (4th
Quarter 1975): 2-16.

Describes the women's novels as "moral " and
"sentimental" but also "quite realistic"; identifies
four basic story lines in the fiction: fall and rise,
pursuit, domestic tragedy, and achievement of female
independence.

Hentz, Caroline Lee
Holmes
Southworth, E.D.E.N.
[Terhune] Harland
Wilson, Augusta Evans

243. _____. THE UNEMBARRASSED MUSE: THE POPULAR
ARTS IN AMERICA. New York: Dial Press, 1970.
497 pp.

Includes cursory discussion of popular
nineteenth-century women writers, mostly in Chapter 1,
"Stories for the People." Finds four basic plots in
the "domestic novel": decline and rise, pursuit,
renunciation, and domestic tragedy.

Cary, Alice
Cary, Phoebe
Cummins
Fern
Fleming
Hentz, Caroline Lee
Holmes
Mowatt
Rowson
Southworth, E.D.E.N.
Victor, Metta Fuller
[Wilson, Augusta Evans] Evans

244. Oberholtzer, Ellis Paxson. THE LITERARY HISTORY
     OF PHILADELPHIA. Philadelphia: George W. Jacobs
     and Co., 1906. 433 pp.

     Some nineteenth-century women are briefly
discussed.

     Alcott
     Hale, Sarah Josepha (P)
     [Haven] Neal (P)
     Leslie (P)
     Lippincott

245. O'Donnell, Thomas F. "Oneida County: Literary
     Highlights." In UPSTATE LITERATURE: ESSAYS IN
     MEMORY OF THOMAS F. O'DONNELL, edited by Frank
     Bergmann, 39-69. Syracuse, N.Y.: Syracuse
     University Press, 1985.

     In the course of a survey of the contributions to
literature of residents of Oneida County, New York,
Frances M. Whitcher and other nineteenth-century women
are discussed.

     Berry
     [Judson] Chubbock
     Whitcher

246. O'Harra, Downing Palmer. "Book Publishing in the
     United States to 1901." PUBLLSHERS' WEEKLY, March
     23, 1929, 1496-1500.

     Includes a list of books published and widely sold
in the U.S. from colonial times to 1860 with the
approximate number of copies sold. Several female
authors of the 1850's are represented. List is less
accurate than the one in Meserole (#224).

     Cummins
     Fern
     Stowe
     [Terhune] Harland
     Warner, Susan

247. OLD MAIDS: SHORT STORIES BY NINETEENTH CENTURY
     U.S. WOMEN WRITERS. Edited by Susan Koppelman.

Boston: Pandora Press, 1984.   237 pp.

Anthology of short fiction about unmarried women.
Contains short biographies of each author,
introduction, and afterword.   Many of the authors
represented wrote before 1870.   As the editor notes,
although most short story collections include only
the most recent female or non-white writers, "a careful
study of the history of the short story genre makes it
clear that women writers predominated in the early
years of its development, creating the bulk of the
stories written from the 1830's to the 1880's."

Carter
Cary, Alice
Cooke
Davis, Rebecca Harding
Graves, Mrs. A.J.
Harper
King
Pindar
Sedgwick, Catharine M.
[Terhune] Harland
Vaughan

248. THE ONE HUNDRED BEST BOOKS BY AMERICAN WOMEN
DURING THE PAST HUNDRED YEARS 1833-1933.   Edited
by Anita Browne.   Chicago: Associated Authors
Service, 1933.   128 pp.

Account of the "best books" in all fields, as
selected by a committee of male and female writers and
academics.   Includes brief biographies of the authors
and one-to-two-page discussions of the books.   Early
nineteenth-century authors are most heavily
represented in the "Juvenile" category; three (Maria
Cummins, Harriet Beecher Stowe, and Augusta Evans
Wilson) appear under "Fiction" and others in other
sections.

Alcott
Cary, Alice
Cary, Phoebe
Child
Clarke, Rebecca Sophia
Cummins
Dodge, Mary Mapes
Finley

Hale, Lucretia P.
Hale, Sarah Josepha
Larcom
Livermore, Mary A.
Moulton
[Mowatt] Ritchie
Stowe
Terhune
Warner, Susan
Wilson, Augusta Evans

249. Orgain, Kate Alma. SOUTHERN AUTHORS IN POETRY AND
     PROSE. New York: Neale Publishing Co., 1908.
     233 pp.

     Contains three-to-four-page biographical sketches
and short selections from the works of several writers.
Has no introduction or explanation of the choice of
authors or selections.

Bellamy
French
[Jeffrey] Johnson
McIntosh
[Shindler] Dana-Shindler
Terhune
Warfield
[Wilson, Augusta Evans] Evans

250. Orians, G. Harrison. "Censure of Fiction in
     American Romances and Magazines, 1789-1810." PMLA
     52 (March 1937): 195-214.

     Several early female novelists are quoted as
either defending or attacking fiction in their works.
The author's thesis is that novels were an anathema to
a large part of the public, particularly that part
outside the circle of female readers, creating a frigid
atmosphere for the ambitious novelist.

Foster
Rowson
Tenney
Warren
[Vicery] Vicery, Eliza
Wood, Sally

251. _____. A SHORT HISTORY OF AMERICAN
LITERATURE: ANALYZED BY DECADES. New York: F.S.
Crofts and Co., 1940. 314 pp.

Outline-style American literary history presented
decade by decade. Descriptive paragraphs on female
authors are generally found under "Lesser Writers."
Only partially indexed.

Bacon, Delia
Brooks, Maria Gowen
Child
Cooke
Cummins
Davis, Rebecca Harding
Dupuy
Fern
Hale, Sarah Josepha
Hentz, Caroline Lee
Holmes
Kirkland
Leslie
Rowson
Rush, Rebecca
Sedgwick, Catharine M.
Sigourney
Southworth, E.D.E.N.
Spofford
Stoddard
Stowe
Tenney
[Terhune] Harland
Warren
Warner, Susan
Whitcher
Wilson, Augusta Evans
Wood, Sally

252. OUR FAMOUS WOMEN: AN AUTHORIZED RECORD OF THE
LIVES AND DEEDS OF DISTINGUISHED AMERICAN WOMEN OF
OUR TIMES. Edited by Elizabeth Stuart Phelps
Ward. Hartford: A.D. Worthington, 1883. 715 pp.

About half the women are authors. The
biographical sketches range from fifteen to twenty-five
pages and emphasize life over works; they were composed
by women who were themselves famous writers, so that
Rose Terry Cooke writes on Harriet Beecher Stowe, Stowe

on A.D.T. Whitney, Whitney on Lucy Larcom, etc.

Alcott (P)
Booth
Child
Cooke (P)
Dodge, Mary Mapes (P)
Larcom (P)
Livermore, Mary A. (P)
Moulton (P)
Prentiss
Spofford (P)
Stowe (P)
Terhune (P)
Whitney (P)

253. OUR HIDDEN HERITAGE: PENNSYLVANIA WOMEN IN
HISTORY. Edited by Janice H. McElroy. Allentown:
Pennsylvania Division of the American Association
of University Women, 1983. 440 pp.

Consists of one-to-two-page biographical sketches;
several writers are included.

Hale, Sarah Josepha
[Lippincott] Greenwood, Grace (P)
Preston (P)
Royall

254. THE OVEN BIRDS: AMERICAN WOMEN ON WOMANHOOD,
1820-1920. Edited by Gail Parker. Garden City,
N.Y.: Doubleday and Co., 1972. 387 pp.

Early but still useful collection of writings by
nineteenth-century women, including prose by Lydia
Sigourney, Lydia Maria Child, and Harriet Beecher
Stowe. Lengthy and insightful introduction tries to
show that "the history of American feminism and
literary history must be studied simultaneously if any
sense is to be made of the rise and fall of the women's
movement in America." The literary "ideology of
Sentimentalism" is viewed as leading to the "crippling
gentility" that was vitiating the women's movement at
the end of the century.

Child
Sigourney

255. THE OXFORD COMPANION TO AMERICAN LITERATURE.
     Edited by James David Hart. New York: Oxford
     University Press, 1983 (1st ed. 1941). 896 pp.

     Dictionary-style handbook with short biographies
of authors and summaries of literary works.
Evaluations are conventional (Lydia Maria Child's
fiction is "didactic rather than creative"; Lydia
Sigourney's "lugubrious preoccupation with death caused
her to look at every sick child as a potential angel").
Coverage is more comprehensive than in the standard
literary histories. One wonders, however, why the
recent edition, which contains many new entries, omits
important African-American writers like Frances E.W.
Harper and Harriet A. Jacobs.

      Alcott
      Andrews
      Austin
      Bacon, Delia
      Bleecker
      Brooks, Maria Gowen
      Cary, Alice
      Cary, Phoebe
      Child
      Cooke
      Cooper, Susan Fenimore
      Cummins
      Davis, Rebecca Harding
      Dodge, Mary Abigail
      Dodge, Mary Mapes
      Dupuy
      Embury
      Farley
      Finley
      Foster
      Hale, Sarah Josepha
      Holmes
      Judson
      Kirkland
      Larcom
      Lee, Eliza Buckminster
      Leslie
      Lippincott
      Morton
      Moulton

Mowatt
Parker
Phelps, Elizabeth Stuart
Pike
Prentiss
Preston
Rowson
Royall
Rush, Rebecca
Sedgwick, Catharine M.
Sedgwick, Susan Ridley
Sigourney
Smith, Elizabeth Oakes
Smith, Margaret Bayard
Southworth, E.D.E.N.
Spofford
Stephens, Ann S.
Stoddard
Stowe
Tenney
Terhune
Townsend, Mary Ashley
Victor, Frances Fuller
Victor, Metta Fuller
Warner, Anna B.
Warner, Susan
Warren
Wells
Whitcher
[Wilson, Augusta Evans] Evans
Wood, Sally

256. Page, Thomas Nelson. "Authorship in the South
     before the War." LIPPINCOTT'S MAGAZINE 44 (July
     1889): 105-20. Reprinted in THE OLD SOUTH:
     ESSAYS SOCIAL AND POLITICAL, 57-92. New York:
     Charles Scribner's Sons, 1892.

     Women are treated as an inferior "class of
writers" who portray southern life in an unreal
romantic light. An exception is made for Mary Virginia
Terhune, who uses more artistry and is "entitled to
stand in a class by herself."

     Hentz, Caroline Lee
     Southworth, E.D.E.N.
     Terhune

257. Papashvily, Helen Waite. ALL THE HAPPY ENDINGS: A
     STUDY OF THE DOMESTIC NOVEL IN AMERICA, THE WOMEN
     WHO WROTE IT, THE WOMEN WHO READ IT, IN THE
     NINETEENTH CENTURY. New York: Harper & Brothers,
     1956. 231 pp.

        Competent study of popular novels written by women
   of the century. Asserts, without providing much
   evidence, that the domestic novels were "handbooks of
   feminine revolt," communicating female grievances
   beneath the surface. Focus is on Martha Finley,
   Caroline Lee Hentz, Mary Jane Holmes, Susanna Rowson,
   E.D.E.N. Southworth, Harriet Beecher Stowe, Mary
   Virginia Terhune, Susan Warner, and Augusta Evans
   Wilson.

            Cummins
            Fern
            Finley
            Fleming
            Follen
            Foster
            Gilman
            Hale, Sarah Josepha
            Hentz, Caroline Lee
            Holmes
            [Judson] Chubbuck
            Lee, Hannah Farham
            Manvill
            Rowson
            Sedgwick, Catharine M.
            Sigourney
            Southworth, E.D.E.N.
            Stephens, Ann S.
            Stowe
            Tenney
            [Terhune] Harland
            Victor, Metta Fuller
            Warner, Anna B.
            Warner, Susan
            [Wilson, Augusta Evans] Evans

258. "A Patchwork Piece: The Nineteenth-Century
     American Women's Fiction Project." WOMEN'S
     STUDIES QUARTERLY 10 (Fall 1982): 35-40.

        Description by Wellesley College students and
   Peggy McIntosh, project director, of a two-year project

in which students examined nineteenth-century American
literature anthologies and syllabi and then read works
by women that might expand the male-dominated canon.
Accounts by the participants emphasize their initial
difficulty in reading these works and the necessity of
"unlearning" much of their training in literary
criticism.

Cary, Alice
Davis, Rebecca Harding

259. Pattee, Fred Lewis. THE DEVELOPMENT OF THE
     AMERICAN SHORT STORY. New York: Harper and
     Brothers, 1923. 388 pp.

Characterizes literature between 1849 and 1860 as
"an orgy of feminine sentimentalism and emotionalism."
Female writers had a "cheapening and retrogressive"
effect on fiction: the women lacked "constructive art"
and "vitality," and "sadly they degraded diction and
style." Caroline Kirkland is viewed as the only
exception. The book is of interest despite the biases
because of the bibliographies. For each decade there
is a list of "leading short stories of the decade";
"leading" is unfortunately not defined but may mean
"popular" since the works of numerous women (several in
addition to those discussed by Pattee and listed below)
are included.

Cooke
Davis, Rebecca Harding
Hale, Sarah Josepha
Holmes
Kirkland
Leslie
[Lippincott] Greenwood
Sedgwick, Catharine M.
Spofford
Stowe

260. _____. THE FEMININE FIFTIES. Port
     Washington, N.Y.: Kennikat Press, 1966 (1st ed.
     1940). 339 pp.

Social and literary history of the 1850's in the
U.S. Considers the decade "feminine" because it was
"fervid, fevered, furious, fatuous, fertile, feeling,

florid, furbelowed, fighting, and funny." In Chapters
5 and 9, which deal exclusively with women writers,
"scribbling women" are alternately patronized and
attacked. The book is full of erroneous judgments,
such as the comment that Caroline Kirkland
"romanticized new Western settlements" in her fiction.

> Cary, Alice (P)
> Cary, Phoebe (P)
> Cooke
> Cummins
> Fern (P)
> Hale, Sarah Josepha (P)
> [Haven] Neal
> Hentz, Caroline Lee
> Holmes
> [Judson] Forester
> Kirkland
> Larcom
> [Lippincott] Greenwood (P)
> Sigourney
> Smith, Elizabeth Oakes
> Southworth
> Stephens, Ann S. (P)
> Stowe (P)
> Warner, Anna B. (P)
> Warner, Susan (P)
> Whitcher
> Wilson, Augusta Evans (P)

261. _____. THE FIRST CENTURY OF AMERICAN
     LITERATURE, 1770-1870. New York: D. Appleton-
     Century Co., 1935. 613 pp.

Repeats the author's earlier judgments of female
writers, particularly in Chapter 35, "The Feminine
Fifties." Women polluted the literary air: "And to
think of the masculine Melville and Hawthorne and
Thoreau condemned to work through their literary lives
in an atmosphere like that."

> Cary, Alice
> Cary, Phoebe
> Foster
> Hale, Sarah Josepha
> Morton
> Rowson
> Sedgwick, Catharine M.

Stowe

262. _____. A HISTORY OF AMERICAN LITERATURE.
New York: Silver, Burdett and Co., 1899. 475 pp.

Hardly mentions women before the Civil War, except
for one page on Catharine M. Sedgwick and four on
Harriet Beecher Stowe (as opposed to five on Nathaniel
Willis and six on E.C. Stedman). Then, Chapter 28,
entitled "Woman in Literature," claims that women made
a great advance in literature after the war so that
their work can now "command equal respect and equal
compensation."

    Austin
    Cary, Alice
    Cooke
    Larcom
    Preston
    Sedgwick, Catharine M.
    Sigourney
    Spofford
    Stowe

263. Pearce, Roy Harvey. "Red Gifts and White: The
Image in Fiction." In THE SAVAGES OF AMERICA: A
STUDY OF THE INDIAN AND THE IDEA OF CIVILIZATION,
196-236. Baltimore: Johns Hopkins Press, 1953.

Analysis of portrayal of Native Americans in
fiction between 1790 and 1850 stressing the idea of
savagism (the assumption of a total opposition between
savage and civilized life with the former being morally
inferior). Emphasis on male writers with brief
discussion of female novelists.

    Bleecker
    Child
    Cushing
    Sedgwick, Catharine M.

264. Pearson, Edmund. DIME NOVELS; OR, FOLLOWING AN
OLD TRAIL IN POPULAR LITERATURE. Boston: Little,
Brown and Co., 1929. 280 pp.

Account of the popular "dime novels," first
published in 1860 by Beadle and Adams. Includes

excerpts from Ann S. Stephens' MALAESKA, the first dime
novel, and information about Stephens and Metta Fuller
Victor.

> Fleming
> Stephens, Ann S.
> Victor, Metta Fuller

265. THE PENGUIN COMPANION TO AMERICAN LITERATURE.
Edited by Malcolm Bradbury, Eric Mottram, and Jean
Franco. New York: McGraw-Hill Book Co., 1971
384 pp.

Dictionary-style handbook on U.S. and Latin
American literature. Emphasizes the twentieth century.
Selection of writers from the earlier periods is very
odd.

> Alcott
> Cary, Phoebe
> Clare
> Rowson
> Stowe

266. Petter, Henri. THE EARLY AMERICAN NOVEL.
Columbus: Ohio State University Press, 1971.
500 pp.

Survey of American novels from 1775 to 1820.
Updates Loshe's study (#212) and also includes much
material on female writers. There is a whole chapter
devoted to Susanna Rowson and another on Tabitha
Tenney's FEMALE QUIXOTISM. Contains a useful appendix
of plot synopses.

> Bleecker
> Botsford
> Foster
> Manvill
> Murray
> Patterson
> Pope
> Read, Martha
> Rowson
> Rush, Rebecca
> Sansay
> Savage

Sigourney
Tenney
Vickery
Warren
Wells
Wood, Sally

267. Pickett, LaSalle Corbell. ACROSS MY PATH:
     MEMORIES OF PEOPLE I HAVE KNOWN. Freeport, N.Y.:
     Books for Libraries Press, 1970 (1st ed. 1916).
     148 pp.

     Short (five to ten pages) anecdotal sketches of
nineteenth-century women with whom the author was
acquainted.

     Alcott
     Larcom
     Livermore, Mary A.
     Moulton
     Mowatt

268. Pierson, Ralph. "A Few Literary Highlights of
     1851-52." AMERICAN BOOK COLLECTOR 2 (Aug./Sept.
     1932): 156-60.

     Mainly a discussion of the sales and reception of
UNCLE TOM'S CABIN; includes brief descriptions of
other North-South novels by women.

     Eastman
     Hale, Sarah Josepha
     Stowe

269. Poe, Edgar Allan. "The Literati of New York
     City." In THE COMPLETE WORKS OF EDGAR ALLAN POE,
     edited by James A. Harrison, vol. 15, 1-137. New
     York: Thomas Y. Crowell and Co., 1902. (First
     published in GODEY'S LADY'S BOOK, May-October
     1846.)

     Poe gives his "unbiased opinion" of thirty-eight
New York writers, about a third of them female. The
sketches, usually two to three pages in length,
evaluate the author's work and then briefly describe
his/her character and physique.

  Bogart
  [Botta] Lynch
  Child
  Embury
  Kirkland
  Mowatt
  [Nichols] Gove
  Sedgwick, Catharine M.
  Stephens, Ann S.

270. Powers, Alfred. A HISTORY OF OREGON LITERATURE.
  Portland, Ore.: Metropolitan Press, 1935.   809 pp.

  Comprehensive treatment of the subject. Notes the
rapid growth of fiction in Oregon in the second decade
of settlement and discusses three female pioneers.
Includes excerpts from fiction by Abigail Scott
Duniway.

  Bailey
  Duniway (P)
  Victor, Frances Fuller (P)

271. PROVISIONS: A READER FROM 19TH-CENTURY AMERICAN
  WOMEN. Edited by Judith Fetterley. Bloomington:
  Indiana University Press, 1985.   467 pp.

  Anthology of prose written by American women
between 1830 and 1865. Includes some short pieces in
their entirety and some excerpts from longer works.
Introduction contains lengthy discussion of the
exclusion of these authors from standard literary
histories, exposing supposedly aesthetic criteria as
ideological in nature. Editor disagrees with critics
who have emphasized "anxiety of authorship" in these
writers: "On the contrary, many of the writers I read
seemed to manifest a considerable degree of comfort
with the act of writing ... and relatively little sense
of disjunctiveness between 'woman' and 'pen.'"

  Cary, Alice
  Child
  Cooke
  Davis, Rebecca Harding
  Dodge, Mary Abigail
  [Fern] Parton
  Jacobs

Kirkland
Leslie
Parton
Phelps, Elizabeth Stuart
Sedgwick, Catharine M.
Sigourney
Spofford
Stowe

272. Quinn, Arthur Hobson. AMERICAN FICTION: AN
     HISTORICAL AND CRITICAL SURVEY. New York: D.
     Appleton-Century Co., 1936. 805 pp.

     Influential history of American fiction. The
author's treatment of female writers reflects his
preference for realism; "sentimentalists" are referred
to only in passing, whereas writers he considers
pioneering realists, such as Rebecca Harding Davis,
receive serious treatment.

     Bleecker
     Child
     Cooke
     Cushing
     Davis, Rebecca Harding
     Foster
     Kirkland
     Mowatt
     Rowson
     Sedgwick, Catharine M.
     Spofford
     Stoddard
     Stowe
     Warren
     Wells
     Wood, Sally

273. Quissell, Barbara C. "The New World that Eve
     Made: Feminist Utopias Written by Nineteenth-
     Century Women." In AMERICA AS UTOPIA, ed.
     Kenneth M. Roemer, 148-74. New York: Burt
     Franklin, 1981.

     Discusses ten feminist utopias, three from the
earlier part of the century. Argues that the authors
were impatient with narrow objectives and sought a
complete reordering of society; "their views were at

once more fundamentally radical and more idiosyncratic
than the issues debated by other nineteenth-century
feminists."

    Appleton, Jane Sophia
    Cridge
    Griffith, Mary

274. Rather, Lois. "Were Women Funny? Some 19th
    Century Humorists." AMERICAN BOOK COLLECTOR 21
    (February 1971): 5-10.

    Survey of female humor, with brief mention of many
nineteenth-century writers and fuller consideration of
the authors listed below. Notes that female humorists
have seldom been represented in anthologies and
vacillates between concluding that women lack humor and
pointing out editors' androcentric bias.

    Mowatt
    Stephens, Ann S.
    Stowe
    [Whitcher] Berry

275. Raymond, Ida [Mary T. Tardy]. THE LIVING FEMALE
    WRITERS OF THE SOUTH. Philadelphia: Claxton,
    Remson and Haffelfinger, 1872. 568 pp.

    Condensed version of the item below. Actually
includes more authors than the earlier work, but
biographical and critical sketches are shorter and
extracts greatly reduced. Contains an introduction
discussing writers who were not living at the time or
about whom very little was known.

    Bacon, Julia
    Ball, Caroline A.
    Bellamy
    Blount
    Bright
    [Butt] Bennett
    Canfield
    Clack
    Clarke, Mary Bayard
    Cowden
    Crane
    Creswell

Cross
Cruse
Cutler
Davidson
Dickson
Dinnies
Dorr
Dorsey, Anna Hanson
Dorsey, Sarah Anne
Downing
DuBose
Dupuy
Eastman
Ford
French
Gilman
Graves, Adelia C.
Gwyn
Hardenbrook
Hentz, Caroline Lee
[Hentz, Caroline Therese] Branch
Homes
Hunter
Jacobus
Jeffrey
Jervey
Ketchum
King
Ladd
Lee, Mary Elizabeth
Lewis
Loughborough
[McAdoo] McAdo
McIntosh
McLeod
Martin
Mason
Means
[Mowatt] Ritchie
Preston
Rives
Saxon
Shindler
Southworth, E.D.E.N.
Terhune
Towles
Townsend, Mary Ashley
Upshur
[Walsingham] Crean

Warfield
Westmoreland
Whitaker
Whittlesey
Williams, Mary Bushnell
[Wilson, Augusta Evans] Evans
Worthington

276. _____. SOUTHLAND WRITERS: BIOGRAPHICAL AND
CRITICAL SKETCHES OF THE LIVING FEMALE WRITERS OF
THE SOUTH. WITH EXTRACTS FROM THEIR WRITINGS. 2
vols. Philadelphia: Claxton, Remson and
Haffelfinger, 1870. 973 pp.

Sketches range from two pages to twenty pages,
many providing biographies that are quite detailed
(though skimpy on dates), plus extensive extracts.
Arrangement is by state. Compiler writes in a flowery,
inflated style and frequently accuses the North of
prejudice against southern writers.

Bellamy
Blount
[Butt] Bennett
Canfield
Clarke, Mary Bayard
Crane
Creswell
Cross
Cruse
Cutler
Davidson
Dinnies
Dorsey, Sarah Anne
Downing
DuBose
Dupuy
Ford
French
Graves, Adelia C.
Homes
Jacobus
Jeffrey
Jervey
Ketchum
King
Ladd
McLeod

Martin
Preston
Shindler
Towles
Townsend, Mary Ashley
[Walsingham] Crean
Warfield
Westmoreland
Whitaker
Whittlesey
Williams, Mary Bushnell
[Wilson, Augusta Evans] Evans

277. THE READER'S ENCYCLOPEDIA OF AMERICAN LITERATURE.
Edited by Max J. Herzberg. New York: Thomas Y.
Crowell Co., 1962. 1280 pp.

Literary encyclopedia with entries varying in
length from a paragraph to a page. In addition to the
author entries, there are entries for titles,
characters, and subjects.

Alcott (P)
Andrews
Austin
Bacon, Delia
Bleecker
Brooks, Maria Gowen
Cary, Alice
Cary, Phoebe
Child
[Clare] McElheney
Cooke
Cooper, Susan Fenimore
Crosby
Cummins
Davis, Rebecca Harding
Dodge, Mary Mapes
Dupuy
Eastman
Farley
[Fern] Willis, Sarah Payson
Finley
Foster
Gage
Gilman
Hale, Lucretia P.
Hale, Sarah Josepha (P)

Sources   155

Hentz, Caroline Lee
Holmes
Judson
Kinney
Kirkland
Larcom
Lee, Hannah Farnham
Leslie
Lewis
Logan
Morton
Moulton
Mowatt
Phelps, Elizabeth Stuart
Preston
Rowson
Royall
Sedgwick, Catharine M. (P)
Sigourney (P)
Smith, Elizabeth Oakes
Southworth, E.D.E.N.
Spofford
Stephens, Ann S.
Stowe (P)
Tenney
Terhune
Townsend, Mary Ashley
Victor, Frances Fuller
Victor, Metta Fuller
Warner, Anna B.
Warner, Susan
Whitcher
[Wilson, Augusta Evans] Evans
Wood, Sally

278. Reep, Diana. THE RESCUE AND ROMANCE: POPULAR
NOVELS BEFORE WORLD WAR I. Bowling Green, Ohio:
Bowling Green State University Popular Press,
1982. 144 pp.

Study of the rescue convention in fifty popular
American novels, including several early works by
women. Relies heavily on plot summary but is straight-
forwardly and entertainingly written. Concludes that
the novels support traditional sex roles.

Alcott
Cummins

Read, Martha
Rowson
Sedgwick, Catharine M.
Southworth, E.D.E.N.
Stephens, Ann S.
Wilson, Augusta Evans

279. "Regional Resources: The South." In TEACHING
WOMEN'S LITERATURE FROM A REGIONAL PERSPECTIVE,
edited by Leonore Hoffmann and Deborah Rosenfelt,
196-207. New York: Modern Language Association of
America, 1982.

Includes brief biographical sketches of some
southern writers.

Dorsey, Sarah Anne
Hentz, Caroline Lee
LeGrand
Townsend, Mary Ashley
Wilson, Augusta Evans

280. REPRESENTATIVE WOMEN OF NEW ENGLAND. Edited by
Julia Ward Howe et al. Boston: New England
Historical Publishing Co., 1904. 500 pp.

Two-page biographical sketches of women, most of
whom were still alive at the time of publication and
"engaged in active pursuits." Not many writers are
included. Although there is no seeming order to the
sketches, there is an index.

Hale, Sarah Josepha
Livermore, Mary A.
Moulton (P)
Spofford
Whitney

281. Reynolds, David S. FAITH IN FICTION: THE
EMERGENCE OF RELIGIOUS LITERATURE IN AMERICA.
Cambridge: Harvard University Press, 1981.
269 pp.

Study of American religious fiction published
between 1785 and 1850. Does not distinguish between
male and female authors in their treatment of religion

but discusses several women, especially Lydia Maria
Child, Catharine M. Sedgwick, and Harriet Beecher
Stowe.

>   Allen
>   Brown
>   Bullard, Anne Tuttle
>   Cheney
>   Child
>   Cummins
>   Dorsey, Anna Hanson
>   Evans
>   Follen
>   Hale, Sarah Josepha
>   Hall
>   Hentz, Caroline Lee
>   Lee, Eliza Buckminster
>   Lee, Hannah Farnham
>   Rowson
>   Savage
>   Sedgwick, Catharine M.
>   Sedgwick, Susan Ridley
>   Stowe
>   Warner, Susan
>   [Warren] Thayer
>   Williams, Catharine Read
>   Wilson, Augusta Evans

282. _____. "The Feminization Controversy:
Sexual Stereotypes and the Paradoxes of Piety in
Nineteenth-Century America." NEW ENGLAND
QUARTERLY 53 (March 1980): 96-106.

Reviews the literature about feminization, the
theory advanced by Ann Douglas (#94) and others that in
the nineteenth century, American religion was
"feminized," as manifested in the sentimental novel.
Concludes that the theory is based on sexual
stereotypes and that while popular novels advocate
benevolence and emotion, they also present strong
protagonists who make "a 'tough' assertion of human
capability."

>   Sedgwick, Catharine M.
>   Lee, Hannah Farnham
>   Stowe

283. Reynolds Conference, 2d, University of South
    Carolina, 1975. SOUTH CAROLINA WOMEN WRITERS.
    Spartanburg, S.C.: Reprint Co., 1979. 286 pp.

    Proceedings of a conference that included papers
    on early writers.

        King
        Moragne
        Wells

284. Richardson, Charles F. AMERICAN LITERATURE
    1607-1885. 2 vols. in 1. New York: G.P. Putnam's
    Sons, 1895. 462 pp.

    Early literary history with hardly any references
    to women in Vol. 1, "Development of American Thought,"
    and brief discussions of female novelists in Vol. 2,
    "American Poetry and Fiction."

        Alcott
        Cooke
        Cummins
        Rowson
        Sedgwick, Catharine M.
        Stowe
        Tenney
        Warner, Susan

285. Riegel, Robert E. AMERICAN FEMINISTS. Lawrence:
    University of Kansas Press, 1963. 223 pp.

    In Chapter 6, "The Literary Approach,"
    nineteenth-century women's literature is seen as
    conformist rather than feminist. Lydia Maria Child is
    inaccurately presented as a "very poor writer but an
    even poorer feminist." Elizabeth Oakes Smith becomes
    "the most attractive of the literary feminists": she
    "combined personal beauty with literary success."

        Child
        Dall
        Livermore, Mary A.
        Smith, Elizabeth Oakes

286. Riley, Glenda. "American Influences upon

Frontierswomen's Ideas." In WOMEN AND INDIANS ON
THE FRONTIER 1825-1915, 1-36. Albuquerque:
University of New Mexico Press, 1984.

Briefly summarizes and quotes from several novels
in a survey of nineteenth-century "cult of true
womanhood" ideology and anti-Indian sentiment as these
attitudes influenced westering women.

Child
Cummins
Hale, Sarah Josepha
Hentz, Caroline Lee
Kirkland
Lee, Hannah Farnham
Sedgwick, Catharine M.
Sigourney
Southworth, E.D.E.N.
Stephens, Ann S.
Stowe
[Terhune] Harland
Warner, Susan

287. _____. "The Subtle Subversion: Changes in
the Traditionalist Image of the American Woman."
HISTORIAN 32 (February 1970): 210-227.

Discussion of the "moral guardian theory," the
theory that women are ethically superior to men and
should be the moral keepers of society. Argues that
this theory, articulated principally by Sarah Josepha
Hale in the first half of the nineteenth century and
spread in stories and articles in GODEY'S LADY'S BOOK
and in novels by women writers, was an attempt to
gain power for women under the guise of traditionalism.

Child
Embury
Hale, Sarah Josepha
Hentz, Caroline Lee
Latham
Leslie
Parsons
Sedgwick, Catharine M.
Sigourney
Southworth, E.D.E.N.
Stowe

288. Robinson, Harriet H. LOOM AND SPINDLE OR LIFE
     AMONG THE EARLY MILL GIRLS. Revised ed. Kailua,
     Hawaii: Press Pacifica, 1976. (1st ed. 1898).
     167 pp.

     Reminiscence of life in the Lowell cotton mills in
     the 1840's. Includes an account of THE LOWELL
     OFFERING, a magazine edited and written by female
     factory operatives, and a chapter containing one-to-
     five-page biographies of the leading writers for the
     magazine.

        Bagley
        Cate
        Chamberlain
        Curtis
        Farley
        Larcom

289. Rollins, Alice Wellington. "Woman's Sense of
     Humor." CRITIC, March 29, 1884, 145-46.

     Contends that male writers cannot create humor as
     well as women can and provides examples of humor in
     literature by American and British women.

290. Rosenfelt, Deborah S. "The Politics of
     Bibliography: Women's Studies and the Literary
     Canon." In WOMEN IN PRINT I, edited by Joan E.
     Hartman and Ellen Messer-Davidow, 11-35. New
     York: Modern Language Association, 1982.

     Uses early nineteenth-century women as an example
     in discussing the omission of female writers from
     bibliographies. Particularly interesting is the
     author's account of the selection of writers for Jacob
     Blanck's BIBLIOGRAPHY OF AMERICAN LITERATURE (1955-69);
     she shows that women whose works could be considered
     "domestic" or "sentimental" were excluded, while
     female realists like Caroline Kirkland were included.

291. Ruoff, John C. "Frivolity to Consumption: Or,
     Southern Womanhood in Antebellum Literature."
     CIVIL WAR HISTORY 18 (Sept. 1972): 213-29.

     Analysis of the portrayal of southern women in

American fiction published between 1832 and 1861.
Concludes that women did not play a central role in the
plantation legend: the male authors who developed the
myth wrote of southern men, treating women as
ornamental; the female authors of the 1850's seldom
attempted to portray Southern society at all but
concentrated on "defining role expectations for women
in general."

> Eastman
> Hentz, Caroline Lee
> McIntosh
> Pearson
> [Pike] Langdon
> Rush, Caroline E.
> Schoolcraft
> Southworth, E.D.E.N.

292. Rusk, Ralph Leslie. THE LITERATURE OF THE MIDDLE
     WESTERN FRONTIER. 2 vols. New York: Columbia
     University Press, 1926. 457 pp., 419 pp.

Includes discussion of western prose by Caroline
Lee Hentz, Caroline Kirkland, and (briefly) Harriet
Beecher Stowe.

> Hentz, Caroline Lee
> Kirkland
> Stowe

293. Rutherford, Mildred Lewis. AMERICAN AUTHORS: A
     HAND-BOOK OF AMERICAN LITERATURE. Atlanta:
     Franklin Printing and Publishing Co., 1894.
     750 pp.

Inclusive and well-written early account of
American literature. Although presented as a
"textbook," it consists not of selections from writers
but of one-to-five-page biographical and critical
sketches. These include some commentary on authors'
works, but the emphasis is on quotations by and about
the authors and anecdotes about their lives.

> Alcott (P)
> Cary, Alice (P)
> Cary, Phoebe (P)
> Child

Cooke
Cross
Cummins
Fern
Finley
Larcom
Lippincott
Moulton
Preston (P)
Sigourney
Spofford
Stoddard
Stowe (P)
Terhune
Warner, Anna B.
Warner, Susan
Whitney
Wilson, Augusta Evans (P)

294. _____. THE SOUTH IN HISTORY AND
LITERATURE: A HAND-BOOK OF SOUTHERN AUTHORS.
Athens, Ga.: Franklin-Turner Co., 1907. 866 pp.

Same format as the author's general American
literature text above, but with slightly shorter and
less informative biographical sketches. Many, though
not all, of the female writers are treated in Chapter
5, "Women Writers of the National Era and Era of the
Early Republic."

Ball, Caroline A.
Bellamy
Blake
Cross
Dinnies
Dorsey, Sarah Anne
Dupuy
Ford
French
Gilman
Hentz, Caroline Lee
Jeffrey
Ketchum
Lee, Mary Elizabeth
Preston
Shindler
Southworth, E.D.E.N.
[Terhune] Harland

Townsend, Mary Ashley
Warfield
Wilson, Augusta Evans

295. Ryan, Mary P. THE EMPIRE OF THE MOTHER: AMERICAN
WRITING ABOUT DOMESTICITY, 1830-1860. New York:
Institute for Research in History and the Haworth
Press, 1982. 170 pp.

Treats women's fiction of the 1850's as the
apotheosis of the "cult of domesticity" in American
culture. Includes in discussion many insights of
previous writers, such as the central role of domestic
ideology in UNCLE TOM'S CABIN and other novels about
slavery. Contains brief but interesting discussion of
the discomfort felt by Lydia Maria Child, Catharine M.
Sedgwick, and Lydia Sigourney in the literary
atmosphere of the 1850's.

Cary, Alice
Child
Cummins
Eastman
Fern
Hale, Sarah Josepha
Hentz, Caroline Lee
Holmes
[Judson] Chubbock
[Lippincott] Greenwood
McIntosh
Sedgwick, Catharine M.
Sigourney
Smith, Elizabeth Oakes
Southworth, E.D.E.N.
Stephens, Ann S.
Stowe
[Terhune] Harland
Warner, Susan
[Wilson, Augusta Evans] Evans

296. Sanborn, Kate. "New England Women Humorists."
NEW ENGLAND MAGAZINE 35 (Oct. 1906): 155-59.

Response to a contention that there were few
humorists among the nineteenth-century literary women
of New England. Gives very brief descriptions of the
humorous writings of several such women.

297. _____, ed. THE WIT OF WOMEN. New York:
     Funk & Wagnalls, 1885.   215 pp.

     Disorganized collection of puns, epigrams, and
humorous sketches by women, with introduction and
running commentary. There is little analysis of the
humor or information about the authors provided.
Although some British and post-Civil War writers are
included, emphasis is on early nineteenth-century
American women.

298. Satterwhite, Joseph N.   "The Tremulous Formula:
     Form and Technique in GODEY'S Fiction."   AMERICAN
     QUARTERLY 8 (Summer 1956): 99-113.

     Summarizes short stories in GODEY'S LADY'S BOOK
with the intent of showing that they represent "the
epitome of the sentimental spirit--the triumph of
matter over form, emotion over good sense, and license
over restraint." Nearly all the "second-rate" writers
discussed are female, and all the first-raters are
male.

          Hale, Sarah Josepha
          Hentz, Caroline Lee
          Sedgwick, Catharine M.
          Smith, Elizabeth Oakes
          Stowe

299. Scheick, William J.   THE HALF-BLOOD: A CULTURAL
     SYMBOL IN 19TH-CENTURY AMERICAN FICTION.
     Lexington: University Press of Kentucky, 1979.
     113 pp.

     Discussion of the half-blood (half white, half
Indian) character in nineteenth-century fiction.
Emphasizes regional differences, with southern writers
portraying the half-blood as a "grotesque creature
antithetical to white civilization" and eastern writers
showing more ambivalence; does not make obvious
distinctions, however, between fictional portraits by
women and men.

          Child
          Howard
          Rowson
          Sedgwick, Catharine M.

Stephens, Ann S.

300. Seidel, Kathryn L.   "The Southern Belle as an
     Antebellum Ideal."   SOUTHERN QUARTERLY 15 (July
     1977): 387-401.

     Discusses the image of the belle in some
antebellum plantation novels.   Generalizing from
fiction by only three authors, Sarah Josepha Hale,
Caroline Lee Hentz and Harriet Beecher Stowe, argues
that "writers of the antebellum period were actually
united in their concept of the belle."   However their
politics may have differed, they held an ideal of the
belle as an "untouched Eve in a domestic garden, or a
goddess on a pedestal, unsullied by money, experience,
and vanity."

     Hale, Sarah Josepha
     Hentz, Caroline Lee
     Stowe

301. _____.   THE SOUTHERN BELLE IN THE AMERICAN
     NOVEL.   Tampa: University of South Florida Press,
     1985.   202 pp.

     Chapter 1 is a slightly revised version of "The
Southern Belle as an Antebellum Ideal," above.   Chapter
9, "The Southern Eve," contains an interesting analysis
of the Eden motif in fiction by Caroline Lee Hentz and
E.D.E.N. Southworth.

     Hale, Sarah Josepha
     Hentz, Caroline Lee
     Southworth, E.D.E.N.
     Stowe

302. Sergel, Charles H.   "The Comparative Popularity of
     Authors."   CRITIC, August 27, 1887, 99-100.

     Purports to assess the popularity of British and
American authors based on number of volumes sold.   E.P.
Roe leads the Americans in the prose fiction category,
with six of the next seven writers being female.

     Alcott
     Fleming

Holmes
Southworth, E.D.E.N.
Stowe
[Terhune] Harland

303. Shepherd, Henry E. THE REPRESENTATIVE AUTHORS OF
MARYLAND. New York: Whitehall Publishing Co.,
1911. 234 pp.

Most of the authors are late nineteenth century,
but a few earlier writers are discussed, with Anne
Moncure Crane being given prominence among the women.

[Crane] Crane-Seemuller
Latimer
Lewis
Phelps, Almira H. Lincoln

304. Shumaker, Arthur W. A HISTORY OF INDIANA
LITERATURE. Indianapolis: Indiana Historical
Society, 1962. 611 pp.

Thorough study of literature by Indiana authors.
Includes discussion of several women who wrote fiction
in the nineteenth century.

Beecher
Cary, Alice
Cary, Phoebe
Collins
Dumont
Hayden, Sarah Marshall
Rose

305. Siegel, Adrienne. THE IMAGE OF THE AMERICAN CITY
IN POPULAR LITERATURE 1820-1870. Port Washington,
N.Y.: Kennikat Press, 1981. 211 pp.

Emphasis solely on the image of the city without
attention to or knowledge of individual authors (thus,
Catharine M. Sedgwick is referred to as a "hack
writer"). There seem to be more female authors than
male who inveigh against urban high society and fewer
who are anti-immigrant, but this is hard to determine
since authors are not distinguished by gender.
Includes interesting chapter on working class and mill

fiction.

    Buckley
    Child
    Cummins
    Cutler
    Davis, Rebecca Harding
    Denison
    Eastman
    [Goodwin] Talcott
    [Green] McDougall
    Haven
    Hilbourne
    Lamas
    Lasselle
    Lee, Hannah Farnham
    Maxwell
    Montaigne
    [Mowatt] Ritchie
    Otis
    Rosewood
    Royall
    Savage
    Sedgwick, Catharine M.
    Smith, Elizabeth Oakes
    Smith, Margaret Bayard
    Soule
    Stephens, Ann S.
    Torrey
    Townsend, Mary Ashley
    Tyler
    White
    Williams, Catharine Read

306. SIGNIFICANT AMERICAN AUTHORS, POETS, AND
PLAYWRIGHTS. Chicago: Childrens Press, 1975.
78 pp.

Brief biographies for children of prominent
American authors, including a few early women.
Arranged in chronological order. Includes index and
color portraits.

    Alcott (P)
    Harper (P)
    Rowson (P)
    Stowe (P)
    [Wilson, Augusta Evans] Evans (P)

307. SIGNIFICANT AMERICAN WOMEN. Chicago: Children's
     Press, 1975. 78 pp.

     Same as the item above, except for focus on women
rather than authors.

     Alcott (P)
     Hale, Sarah Josepha (P)
     Rowson (P)
     Stowe (P)

308. Smith, Harrison. "Feminism and the Household
     Novel." SATURDAY REVIEW, March 30, 1957, 22.

     Short summary of women's "monstrous proliferation
of words and manufactured emotions" in the 1850's and
60's. Does not mention feminism and inaccurately
portrays the "household novelists" as having led
"sheltered domestic lives."

     Southworth, E.D.E.N.
     Stowe

309. Smith, Henry Nash. "The Scribbling Women and the
     Cosmic Success Story." CRITICAL INQUIRY 1 (Sept.
     1974): 47-70.

     Examines popular American fiction, mainly novels
by women, between the early 1850's and the early
1870's. Asserts that this fiction expresses the "ethos
of conformity"; unquestioned submission to authority is
shown to lead to success. Does not relate this
thematic pattern to the situation of women. Quotes
lengthy passages from THE WIDE, WIDE WORLD and THE
LAMPLIGHTER as examples.

     Cummins
     Stowe
     Warner, Susan

310. _____. VIRGIN LAND: THE AMERICAN WEST
     AS SYMBOL AND MYTH. Revised ed. Cambridge:
     Harvard University Press, 1970. 305 pp.

     Considers several female novelists in Chapter 21,
"The Agricultural West in Literature." Sees them as

discovering literary value in the agricultural West but
failing to find an adequate form for their materials.

Cary, Alice
Kirkland
Soule
Stephens, Ann S.
[Victor, Frances Fuller] Barritt
[Victor, Metta Fuller] Fuller

311. Smith, Herbert F. THE POPULAR AMERICAN NOVEL,
1865-1920. Boston: Twayne Publishers, 1980.
192 pp.

Discusses several authors who wrote extensively
before 1865, especially in Chapter 2, "Drowning in
Bathos: The Sentimental Novel." Considerable space is
devoted to ridicule of the "homely" E.D.E.N.
Southworth, whom the author sees as the apotheosis of
the "sentimental scribbler."

Alcott
Austin
Bellamy
Chesebro'
Southworth, E.D.E.N.
Terhune
Warner, Susan
Whitney

312. Smith, Leslie. "Through Rose-Colored Glasses:
Some American Victorian Sentimental Novels." In
NEW DIMENSIONS IN POPULAR CULTURE, edited by
Russell B. Nye, 90-106. Bowling Green, Ohio:
Bowling Green University Popular Press, 1972.

Condescending discussion of the "rags to riches"
pattern in some popular American novels of the middle
nineteenth century. Emphasizes novels by Sylvanus
Cobb, E.D.E.N. Southworth, and Mary Jane Holmes.

Holmes
Southworth, E.D.E.N.

313. Smith, Thelma M. "Feminism in Philadelphia,
1790-1850." PENNSYLVANIA MAGAZINE OF HISTORY AND

BIOGRAPHY 68 (July 1944): 243-68.

Survey of the achievements of Philadelphia women
writers in the stated period. Emphasizes their
education and interests and the influence of feminist
thought on their careers and writings.

        Hale, Sarah Josepha
        [Haven] Neal
        Judson
        Lippincott
        Moore, Clara Jessup
        [Sansay] Hassall
        Tuthill, Louisa C.

314. Smyth, Albert H. AMERICAN LITERATURE. Revised
     ed. Philadelphia: Eldredge and Brother, 1894.
     304 pp.

Early history of American literature; includes
female writers. Catharine M. Sedgwick is seen as
"tedious" compared with Lydia Maria Child, a "writer of
much greater force," who is accorded equal stature with
John Pendleton Kennedy and William Gilmore Simms.

        Brooks, Maria Gowen
        Child
        Cooke
        Davis, Rebecca Harding
        Moulton
        Sedgwick, Catharine M.
        Spofford
        Stowe
        Whitney

315. Solomon, Barbara Miller. IN THE COMPANY OF
     EDUCATED WOMEN: A HISTORY OF WOMEN AND HIGHER
     EDUCATION IN AMERICA. New Haven: Yale University
     Press, 1985. 298 pp.

Chapters 2 and 3 include brief discussion of
educated women's entrance into the literary field in
the mid-nineteenth century and of author-educators'
attitudes toward education as expressed in their
fiction.

        Cummins

Hale, Sarah Josepha
Hentz, Caroline Lee
[Judson] Chubbuck
[Lippincott] Greenwood
Phelps, Almira H. Lincoln
Terhune

316. "Some 'Lady Novelists' and Their Works: As Seen
from a Public Library." LITERARY WORLD, June 3,
1882, 184-86.

Advises libraries either not to buy "trashy and
sensational" books by the "lady novelists" or to buy
only one copy "so that the persistent inquirer may be
silenced by the knowledge that what he wants is to be
had, though he may try a year before he gets it." Goes
on to catalog the faults of each novelist individually.

Dupuy
Hentz, Caroline Lee
Holmes
Southworth, E.D.E.N.
Stephens, Ann S.
Warfield

317. THE SOUTH IN THE BUILDING OF THE NATION. Edited
by John B. Henneman et al. 12 vols. Richmond:
Southern Historical Publication Society, 1909.

Female writers are scarcely mentioned in Volume 7,
"History of the Literary and Intellectual Life of the
South," or Volume 8, "History of Southern Fiction," but
are included in the one-to-two-page biographical
sketches of southern whites in Volumes 11 and 12.

Bacon, Julia
Ball, Caroline A.
Clack
Clarke, Mary Bayard
Creswell
Cross
Cruse
Cutler
Dinnies
Dorr
Dorsey, Sarah Anne
Downing

Dupuy
[Elemjay] Ellinjay
Ford
French
Gilman
Hentz, Caroline Lee
Jeffrey
Jervey
Ketchum
King
McIntosh
[Mowatt] Ritchie
Phelps, Almira H. Lincoln
Preston
Southworth, E.D.E.N.
Terhune
Townsend, Mary Ashley
Walsingham
Warfield
Williams, Mary Bushnell
Wilson, Augusta Evans

318. SOUTHERN WRITERS: A BIOGRAPHICAL DICTIONARY.
Edited by Robert Bain, Joseph M. Flora, and Louis
D. Rubin, Jr. Baton Rouge: Louisiana State
University Press, 1979. 515 pp.

A few nineteenth-century women are included in
this collection of brief (one to two pages)
biographical sketches.

Davis, Rebecca Harding
Gilman
Hentz, Caroline Lee
Preston
Southworth, E.D.E.N.
Wilson, Augusta Evans

319. Spingarn, Lawrence P. "The Yankee in Early
American Fiction." NEW ENGLAND QUARTERLY 31
(December 1958): 484-95.

Contends that in novels and tales published before
1870, American fiction writers created a composite
Yankee character type that was realistic and
convincing. Examples are taken from the work of
Nathaniel Hawthorne, Oliver Wendell Holmes, and

several female writers.

    Otis
    Sedgwick, Catharine M.
    Stoddard
    Stowe

320. Staehelin-Wackernagel, Adelheid. THE PURITAN
    SETTLER IN THE AMERICAN NOVEL BEFORE THE CIVIL
    WAR. Cooper Monographs, #7. Bern, Switzerland,
    1961. 165 pp.

    Discusses the portrayal of Puritans in historical
novels, finding an ambivalent attitude that becomes
progressively more critical. Does not distinguish
between men's and women's portrayals.

    Bacon, Delia
    Cheney
    Child
    Lee, Eliza Buckminster
    Sedgwick, Catharine M.

321. Stanton, Theodore. A MANUAL OF AMERICAN
    LITERATURE. New York: G.P. Putnam's Sons, 1909.
    493 pp.

    Early literary history which gives fair treatment
to women and distinguishes one female writer from
another.

    Alcott
    Brooks, Maria Gowen
    Cary, Alice
    Child
    Cummins
    Harris
    Judson
    Kirkland
    Sedgwick, Catharine M.
    Sigourney
    Spofford
    Stephens, Ann S.
    Stoddard
    Stowe
    [Terhune] Harland
    Warner, Susan

Whitcher
Whitney
Wood, Sally

322. Stearns, Bertha Monica. "New England Magazines
     for Ladies 1830-1860." NEW ENGLAND QUARTERLY 3
     (October 1930): 627-56.

Discussion of editorial policy includes
description of three editors' literary contributions to
their own magazines.

     Gilman
     [Mayo] Edgarton
     Stephens, Ann S.

323. Stedman, Edmund Clarence, and Ellen Mackay
     Hutchinson, eds. A LIBRARY OF AMERICAN
     LITERATURE. 11 vols. New York: Charles L.
     Webster & Co., 1888-90.

Collection of "characteristic examples of the
literature of this country," presented without further
selection criteria or critical comment. Important as a
source of writings for authors not included in later
anthologies. Paragraph-length biographies of the
authors, written by Arthur Stedman, appear in Volume
11.

     Alcott
     Austin
     Bacon, Delia
     Bleecker
     Booth
     Bradley
     Brooks, Maria Gowen (P)
     Cary, Alice
     Child (P)
     Cooke
     Davis, Rebecca Harding
     Dodge, Mary Mapes (P)
     Dorr
     Faugeres
     Foster
     Gilman
     Guernsey, Clara F.
     Hale, Sarah Josepha

Harris
Judson
Ketchum
Kinney
Kirkland
Larcom
Leslie
Lippincott
Morton
Moulton
Preston
Putnam
Roberts
Rowson (P)
Sedgwick, Catharine M. (P)
Sigourney
Smith, Elizabeth Oakes
Spofford (P)
Stephens, Ann S.
Stoddard (P)
Stowe (P)
Tenney
Terhune
Townsend, Mary Ashley
Walker
Warner, Susan
Whitcher
Whitney
Wilson, Augusta Evans

324. Sterling, Dorothy, ed. WE ARE YOUR SISTERS:
BLACK WOMEN IN THE NINETEENTH CENTURY. New York:
W.W. Norton and Co., 1984. 535 pp.

Excellent collection of writings by and about
nineteenth-century black women. Contains much
information about Frances E.W. Harper and Harriet A.
Jacobs and about the lives and works of other women who
may eventually be discovered to have written fiction in
nineteenth-century African-American periodicals.

Child
Harper (P)
Jacobs
Stowe

325. Stern, Madeleine B. BOOKS AND BOOK PEOPLE IN

19TH-CENTURY AMERICA. New York: R.R. Bowker Co., 1978. 341 pp.

Includes chapters on Louisa May Alcott, Ann S. Stephens, and publisher G.W. Carleton, discussing his relationship with female authors.

Alcott
Fleming
Stephens, Ann S.
Wilson, Augusta Evans

326. _____. "Notable Women of 19th Century America." MANUSCRIPTS 34 (Winter, Spring, Summer 1982): 7-20, 89-98, 169-84.

Provides biographical sketches and discussion of the letters of women, including several writers, whom the rare book and manuscript dealer considers collectible.

Alcott
Child
Livermore, Mary A.
Stowe

327. _____. PUBLISHERS FOR MASS ENTERTAINMENT IN NINETEENTH CENTURY AMERICA. Boston: G.K. Hall and Co., 1980. 358 pp.

Account of nineteenth-century American publishers, arranged alphabetically by publisher. Mentions the names of numerous female authors, with more substantial information about those listed below.

Alcott
Holmes
Southworth, E.D.E.N.
Stephens, Ann S.
Victor, Metta Fuller
Whitney
Wilson, Augusta Evans

328. _____. "Queens of Literature." In PAGES: THE WORLD OF BOOKS, WRITERS, AND WRITING, edited by Matthew J. Bruccoli and C.E. Frazer Clark, Jr.,

291-95. Detroit: Gale Research Co., 1976.

Brief discussion of the eight English and American authors represented in a nineteenth-century card game, "Queens of Literature."

    Alcott (P)
    Larcom (P)
    Stowe (P)
    Whitney (P)

329. Stevens, William Oliver. FAMOUS WOMEN OF AMERICA. New York: Dodd, Mead & Co., 1950. 174 pp.

Three writers are included in this collection of four-to-five-page biographical sketches. There are no footnotes or bibliographies.

    Alcott (P)
    Dodge, Mary Mapes (P)
    Stowe (P)

330. STORY AND VERSE FOR CHILDREN. Edited by Miriam Blanton Huber. New York: Macmillan Co., 1940. 857 pp.

Anthology of children's literature that concludes with a section entitled "The Makers of Children's Books"; the biographies are brief, usually less than half a page in length. The Cary sisters and Mary Mapes Dodge are dropped from the second (1955) and third (1965) editions.

    Alcott
    Cary, Alice
    Cary, Phoebe
    Child
    Dodge, Mary Mapes
    Follen

331. Stout, Janis P. "Charity and the Redemption of Urban Society in American Popular Fiction before 1860." RESEARCH STUDIES 43 (September 1975): 162-74.

Claims that the response of popular (unfortunately

termed "subliterary") fiction to social inequity in the
nineteenth century was sentimental and inadequate.
Urban society was deemed wicked and its redeemer
imagined as "a man who enjoys both wealth and--through
charity--a vicarious participation in virtuous
poverty."

> Cummins
> Sedgwick, Catharine M.
> Smith, Elizabeth Oakes

332. _____. "'Wo unto Sodom': Urban
Stereotypes in Popular Fiction." Chap. 2 in
SODOMS IN EDEN: THE CITY IN AMERICAN FICTION
BEFORE 1860. Westport, Conn.: Greenwood
Press, 1976.

Survey of popular novels about the city. Rather
quickly dismisses fiction by women as stereotyping
country and city, as good/evil, and as exalting "home,
virtuous womanhood, and charity."

> Child
> Cummins
> Read, Martha
> Sedgwick, Catharine M.
> Smith, Elizabeth Oakes

333. Stovall, Floyd. "The Decline of Romantic Idealism
1855-1871." In TRANSITIONS IN AMERICAN LITERARY
HISTORY, edited by Harry Hayden Clark, 317-78.
New York: Octagon Books, 1967 (1st ed. 1954).

Sees the "negative" manifestation of the decline
as an increase in sentimental and sensational fiction
written primarily by women. Does, however, praise the
realism of some minor characters in popular fiction and
discusses some female writers as exemplars of the
"positive" result of the decline of romantic idealism,
the growth of humor and realism.

> Cary, Alice
> Cooke
> Davis, Rebecca Harding
> [Fern] Parton
> Hentz, Caroline Lee
> Kirkland

Sedgwick, Catharine M.
Stowe
Warner, Susan
Whitcher

334. Tandy, Jeannette Reid. "Pro-Slavery Propaganda in American Fiction of the Fifties." SOUTH ATLANTIC QUARTERLY 21 (January 1922): 41-50; (April 1922): 170-78.

Discussion of responses to UNCLE TOM'S CABIN published in the 1850's. Includes plot summaries of pro-slavery novels by women.

Eastman
Flanders
Hale, Sarah Josepha
Rush, Caroline E.
Schoolcraft

335. Thompson, Adele E. "Woman's Place in Early American Fiction." ERA 12 (November 1903): 472-74.

Brief attempt to assess the contributions of women writing before the Civil War. Considers the earliest writers, who concentrated on poetry and religious prose, "a little thin and somewhat lacking in originality." Claims that when women began writing fiction they were more successful and built the foundation for later novelists.

[Child] Childs
Sedgwick, Catharine M.
Stowe

336. Thompson, Lawrence S. "The War between the States in the Kentucky Novel." REGISTER OF THE KENTUCKY HISTORICAL SOCIETY 50 (January 1952): 26-34.

Discusses the novels only very briefly but includes checklist of novels that gives plot summaries and explains how the work relates to Kentucky.

Davis, Rebecca Harding
Ford

Holmes
Remick
Spencer

337. Thompson, Lawrence S., and Algernon D. Thompson.
     THE KENTUCKY NOVEL. Lexington: University of
     Kentucky Press, 1953. 172 pp.

     Annotated bibliography of fiction set in Kentucky;
     arranged alphabetically by author. Includes one-
     paragraph plot summaries and evaluations of the novels.

          Ford
          Harlan
          Holmes
          Ketchum
          Roe
          Spencer
          Stowe
          Victor, Metta Fuller

338. Thorp, Willard. "Catholic Novelists in Defense of
     Their Faith, 1829-1865." PROCEEDINGS OF THE
     AMERICAN ANTIQUARIAN SOCIETY 78, pt.1 (1968):
     25-117. Reprinted, New York: Arno Press, 1978.

     Discussion of early Catholic novels. Devotes
     several pages to Anna Hanson Dorsey and Mrs. Sadlier
     and includes brief descriptions of novels by lesser
     known women.

          [Brownson] Tenney
          Dorsey, Anna Hanson
          Sadlier

339. Tompkins, Jane. SENSATIONAL DESIGNS: THE CULTURAL
     WORK OF AMERICAN FICTION, 1790-1860. New York:
     Oxford University Press, 1985. 236 pp. Shorter
     versions of Chapter 6, "The Other American
     Renaissance," appear in GENRE 16 (Winter 1983):
     423-36 and in AMERICAN RENAISSANCE RECONSIDERED:
     SELECTED PAPERS FROM THE ENGLISH INSTITUTE,
     1982-83, edited by Walter Benn Michaels and Donald
     E. Pease, 34-57. Baltimore: Johns Hopkins
     University Press, 1985.

   Argues that American literary classics have
achieved their status not by "intrinsic merit" but by
their embodiment of the interests and beliefs of a
cultural hierarchy.
   Discusses in the context of their historical
circumstances works by Charles Brockden Brown, James
Fenimore Cooper, Harriet Beecher Stowe, and Susan
Warner. In the chapters on Stowe and Warner, the
author contends that the exclusion of
"sentimental novels" from the American literary canon
has been a mistake and shows how the women used the
ideology of evangelical Christianity to reorganize
culture from women's point of view, elaborating "a myth
that gave women the central position of power and
authority in the culture."

       Stowe
       Warner, Susan

340. _____. "Sentimental Power: UNCLE TOM'S
       CABIN and the Politics of Literary History."
       GLYPH 8 (1981): 79-102.

   Landmark essay questioning critics' wholesale
denigration of the nineteenth-century "sentimental" or
"domestic" novel. "If the fiction written in the
nineteenth century by women whose works sold in the
hundreds of thousands has seemed narrow and parochial
to the critics of the twentieth century," the problem
lies with modernist assumptions about the nature and
function of literature; these assumptions prevent
critics from appreciating the complexity of novels like
UNCLE TOM'S CABIN.

       Stowe

341. Townsend, John Wilson, ed. KENTUCKY IN AMERICAN
       LETTERS, 1784-1912. 2 vols. Cedar Rapids, Iowa:
       Torch Press, 1913.

   Collection of writings by Kentucky residents,
chronologically arranged by birth date. Entries
consist of a one-to-two-page biographical sketch and
two to three pages of selections from the writer's
works.

       Ford

Hentz, Caroline Lee
Holmes
Jeffrey
Ketchum
Shindler
Warfield

342. Trensky, Anne Tropp. "The Saintly Child in
     Nineteenth-Century American Fiction." In
     PROSPECTS, edited by Jack Salzman, 389-413
     (Vol.1, 1975).

     Analyzes a number of works, most of them by women
     (although gender is never discussed). Claims that the
     saintly child story "reflects a religiosity that is so
     obsessive as to appear sick to a modern reader"; the
     fiction also has erotic overtones, often portraying a
     "repressed, incestuous eroticism" between a father or
     father-surrogate and his daughter.

     Alcott
     Cummins
     Fern
     Finley
     Smith, Elizabeth Oakes
     Stowe
     Warner, Susan
     [Wilson, Augusta Evans] Evans

343. Trent, William P. A HISTORY OF AMERICAN
     LITERATURE, 1607-1865. New York: D. Appleton and
     Co., 1903. 608 pp.

     Standard literary history that mentions some
     female writers. The didacticism of their work is
     emphasized, with the women being seen as "do-gooders."

     Brooks, Maria Gowen
     Child
     Leslie
     Morton
     Rowson
     Sedgwick, Catharine M.
     Sigourney
     Stowe
     Warner, Susan

344. Tuchman, Gaye. "Some Thoughts on Public and
      Private Spheres." CENTERPOINT 3, no. 3-4 (1980):
      111-13.

      Brief discussion of the changing meanings of the
terms "public" and "private" from the eighteenth
century to the present, with nineteenth-century
"sentimentalists" used as an extended example. Notes
that the female authors were seen as "entitled to
neither public nor private space."

345. Underwood, Francis H. THE BUILDERS OF AMERICAN
      LITERATURE. Boston: Lee and Shepard, 1893.
      302 pp.

      Contains two-to-three-page biographical sketches
of American authors who were born before 1826,
including several women.

      Cary, Alice
      Child
      Dorr
      Sedgwick, Catharine M.
      Sigourney
      Stowe
      Whitney

346. _____. A HAND-BOOK OF ENGLISH LITERATURE:
      AMERICAN AUTHORS. Boston: Lee & Shepard, 1872.
      637 pp.

      In spite of its title, this is an anthology, with
short selections (five to six pages) and one-to-two-
page biographical sketches of the authors.

      Cary, Alice
      Child
      [Cooke] Terry
      [Dodge, Mary Abigail] Hamilton
      Larcom
      Moulton
      Sedgwick, Catharine M.
      Sigourney
      Spofford
      Stowe
      Whitney

347. Urann, C.A.   "Early Women Writers in America."
     CHAUTAUQUAN 30 (Jan. 1900): 377-80.

     Positive, though occasionally inaccurate, review
of women's literary accomplishments in the nineteenth
century ("early" means early 1800's). Claims that, as
the century progressed, women learned to handle their
subjects more skillfully and "to be less easily swayed
by their emotions."

     Cary, Alice
     Cary, Phoebe
     [Fern] Eldredge
     Hale, Sarah Josepha
     Leslie
     [Lippincott] Clarke
     Mowatt
     Spofford
     Terhune
     Whitcher
     Whitney

348. Van Doren, Carl. THE AMERICAN NOVEL 1789-1939.
     New York: Macmillan Co., 1940. 406 pp.

     Typical history which mentions a few female
authors very briefly. In the entire book there is one
reference to Louisa May Alcott and one to Kate Chopin
as the author of BAYOU FOLK.

     Cooke
     Foster
     Rowson
     Stowe
     Warner, Susan

349. Venable, W.H.   BEGINNINGS OF LITERARY CULTURE IN
     THE OHIO VALLEY: HISTORICAL AND BIOGRAPHICAL
     SKETCHES. Cincinnati: R. Clarke and Co.,
     1891. 519 pp.

     Several female authors are discussed in this
survey of culture in the West before the Civil War.

     Cary, Alice
     Cary, Phoebe
     Dumont

Gage
Hentz, Caroline Lee
Stowe
Victor, Metta Fuller
Warfield

350. VIRGINIA AUTHORS, PAST AND PRESENT. Edited by
Welford Dunaway Taylor and Maurice Duke.
Richmond: Virginia Association of Teachers of
English, 1972. 125 pp.

Includes one-page biographical sketches with
bibliographies of the authors' works.

Eastman
Preston
Terhune

351. Voloshin, Beverly. "A Historical Note on Women's
Fiction: A Reply to Annette Kolodny." CRITICAL
INQUIRY 2 (Summer 1976): 817-20.

Argues that Kolodny is mistaken in implying (in
"Some Notes on Defining a 'Feminist Literary
Criticism,'" 1975) that Nathaniel Hawthorne eventually
reversed his negative judgment of the fiction of his
female contemporaries. In fact, he praised only RUTH
HALL, and few readers today will appreciate the other
women's novels.

Fern

352. _____. "The Limits of Domesticity: The
Female BILDUNGSROMAN in America, 1820-1870."
WOMEN'S STUDIES 10, no. 3 (1984): 283-302.

Analyzes five popular novels (Catharine M.
Sedgwick's A NEW-ENGLAND TALE, Susan Warner's THE WIDE,
WIDE WORLD, Maria Cummins' THE LAMPLIGHTER, and Augusta
Evans Wilson's BEULAH and ST. ELMO) in an attempt to
demonstrate a tension between their expressed approval
of domestic values and covert interest in the opposing
values of female independence and equality.

Cummins
Hale, Sarah Josepha

> Sedgwick, Catharine M.
> Sigourney
> Warner, Susan
> [Wilson, Augusta Evans] Evans

353. Wagenknecht, Edward. CAVALCADE OF THE AMERICAN
     NOVEL. New York: Holt, Rinehart and Winston,
     1952. 575 pp.

     History of the American novel, unusually inclusive
for its time. Several nineteenth-century women are
discussed in Chapter 5, "Mrs. Stowe and Some
Contemporaries," and others are treated in the
Appendix. The author notes the "quiet realism" in the
works of some "sentimentalists."

> Alcott
> Child
> Cummins
> Davis
> Fern
> Foster
> Rowson
> Sedgwick, Catharine M.
> Southworth, E.D.E.N.
> Stowe
> Terhune
> Warner, Susan
> Wilson, Augusta Evans

354. Walker, Nancy. THE TRADITION OF WOMEN'S HUMOR IN
     AMERICA. Huntington Beach, Calif.: American
     Studies Publishing Co., 1984. 34 pp.

     Survey of women's humor that follows Kate
Sanborn's 1885 collection, THE WIT OF WOMEN (#297), in
discussing nineteenth-century women's humor. Views
women's humor of the period as differing from the
dominant male tradition in its focus on personal rather
than public life and its protest against the status of
women in American society.

> Cary, Phoebe
> Dodge, Mary Abigail
> Kirkland
> Whitcher

355. _____. "Wit, Sentimentality and the
     Image of Women in the Nineteenth Century."
     AMERICAN STUDIES 22 (Fall 1981): 5-22.

     Best essay available on nineteenth-century female
humorists. Argues that they satirized sentimentality
and the sentimental female writer in attempt "to deny
the image of woman as a weak, frail vessel of Christian
piety, and to posit instead an image of the 'witty'
woman: one who sees through sham and stereotype, for
whom courage and strength of mind are positive
virtues."

     Dodge, Mary Abigail
     [Fern] Parton
     Kirkland
     [Whitcher] Whicher

356. Walser, Richard. LITERARY NORTH CAROLINA: A BRIEF
     HISTORICAL SURVEY. Raleigh, N.C.: State Dept. of
     Archives & History, 1970. 137 pp.

     Includes short discussion of fiction by some early
women writers.

     Downing
     Gales
     Mason
     Stowe
     Whittlesey (P)

357. Wamsley, James S., and Anne M. Cooper. IDOLS,
     VICTIMS, PIONEERS: VIRGINIA'S WOMEN FROM 1607.
     Richmond: A Bicentennial Project of the Virginia
     State Chamber of Commerce and the Virginia
     Commission on the Status of Women, 1976. 307 pp.

     Discussion of early writers can be found in
Chapter 23, "Virginia's Penwomen."

     Eastman
     [Mowatt] Ritchie (P)
     Preston
     Rives
     Royall
     [Terhune] Harland (P)

358. Waterbury, Willard E. "Leading Women of the
     Nineteenth Century." In WOMAN: HER POSITION,
     INFLUENCE, AND ACHIEVEMENT THROUGHOUT THE
     CIVILIZED WORLD, edited by William C. King,
     343-490. Springfield, Mass.: King-Richardson
     Co., 1903.

     Includes one-page biographical sketches of
authors.

     Alcott
     Cary, Alice
     Cary, Phoebe
     Child
     Crosby
     Dodge, Mary Abigail
     Fern
     Larcom (P)
     [Lippincott] Greenwood
     Livermore, Mary A.
     Moulton
     Sedgwick, Catharine M. (P)
     Sigourney (P)
     Spofford (P)
     Stowe (P)
     [Terhune] Harland (P)

359. Wauchope, George Armstrong. THE WRITERS OF SOUTH
     CAROLINA. Columbia, S.C.: State Co., 1910.
     420 pp.

     Consists of a long introductory essay, one-page
biographical notices, and selections from the writers.

     Dinnies
     Gilman
     Gwyn
     King
     Lee, Mary Elizabeth
     Shindler
     Whitaker

360. Weibel, Kathryn. "Images of Women in Fiction."
     Chap. 1 in MIRROR MIRROR: IMAGES OF WOMEN
     REFLECTED IN POPULAR CULTURE. Garden City, N.Y.:
     Anchor Press, 1977.

Discusses CHARLOTTE TEMPLE, THE WIDE, WIDE WORLD,
UNCLE TOM'S CABIN, and works by E.D.E.N. Southworth as
representative popular novels. Views them as
supporting the book's thesis, that American popular
culture has consistently portrayed women as
"housewifely, passive, wholesome, and pretty."

 Rowson
 Southworth, E.D.E.N.
 Stowe
 Warner, Susan

361. Welter, Barbara. DIMITY CONVICTIONS: THE AMERICAN
WOMAN IN THE NINETEENTH CENTURY. Athens: Ohio
University Press, 1976. 230 pp.

Women's fiction is used to illustrate the four
virtues--piety, purity, submissiveness, and domesticity
--that Welter sees as attributes of nineteenth-century
True Womanhood. The well-known essay, "The Cult of
True Womanhood, 1820-1860," originally published in
AMERICAN QUARTERLY in 1966, is Chapter 2 in this book.
Chapter 7, "Defenders of the Faith: Women Novelists of
Religious controversy in the Nineteenth Century,"
includes consideration of Augusta Evans Wilson.
Chapter 1, "Coming of Age in America: The American
Girl in the Nineteenth Century," is also relevant.

 Alcott
 Child
 Dall
 Doten
 Embury
 Farnham
 Finley
 Gilman
 Graves, Mrs. A.J.
 Hale, Sarah Josepha
 [Hubbell] Linwood
 [Judson] Forester
 [Lippincott] Clarke
 Martyn
 Stowe
 [Wilson, Augusta Evans] Evans

362. Wendell, Barrett. A LITERARY HISTORY OF AMERICA.
New York: Charles Scribner's Sons, 1901. 574 pp.

Fails to mention many female writers who were very
well known in the nineteenth century (for instance,
Catharine M. Sedgwick, Susan Warner, and Lydia Maria
Child), but does discuss Louisa May Alcott and Caroline
Kirkland and devotes several pages to Harriet Beecher
Stowe.

    Alcott
    Kirkland
    Stowe

363. Westbrook, Perry D. THE NEW ENGLAND TOWN IN FACT
     AND FICTION. East Brunswick, N.J.: Associated
     University Presses, 1982. 286 pp.

A study of the mythology of the small New England
town as it appears in both fiction and non-fiction.
Highly selective, analyzing works by some nineteenth-
century women and omitting relevant authors such as
Sarah Josepha Hale.

    Dorr
    Sedgwick, Catharine M.
    Stowe

364. Whipple, Edwin P. "A Century of American
     Literature." In THE FIRST CENTURY OF THE
     REPUBLIC: A REVIEW OF AMERICAN PROGRESS, 349-398.
     New York: Harper & Brothers, 1876.

This assessment of the first century of literature
in the U.S. includes very brief mention of many female
writers and more extensive commentary on the authors
listed below.

    Alcott
    Stowe
  . Whitney

365. White, Barbara A. "The Girl Protagonist before
     1920." Chap. 2 in GROWING UP FEMALE: ADOLESCENT
     GIRLHOOD IN AMERICAN FICTION. Westport, Conn.:
     Greenwood Press, 1985.

Discussion of teenaged heroines in nineteenth-
century fiction by women. Contrasts the "Good Good

Girl" in novels by Martha Finley, Susan Warner, and others with the more rebellious protagonists of Hannah Foster, E.D.E.N. Southworth, and Louisa May Alcott.

Alcott
Cummins
[Fern] Parton
Finley
Foster
Southworth
Terhune
Warner, Susan
Wilson, Augusta Evans

366. _____. "Some Sources for the Study of Women's Fiction, 1790-1865." LEGACY 2 no.1 (Spring 1985): 6-8.

Review article summarizing existing scholarship and criticism in the field and suggesting work that needs to be done. Calls for more literary criticism, that is, attention to the fiction itself and more discussion of criteria of evaluation.

367. White, Eliza Orne. "Some New England Authors and Their Stories." HORN BOOK 1 (1925): 11-21.

Appreciation of some works for children; includes many quotations from the stories.

Alcott (P)
Hale, Lucretia P. (P)
Whitney (P)

368. Whiting, Lilian. WOMEN WHO HAVE ENNOBLED LIFE. Philadelphia: Union Press, 1915. 260 pp.

Collection of biographical sketches, about thirty pages each and containing quotations from the subjects' letters and other primary sources. Includes portraits.

Alcott (P)
Livermore, Amry A. (P)
Stowe (P)

369. Whitman, Charles Huntington. THE LITERATURE OF
     NEW JERSEY. New York: American Historical
     Society, 1930. 78 pp.

     Short biographical sketches of New Jersey writers,
alphabetically arranged. Emphasis is on late
nineteenth-century and early twentieth-century authors,
but some earlier writers are included.

     Dodge, Mary Mapes
     Kinney
     Terhune

370. Whitton, Mary Ormsbee. THESE WERE THE WOMEN:
     U.S.A. 1776-1860. New York: Hastings House, 1954.
     288 pp.

     Some writers of fiction are discussed in this
survey of women's accomplishments. Information is
sometimes inaccurate--for instance, Lydia Maria Child
is identified as the "first American woman novelist."

     Child
     Fern
     French
     Hale, Sarah Josepha
     Mowatt
     Royall
     Sigourney
     Stowe
     [Terhune] Hawes
     [Wilson, Augusta Evans] Evans

371. Williams, Benjamin Buford. A LITERARY HISTORY OF
     ALABAMA: THE NINETEENTH CENTURY. Cranbury, N.J.:
     Associated University Presses, 1979. 258 pp.

     Discusses Caroline Lee Hentz and Augusta Evans
Wilson at length, concluding only that their novels
should be seen "merely as products of domestic
sentimentalism."

     Bellamy
     Cruse
     Hentz, Caroline Lee
     Royall
     Wilson, Augusta Evans

372. Williams, Kenny J. THEY ALSO SPOKE: AN ESSAY ON
     NEGRO LITERATURE IN AMERICA, 1787-1930. Nashville:
     Townsend Press, 1970. 319 pp.

     The only nineteenth-century woman treated in depth
is Frances E.W. Harper, who is seen primarily as a
poet. The author views Harriet A. Jacobs' INCIDENTS IN
THE LIFE OF A SLAVE GIRL inaccurately as the work of
Lydia Maria Child and as centering upon "the role of
the white wife."

         Harper
         Jacobs

373. Williams, Stanley Thomas. THE AMERICAN SPIRIT IN
     LETTERS. Vol. 11 of THE PAGEANT OF AMERICA: A
     PICTORIAL HISTORY OF THE UNITED STATES, edited by
     Ralph Henry Gabriel. New Haven: Yale University
     Press, 1926. 329 pp.

     Survey of American literature. Although
discussion of writers is brief (one or two paragraphs
for each), there are numerous photographs, including
illustrations from late eighteenth and nineteenth-
century novels. A group portrait entitled "Authors of
the United States, Mid-Nineteenth Century" includes
nine women with the thirty-five men.

         Alcott (P)
         Bleecker (P)
         Brooks, Maria Gowen (P)
         Cary, Alice (P)
         Cary, Phoebe (P)
         Child (P)
         Foster
         Morton
         Rowson
         Sedgwick, Catharine M. (P)
         Sigourney
         Stowe (P)
         Tenney

374. Wishy, Bernard. THE CHILD AND THE REPUBLIC: THE
     DAWN OF MODERN AMERICAN CHILD NURTURE.
     Philadelphia: University of Pennsylvania Press,
     1968. 205 pp.

Children's literature between 1830 and 1900 is analyzed as evidence of American attitudes toward childhood and child nurture.

Alcott
Child
Finley
Sedgwick, Catharine M.
Sigourney

375. WOMAN: HER POSITION, INFLUENCE, AND ACHIEVEMENT THROUGHOUT THE CIVILIZED WORLD. Edited by William C. King. Springfield, Mass.: King-Richardson Co., 1901. 667 pp.

Consists of page-long biographical sketches, chronologically arranged, of famous women of all eras, followed by essays on women's achievements in various fields. Book Six includes many American writers. Thomas Wentworth Higginson notes in his essay, "Woman in Literature," pp. 493-505, that women's development as authors has been "broken and unequal . . . through the interruptions of war and the lingering prejudice against their work"; greater recognition will lead to higher achievement.

Alcott
Cary, Alice
Cary, Phoebe
Child
Crosby
Dodge, Mary Abigail
Fern
Larcom (P)
[Lippincott] Greenwood
Livermore, Mary Ann (P)
Moulton
Sedgwick, Catharine M. (P)
Sigourney (P)
Spofford (P)
Stowe (P)
[Terhune] Harland (P)

376. A WOMAN OF THE CENTURY. Edited by Frances E. Willard and Mary A. Livermore. 2 vols. Buffalo: Charles Wells Moulton, 1893. 812 pp. Rev. ed. under title AMERICAN WOMEN. New York: Mast,

Crowell & Kirkpatrick, 1897.   824 pp.

Contains 1,470 biographical sketches and portraits, supposedly of American women whose achievements took place during the nineteenth century. However, the focus is on the latter part of the century; most of the women included were born after 1850 and still alive when the book was published. The second edition added thirty biographies of late nineteenth-century women and a useful classified index.

Alcott (P)
Arey (P)
Austin (P)
Baker, Harriette Newell Woods
Barrow
Beauchamp
Bellamy
Blake (P)
Booth (P)
Botta (P)
Boyd (P)
Cary, Alice (P)
Cary, Phoebe (P)
Child (P)
Clarke, Rebecca Sophia (P)
Cooke (P)
Cooper, Sarah Brown Ingersoll (P)
Crosby (P)
Dall (P)
Davis, Minnie S. (P)
Davis, Rebecca Harding
Diaz (P)
Dodge, Mary Abigail
Dodge, Mary Mapes (P)
Dorr (P)
Dorsey, Anna Hanson
Duniway (P)
[Fern] Parton
Finley (P)
Gage
Goodwin, H.B. (P)
Goodwin, Lavinia S.
Graves, Adelia C. (P)
Hanaford (P)
Holmes (P)
Jeffrey (P)
Larcom (P)
Latimer (P)

Lippincott (P)
Livermore, Mary A. (P)
Moore, Clara Jessup (P)
Moulton (P)
[Mowatt] Ritchie (P)
Otis
Preston
Sedgwick, Catharine M.
Sigourney (P)
Smith, Elizabeth Oakes
Southworth, E.D.E.N. (P)
Spofford (P)
Stoddard
Stowe (P)
Terhune (P)
Townsend, Mary Ashley (P)
Victor, Frances Fuller (P)
Victor, Metta Fuller (P)
Whitney
Wilson, Augusta Evans (P)
Wood, Julia Amanda Sargent (P)

377. WOMEN AND LITERATURE: AN ANNOTATED BIBLIOGRAPHY OF
WOMEN WRITERS. 3rd ed. Cambridge, Mass.: Women
and Literature Collective, 1976 (1st ed. 1973).
212 pp.

There are serious omissions from the "United
States, Pre-19th Century" and "United States, 19th
Century" sections of this very fine bibliography, but
the annotations remain useful. Also included are short
biographical sketches of the writers.

Alcott (P)
Cooke
Fern
Foster
Harper
[Jacobs] Brent
Larcom
Sedgwick, Catharine M.
Spofford
Stowe (P)
Victor, Frances Fuller

378. "Women Fiction Writers of Maine." MAINE LIBRARY
BULLETIN (July 1928): 8-24.

Discusses Sally Wood and Sarah Orne Jewett as the two most important Maine writers and then provides short biographical sketches and bibliographies of female authors born in Maine.

[Clarke] Clark, Rebecca Sophia
[Fern] Parton
Goodwin, H.B.
Pike
Prentiss
Smith, Elizabeth Oakes
Spofford
Sweat
Wood, Sally

379. Woodward, Helen Beal. THE BOLD WOMEN. New York: Farrar, Straus and Young, 1953. 373 pp.

Biographies of nineteenth-century American women, including some authors, related informally and in a patronizing tone.

Bacon, Delia
Farnham
Hale, Sarah Josepha
Leslie
Royall

380. Wright, Lyle H. "A Few Observations on American Fiction, 1851-1875." PROCEEDINGS OF THE AMERICAN ANTIQUARIAN SOCIETY 65 (Apr.-Oct. 1955): 75-104.

Comments by the famous bibliographer on forgotten novels he encountered when compiling his bibliography. Fiction on specific themes, such as the Civil War and women's rights, is discussed, along with popularity and sales figures. Women are presented as inferior writers who can "mass-produce tears."

Bullard, Laura J.
Cridge
Greenough
Pearson
Phelps, Elizabeth Stuart
Rush, Caroline E.
Stowe

381. Wright, Nathalia. "The Untrammelled Life." Ch. 2
in AMERICAN NOVELISTS IN ITALY. Philadelphia:
University of Pennsylvania Press, 1965.

Three female novelists are considered among other
writers who were "forerunners of the major fictionists
of the period" in writing about Italy. The author is
primarily concerned with the influence of their
residence in Italy on the novelists' works.

   Brewster
   Greenough
   Stowe

382. THE WRITING WOMEN OF NEW ENGLAND, 1630-1900: AN
ANTHOLOGY. Edited by Arlen Gilman Runzler
Westbrook and Perry D. Westbrook. Metuchen, N.J.:
Scarecrow Press, 1982. 274 pp.

Collection of writings by New England women who
are seen as representative of the region.
Unfortunately, the editors failed to include African-
American women. Selections are interesting and well
chosen; each is prefaced by a two-to-three-page
biographical sketch of the author.

   Alcott
   Cooke
   Larcom
   Livermore, Mary A.
   Morton
   Stowe

383. YESTERDAY'S AUTHORS OF BOOKS FOR CHILDREN. Edited
by Anne Commire. 2 vols. Detroit: Gale Research
Co., 1977-1978. 274 pp., 335 pp.

Consists of "facts and pictures about authors,"
entries ranging from half a page for Maria Cummins to
several pages for Louisa May Alcott and Harriet Beecher
Stowe. The facts are generally lists of editions of
various works and a chronology with excerpts from the
author's diaries or autobiographical writings.

   Alcott (P)
   Cummins
   Stowe (P)

384. YESTERDAY'S CHILDREN: AN ANTHOLOGY COMPILED FROM
THE PAGES OF <u>OUR YOUNG FOLKS</u>, 1865-1873. Edited
by John Morton Blum. Boston: Houghton Mifflin
Co., 1959. 276 pp.

Collection of fiction, poetry and essays from the
New England magazine for youth. Includes pieces by
several women, whose work is briefly discussed by the
editor.

Alcott
[Dodge, Mary Abigail] Hamilton
Hale, Lucretia P.
Larcom
Moulton
Stowe

385. YOUTH'S COMPANION. Edited by Lowell Thompson et
al. Boston: Houghton Mifflin Co., 1984. 1140 pp.

Selections from 100 years of the popular magazine,
YOUTH'S COMPANION. Includes editors' discussion of the
authors and their times

Alcott
Larcom
Sedwick, Catharine M.
Stowe

Abbott, Anne W[ales]   (b.1808)

   7; 216

Alcott, Louisa May   (1832-1888)   Also wrote under:
   L.M.A.; A.M.; A.M. Barnard; Flora Fairfield;
   Tribulation Periwinkle.

   1; 3(P); 7; 8(P); 9; 11; 12(P); 13; 14; 16(P); 20;
   23; 26; 28; 29(P); 31; 35; 39(P); 42; 49; 50; 52;
   53; 54; 55; 57; 58; 64; 65; 66(P); 72; 75; 77(P);
   79; 88; 93; 94; 99(P); 103; 104; 110; 115; 118;
   126; 133; 138; 143; 144; 146; 149; 153; 155; 156;
   158; 159; 161; 165; 171(P); 173; 177; 183; 185(P);
   190; 199; 200; 202(P); 203; 204; 206; 208; 210(P);
   215; 220(P); 223; 227; 234(P); 236; 239; 241; 244;
   248; 252(P); 255; 265; 267; 277(P); 278; 284;
   293(P); 302; 306(P); 307(P); 311; 321; 323; 325;
   326; 327; 328(P); 329(P); 330; 342; 353; 358; 361;
   362; 364; 365; 367(P); 368(P); 373(P); 374; 375;
   376(P); 377(P); 382; 383(P); 384; 385

Allen, Elizabeth   (fl. 1846)

   134; 281

Andrews, Jane   (1833-1887)

   7; 13; 14; 42; 53; 93; 126 (b.1835); 156; 226;
   239; 255 (b.1835); 277

Appleton, Anna E.   (b.1825)

    7; 149

Appleton, Elizabeth Haven   (1815-1890)

    7; 65; 74

Appleton, Jane Sophia   (fl. 1848, d.1884)

    79; 273

Arey, H[arriet] E[llen] G[rannis]   (1819-1901)

    7; 74; 180(P); 376(P)

Austin, Jane Goodwin   (1831-1894)

    7; 8(P); 13; 23; 35; 52; 88; 93; 100; 115; 185(P);
    230(P); 255; 262; 277; 311; 323; 376(P)

Bache, Anna   (fl.1840's)

    7; 155; 164

Bacon, Delia [Salter]   (1811-1859)

    7; 8; 12(P); 13; 23; 30; 43; 66; 74; 88; 94; 141;
    155; 175(P); 199; 200; 239; 251; 255; 277; 320;
    323; 379

Bacon, Julia   "Mollie Myrtle"   (b.ca.1835)

    7; 83; 275; 317

Bagley, Sarah [G.]   (fl.1840-1845)   Also wrote under:
    S.G.B.

    4; 13; 112; 184; 199; 213; 215; 239; 288

Bailey, Margaret J[ewett Smith]   (fl.1854)

   270

Baker, Harriette Newell Woods   "Madeline Leslie,"
"Aunt Hattie"   (1815-1893)

   7 (Leslie); 28; 35; 52; 93; 152; 155; 216; 226;
376(P)

Baker, Sarah S[choonmaker Tuthill]   "Aunt Friendly"
(1824-1906)

   7; 52; 152; 216 (Aunt Friendly)

Ball, Caroline A[ugusta Rutledge]   (b.1825)

   83; 155; 201; 275; 294; 317 (b.ca.1835)

Ball, Pamilla W.   (fl.1835)

   107

Barrow, Frances Elizabeth [Mease]   "Aunt Fanny"
(1822-1894)

   7; 52; 93; 201; 376

Beauchamp, Mary Elizabeth   (b.1825)   Also wrote under:
Filia Ecclesiae.

   7; 376(P)

Beecher, Eunice White Bullard   (1813-1897)   Also wrote
under: A Minister's Wife; Mrs. Henry Ward Beecher.

   7; 304 (b.1812)

Belisle, Orvilla S.   (fl.1855)

   21

Bell, Alfreda Eva   (fl.1855)

    21

Bellamy, Elizabeth Whitfield [Croom]   "Kamba Thorpe"
    (1837-1900)

    7; 8; 88; 155; 201 (b.1839); 249 (b.1838); 275;
    276; 294; 311; 371; 376 (b.1839)

Berry, Kate   (1817-1865)

    245

Blake, Lillie Devereux [Umsted]   (1833-1913) Also
    wrote under: Aesop; Tiger Lily; Lillie Devereux
    Umsted.

    3; 7 (Umsted, b.1834); 8 (b.1835); 13; 14; 35
    (b.1835); 88 (b.1835); 149; 180; 199; 201; 210;
    239; 294 (b.1835); 376 (b.1835) (P)

Bleecker, Ann Eliza [Schuyler]   (1752-1783)

    7; 8; 13; 15; 22; 32; 44; 72; 77(P); 78; 88;
    89; 102; 126; 145; 153; 160; 166(P); 193; 196;
    212; 214 (Bleeker); 221; 239; 255; 263; 266;
    272; 277; 323; 373(P)

Blount, Annie R.   (b.1839)   Also wrote under: Jenny
    Woodbine.

    83; 121; 155; 201; 275; 276

Bogart, Elizabeth   (b.1806)   Also wrote under:
    Adelaide; Estelle.

    7; 145; 154; 155; 269

Booth, Mary L[ouise]   (1831-1889)

    7; 69; 77; 88; 149; 199; 239; 252; 323; 376(P)

Botsford, Margaret (fl.1812-1828) Also wrote under:
Mrs. M; A Lady of Philadelphia.

38; 44; 266

Botta, Anne C[harlotte] Lynch (1815-1891) Also
wrote under: Anne Lynch.

3; 7 (Lynch); 8; 13; 19(P); 35; 40; 77(P); 78
(Lynch); 88; 93; 134; 149; 155; 160; 239; 269
(Lynch); 376 (b.1820) (P)

Boyd, Louise Esther Vickroy (1827-1909)

7; 74; 176; 376(P)

Bradley, Mary E[mily Neely] (1835-1898) Also wrote
under: Cousin Alice; Kate J. Neely.

7; 44; 128; 201; 323

Brewster, Anne [Maria] Hampton (b.1818)

7; 381

Briggs, Emily E[dson Pomona] "Olivia" (1830-1910)

13; 28 (b.1831); 199; 217; 239

Bright, Amanda [Metcalf] (b.1822)

7; 201; 275

Brooks, Maria Gowen (1794/95-1845) Also wrote under:
A Lover of the Fine Arts; Maria del Occidente.

7; 8(P); 13; 14; 23; 66; 77(P); 78; 87; 88; 110;
126; 137; 145; 155; 199; 225; 239; 251; 255; 277;
314; 321; 323(P); 343; 373(P)

Brooks, M[arie] Sears (fl.1850's and 1860's, d.1893)

176; 376

Brown, Phoebe H[insdale]   (1783-1861)

    88; 281

Browne, Maria J.B.   (fl.1850)

    7; 154; 155; 226

Browne, Sara H.   (fl.1847-1850)   Also wrote under: A
    S.S. Teacher.

    7; 154; 155; 226

Brownson, Sarah M[aria] Nicolena   [married name Tenney]
    (1839-1876)   Also wrote under: An American; One of
    Themselves.

    7; 13; 338 (Tenney)

Buckley, Maria L.   (fl.1852-1856)

    44; 305

Bullard, Anne Tuttle [Jones]   "Mrs. Caustic"
    (fl.1830-1852)

    7; 281

Bullard, Laura J. [Curtis]   (fl.1854-1856)

    7; 48; 380

Butt, Martha Haines [married name Bennett]   (1834-1871)

    7; 83 (Bennett); 98; 130; 167; 201 (Bennett);
    275 (Bennett); 276 (Bennett)

Campbell, Jane C.   (fl.1854-1859)

7; 13; 86

Campbell, Juliet H. L[ewis] (b.1823) Also wrote
    under: Judith Canute.

    7; 13; 145

Canfield, Gertrude A. (b.1836)

    275; 276

Carter, Alice Ann (fl.1840's)

    247

Cary, Alice (1820-1871) Also wrote under: Alice
    Carey; Patty Lee.

    1; 3; 7 (Carey); 8(P); 13; 14; 23; 25 (Carey); 28;
    34; 35; 50; 52; 57; 58; 74; 77 (b.1822); 78
    (Carey); 86; 88; 91; 92; 93; 94; 97; 108; 109;
    110; 126; 145 (Carey) (P); 146; 149 (P); 151; 153;
    154 (Carey); 155; 160; 173; 190; 196; 199; 200;
    210(P); 236; 239; 243; 247; 248; 255; 258; 260(P);
    261; 262; 271; 277; 293(P); 295; 304; 310; 321;
    323; 330; 333; 345; 346; 347; 349; 358; 373(P);
    375; 376(P)

Cary, Phoebe (1824-1871)

    1; 3; 7 (Carey, b.1825); 8(P); 13; 23 (b.1825);
    34; 35; 57; 58; 74; 77; 78 (Carey); 86; 88; 91;
    93; 108; 109; 110; 126; 145 (Carey); 146; 149 (P);
    151; 155; 160; 173; 190; 199; 200; 210 (P); 239;
    243; 248; 255; 260 (P); 261; 265; 277; 293(P);
    304; 330; 347; 349; 354; 358; 373(P); 375; 376(P)

Cary, Virginia Randolph (1786-1852)

    7; 18

Cate, Eliza J[ane] (1812-1884) Also wrote under: D.

184; 213; 288

Chamberlain, Betsey   (fl.1840's)   Also wrote under:
    Jemima; Tabitha.

288

Chaplin, Jane Dunbar   (1819-1884)   Also wrote under:
    Hyla.

7; 13; 155

Cheney, Harriet V [aughan Foster]   (b.1796)

    7; 22; 30; 78; 141; 145; 149; 155; 212; 226; 281;
    320

Chesebro', Caroline [real name Caroline Chesebrough]
    (1825-1873)

    7; 8 (Chesebrough); 13 (Chesebrough); 25; 28; 44;
    65; 77; 88 (Chesebrough); 126; 154; 155; 166(P);
    174; 217; 311 (b.1828?)

Child, Lydia Maria [Francis]   (1802-1880)   Also wrote
    under: L.M.C.; An American; A Lady of Massa-
    chusetts; Mrs. D.L. Child.

    2; 3; 7; 8(P); 12(P); 13; 14; 22; 23; 25; 28; 29
    (P); 30; 35; 38; 40; 41; 43; 44; 50; 52; 53; 55;
    57; 62; 67; 69(P); 70; 72; 77; 78; 87; 88; 92; 93;
    94; 100; 108; 110; 120; 126; 137 (Mrs. David L.
    Child); 138; 140; 141; 145; 146; 149; 152;
    154; 155; 156; 160; 161; 163; 164; 166(P); 177;
    182 (Childs); 183; 196; 198; 199; 200; 203; 204;
    205; 208; 210; 212; 215; 216; 217; 226; 229; 231;
    233; 234(P); 235; 239; 248; 251; 252; 254; 255;
    263; 269; 271; 272; 277; 281; 285; 286; 287; 293;
    295; 299; 305; 314; 320; 321; 323(P); 324; 326;
    330; 332; 335 (Childs); 343; 345; 346; 353; 358;
    361; 370; 373(P); 374; 375; 376(P)

Church, Ella Rodman [McIlvane]   (b.1831)   Also wrote

under: Ella Rodman.

7; 13; 35; 38

Clack, [Marie] Louise [Babcock]   (b.ca.1835)

7; 83; 201; 275; 317

Clare, Ada   [real name Jane McElhinney]   (ca. 1836-
1874)   Also wrote under: Clare; Queen of Bohemia.

7 (Julia MacElhinney); 199; 239; 265; 277
(McElheney)

Clark, Mary L[atham]   (b.1831)

155; 226

Clarke, Mary Bayard [Devereux] "Tenella"   (1827-1886)

7 (b.1830); 8; 83; 88; 155; 201; 237; 239; 275;
276; 317 (b.1822 or 1830)

Clarke, Rebecca Sophia   "Sophie May"   (1833-1906)

5(P); 7; 8; 13; 16; 42; 48; 52; 53 (May); 88; 93;
104; 123 (Clark); 126; 156; 183 (May); 199; 239;
248; 376(P); 378 (Clark)

Collins, A[ngelina] Maria [Lorraine]   (1805-1885)   Also
wrote under: Lady of the West; Young Lady of
Virginia; A.M. Lorraine.

47 (Lorraine); 176 (b.1820); 304

Comstock, Elizabeth A.   (1817-1860)   Also wrote under:
Elizabeth Emmet.

77

Cook, Martha [Elizabeth Duncan] Walker   (1806-1874)

7; 88

Cooke, Rose Terry (1827-1892) Also wrote under:
    A.W.H.; Rose Terry.

    7 (Terry); 8 (b.1837) (P); 13; 14; 35; 50; 51; 65;
    66; 71; 88; 92; 93; 96; 115; 126; 146; 162;
    171(P); 197; 199; 202; 239; 247; 251; 252(P); 255;
    259; 260; 262; 271; 272; 277; 284; 293; 314; 323;
    333; 346 (Terry); 348; 376(P); 377; 382

Cooper, Sarah Brown Ingersoll (1835-1896)

    88 (b.1836); 199; 239; 376 (b.1836) (P)

Cooper, Susan [Augusta] Fenimore (1813-1894)
    Also wrote under: A Lady; Anabel Penfeather.

    7; 8; 13; 28; 44; 78; 88; 145 (Miss Cooper);
    149; 154; 155 (b.1825); 199; 239; 255; 277

Corwin, Jane Hudson (1809-1881)

    74

Cowdin, Mrs. V.G. (fl.1860-1861)

    105; 106; 130; 136; 201; 275 (Cowden)

Coxe, Margaret (b.1800)

    7; 74; 78; 145; 149

Crane, Anne Moncure [married name Seemuller] (1838-
    1872) Also wrote under: Anne Moncure Crane
    Seemuller.

    7 (Seemuller); 8; 88; 155 (Seemuller); 201; 275;
    276; 303 (Crane-Seemuller)

Creswell, Julia P[leasants] (1821 or 1827-1886) Also

wrote under: Adrienne; Julia Pleasants.

83; 155; 201; 275; 276; 317

Cridge, Annie Denton (b.1801-1805)

7; 79; 273; 380

Crosby, [Frances] Fanny J[ane] [married name Van
    Alstyne] (1820-1915)

3; 13 (Van Alstyne); 14 (Van Alstyne); 88; 93;
199; 215; 239; 277; 358; 375; 376 (b.1823)

Cross, Jane T[andy Chinn Hardin] (1817-1870)

13; 83; 121; 155; 201; 275; 276; 293; 294; 317

Cruse, Mary Anne (ca.1835-ca.1910) Also wrote under:
    M.A.C.

7; 83; 105; 155; 201; 208; 275; 276; 317; 371

Cummins, Maria [Susanna] (1827-1866) Also wrote
    under: M.C.

7 (Cummings); 8; 13; 14; 16; 25; 28; 31; 35; 37;
43; 44; 45; 53; 57; 72; 73; 88; 93; 94; 96; 99;
101; 103 (Cummings); 110; 115; 117; 118; 120; 122;
124; 126; 132; 143; 150; 153; 155 (Cummings); 164;
166(P); 175; 183; 186; 187; 188; 194; 195; 196;
199; 217; 219; 223; 227; 229; 232; 239; 243; 246;
248; 251; 255; 257; 260; 277; 278; 281; 284; 286;
293; 295; 305; 311; 315; 321; 331; 332; 342; 352;
353; 365; 383

Curtis, Harriot F. (1813-1889) Also wrote under: A
    Lady Chrysalis; Mina Myrtle.

38; 112; 184; 288

Cushing, Eliza Lanesford [Foster] (b.1794)

7; 22; 189; 263; 272

Cutler, Lizzie Petit (1831-1902) Also wrote under:
Mrs. P.Y. Cutler; Lizzie Petit.

7 (Petit); 8; 83; 88; 121 (Petit); 128 (Petit);
155; 201 (b.1836); 275; 276; 305; 317 (b.1836)

Dall, Caroline [Wells] H[ealey] (1822-1912)

7; 12(P); 13; 14; 69; 88; 108; 149; 155; 163; 198;
199; 239; 285; 361; 376(P)

Davidson, Virginia E.   (fl.1836) Also wrote under:
Virginia.

275; 276

Davis, Caroline E. [Kelly]   (b.1831)   Also wrote under:
Caroline E. Kelly.

7; 155; 226

Davis, Minnie S.   (b.1835)

7; 149; 201; 376(P)

Davis, Rebecca [Blaine] Harding   (1831-1910)

3; 7; 8; 9; 13; 14; 31; 33; 35; 36; 46; 64; 65;
79; 88; 101; 120; 122; 143; 171; 173; 177; 178;
191; 199; 203; 205; 206; 207; 223; 238; 239; 240;
241; 247; 251; 255; 258; 259; 271; 272; 277; 305;
314; 318; 323; 333; 336; 353; 376

Denison, Mary [Ann] Andrews   (1826-1911) Also wrote
under: A.M.D.; M.A.D.; Mrs. C.W. Denison; N.I.
Edson; Clara Vance.

7; 13; 28; 141; 155; 180(P); 239; 305

Diaz, A[bby] M[orton] (1821-1904)

    7; 8; 13; 14; 35; 52; 53; 88; 104; 199; 239;
    376(P)

Dickson, Jeanie A. (fl.1850)

    275

Dinnies, Anna Peyre [Shackelford] (1805-1886) Also
    wrote under: Moina; Rachel; Anna Peyre.

    7; 13; 59 (b.1816); 62; 78; 83; 85 (b.1807); 121;
    145; 149; 155; 201 (b.1816); 275; 276; 294
    (b.1816); 317 (b.1816); 359 (b.1816)

Dodge, Mary Abigail "Gail Hamilton" (1833-1896)
    Also wrote under: Cunctare.

    7 (b.1830); 8; 13; 14; 23 (b.1838); 35 (b.1838);
    58; 64; 71; 88; 93 (b.1830); 108 (Hamilton); 109;
    145 (Hamilton); 146; 155 (b.1838); 183; 197; 199;
    200; 220; 239; 255; 271; 346 (Hamilton); 354; 355;
    358; 375; 376 (b.1830); 384 (Hamilton)

Dodge, Mary [Elizabeth] Mapes (1831-1905) Also wrote
    under: M.M.D.; Nathaniel Shotwell; Joel Stacy.

    3; 7 (b.1838); 8(P); 13; 14; 16(P); 20; 31; 35
    (b.1838); 49; 50; 52; 53; 65; 88; 93 (b.1838); 99;
    104; 126 (b.1836); 138; 149; 156; 158; 161; 165;
    183; 185(P); 197; 199; 202 (b.1840?) (P); 210
    (b.1838); 227; 230(P); 239; 248; 252(P); 255; 277;
    323 (b.1838) (P); 329(P); 330; 369 (b.1838); 376
    (b.1838) (P)

Dorr, Julia C[aroline] R[ipley] (1825-1913) Also
    wrote under: Sibyl Huntington; Lanmere; Isabel
    Leslie; Caroline Thomas.

    7; 8; 13; 14; 28; 35; 77(P); 88; 93; 134(P); 146;
    154; 155; 171(P); 199; 201; 220(P); 275; 317; 323;
    345; 363; 376(P)

Dorsey, Anna Hanson [McKenney] (1815-1896)

    7; 8; 13; 88; 201; 275; 281; 338; 376 (b.1816)

Dorsey, Sarah Anne [Ellis] (1829-1879)   Also wrote
    under: Filia.

    7; 8; 13; 83; 85; 88; 128; 155; 170; 201; 209;
    210; 218; 239; 275; 276; 279; 294; 317

Doten, Elizabeth (b.1829)

    7; 40; 361

Downing, [Frances] Fanny Murdaugh (1835-1894)   Also
    wrote under: Frank Dashmore; Viola.

    7; 83; 155; 201; 217; 275; 276; 317; 356

DuBose, [Catherine] Kate A[nne Richards] (1828-1906)

    7; 83; 121; 155; 201 (b.1826); 275; 276

Dumont, Julia L[ouisa Cory] (1794-1857)

    7; 74; 91; 107; 155; 176; 349

Duniway, Abigail [Jane] Scott (1834-1915)

    7; 8; 13; 14; 88; 199; 239; 270(P); 376(P)

Dunning, Annie K[etchum] (b.1831)   Also wrote under:
    Nellie Grahame.

    7; 155

Dupuy, Eliza A[nn] (1814-1880)   Also wrote under: A.E.
    Dupuy; Annie Young.

    7; 8(d.1881); 13; 28; 38; 83; 88(d.1881); 121;
    128; 141; 155; 201 (d.1881); 209; 236; 239; 251;

255 (d.1881); 275; 276; 277 (d.1881); 294
(d.1881); 316; 317 (d.1881)

Eames, Jane A[nthony] (1816-1894) Also wrote under: A
    Layman.

    7; 145

Eastman, Mary H[enderson] (1818-1887) Also wrote
    under: Matilda.

    7; 13; 18; 38; 44; 46; 98; 128; 130; 136; 142;
    154; 155; 167; 199; 201; 231; 239; 268; 275; 277
    (d.1880); 291; 295; 305; 334; 350 (d.1880); 357

Elemjay, Louise [Wright] (fl.1852-1858)

    83 (Elenjay); 155 (Elenjay); 201 (Ellemjay); 317
    (Ellinjay, b.ca.1840)

Ellet, Elizabeth F[ries Lummis] (ca.1812-1877) Also
    wrote under: E.F.E.

    7; 8 (b.1818); 13; 35 (b.1818); 40; 69; 77
    (b.1818); 78; 88 (b.1818); 145; 149; 154 (b.1818);
    155 (b.1818); 180; 199; 239

Embury, Emma C[atherine Manley] (1806-1863) Also
    wrote under: Ianthe.

    7; 8; 13; 28; 35; 40; 62; 77; 78; 88; 102; 126;
    145(P); 148; 149; 154; 155; 173; 255; 269; 287;
    361

Evans, Sarah Ann (fl.1825) Also wrote under: A Lady.

    13; 44; 281

Farley, Harriet [married name Donlevy] (1813?-1907)
    Also wrote under: H.F.; Adelia; Ella; Susan.

    4; 7; 8 (b.1817) (P); 13; 14; 35 (b.1815?); 52

(b.1817); 77; 78; 88 (b.1817); 94; 112; 145(P);
149; 154; 155; 184; 199; 213; 239; 255 (b.1817);
277 (b.1817); 288

Farnham, Eliza W[ood Burhans]   (1815-1864)   Also wrote
under: Mrs. T.J. Farnham; Eliza Woodson.

3; 7; 8; 13; 14; 35; 77; 88; 94; 155; 196; 199;
239; 361; 379

Faugeres, Margaretta V. [Bleecker]   (1771-1801)

7; 13; 14; 15; 44; 77; 78 (b.1777); 89; 102; 145;
193; 323

Fern, Fanny   [real name Sara Payson Willis Eldredge
Parton]   (1811-1872)

5 (Parton) (P); 7 (Parton); 8 (Parton); 10
(Parton) (P); 13 (Parton); 14 (Parton); 23
(Parton); 28; 35; 37; 38 (Parton); 41; 44
(Parton); 45 (Parton); 48 (Parton); 69 (Willis);
72 (Parton); 77; 80; 86; 88 (Parton); 93 (Parton);
94 (Willis, b.1812); 96; 97; 103 (Parton); 108;
113 (Parton); 118; 124 (Willis); 126 (Parton);
132; 133; 135 (Parton); 137; 143 (Willis); 146
(Parton); 153 (Willis); 154; 155 (Parton); 159;
166 (Parton) (P); 174; 175; 186 (Parton); 187
(Parton); 188 (Parton); 195; 197 (Parton); 199
(Parton); 216; 217; 220 (Parton) (P); 224
(Parton); 236; 239 (Parton); 243; 246; 251; 257;
260(P); 271 (Parton); 277 (Willis); 293; 295;
333 (Parton); 342; 347 (Eldredge); 352; 353;
355 (Parton); 358; 365 (Parton); 370; 375; 376
(Parton); 377; 378 (Parton)

Finley, Martha [Farquharson]   (1821 or 1828-1909)   Also
wrote under: Martha Farquharson.

2; 7; 8(P); 13; 14; 16(P); 20; 28; 42; 49; 52; 53;
54; 66; 74; 88; 93; 94; 99; 104; 126; 138; 155;
156; 166(P); 176; 183; 199; 201; 219; 239; 248;
255; 257; 277; 293; 342; 361; 365; 374; 376(P)

Flanders, Mrs. G.M.   (fl.1860's)

    13; 44; 128; 136; 167; 191; 231; 334

Fleming, May Agnes [Early]   (1840-1880)   Also wrote
    under: Cousin May Carleton; Mary Agnes Fleming.

    7; 93; 173; 180(P); 195; 236; 243; 257; 264; 302;
    325

Follen, Eliza Lee [Cabot]   (1787-1860)   Also wrote
    under: A Lady.

    7; 8; 12; 13; 14; 28 (d.1867); 53; 77; 78; 88;
    94; 104; 145; 149; 155 (d.1859); 216; 239; 257;
    281; 330

Ford, Sallie R[ochester]   (1828-1910)   Also wrote
    under: Mrs. Samuel Howard Ford.

    7; 13; 83; 121; 155; 201; 208; 224; 275; 276; 294
    (d.1903); 317 (d.1902); 336; 337; 341

Foster, Hannah [Webster]   (1758 or 1759-1840)   Also
    wrote under: A Lady of Massachusetts; Mrs. John
    Foster.

    7; 8; 9; 13; 14; 15; 17; 24; 28; 31; 32; 44; 50;
    66; 72; 81; 82; 87; 88; 89; 103; 117; 123; 126;
    141; 153; 166; 189; 199; 203; 212; 214; 217; 221;
    222; 227; 229; 239; 241; 250; 255; 257; 261; 266;
    272; 277; 323; 348; 353; 365; 373; 377

Fowler, Lydia Folger   (1822-1879)   Also wrote under:
    Mrs. L.N. Fowler.

    7 (b.1823); 199; 239

French, L[ucy] Virginia [Smith]   (1825-1881)   Also
    wrote under: L'Inconnue; Lucy Smith.

    7 (b.1830); 8; 13; 18; 83; 88; 121(P); 155; 201;
    249 (Virginia L. French, b.1830); 275; 276; 294

(b.1830); 317   (b.1830); 370

Gage, Frances Dana [Barker]   (1808-1884)   Also wrote
    under: Aunt Fanny.

    7; 8; 13 (d.1880); 14 (d.1880); 74; 88; 149; 151;
    155; 163; 220(P); 239; 277; 349; 376

Gales, Winifred Marshall   (1761-1839)   Also wrote
    under: A female.

    237; 356

Gilman, Caroline Howard   (1794-1888)   Also wrote under:
    A New England Bride; A New England Housekeeper;
    A Southern Matron; Clarissa Packard.

    7; 13; 14; 19; 28; 44; 59; 77(P); 78; 83; 88;
    121; 128; 139; 145(P); 149; 154; 155; 168; 172;
    186; 187; 188; 199; 201; 217; 225; 226; 231; 239;
    257; 275; 277; 294; 317; 318; 322; 323; 359; 361

Goodwin, H[annah Elizabeth] B[radbury] [married name
    Talcott]   (1827-1893)   Also wrote under: H.B.G.;
    Mrs. Goodwin-Talcott.

    7 (Talcott); 36 (Talcott); 72; 305 (Talcott);
    376(P); 378

Goodwin, Lavinia S[tella Tyler]   (1833-1911)

    7; 376

Graves, Adelia C[leopatra Spencer]   (1821-1895)   Also
    wrote under: Aunt Alice.

    7; 74 (d.1894); 201; 275; 276; 376(P)

Graves, Mrs. A.J.   (fl.1844)

    7; 28; 247; 361

Green, Frances H[arriet Whipple] [married name
    McDougall] (1805-1878)   Also wrote under: An
    American Citizen; A Rhode Islander; Fanny Green;
    Frances Harriet Whipple.

    7; 8; 78; 88; 112 (Whipple); 145; 155 (Greene);
    191 (McDougall); 305 (McDougall)

Greenough, Sarah Dana Loring   (1827-1885)   Also wrote
    under: Mrs. Richard S. Greenough.

    7; 380; 381

Griffith, Mary   (fl.1831-1842, d.1877)

    13; 38; 44; 79; 273

Griffith, [Martha] Mattie [married name Browne]
    (fl.1857- 1860, d.1906)   Also wrote under: Martha
    Griffith.

    7; 13 (Browne); 44 (Griffiths); 61 (Browne); 128
    (Griffin); 157; 201; 211 (Griffiths); 231

Guernsey, Clara F[lorida]   (1836-1893)

    7 (b.1839); 13; 155; 323 (b.1839)

Guernsey, Lucy Ellen   (1826-1899)

    7; 13; 76; 155

Gwyn, Laura   (b.1833)

    83; 201; 275; 359

Hale, Lucretia P[eabody]   (1820-1900)

    7; 8; 13; 14; 16(P); 20; 52; 53; 88; 93; 99; 126;
    156; 158; 165; 185(P); 199; 239; 248; 277; 367(P);
    384

Hale, Sarah Josepha [Buell] (1788-1879) Also wrote
    under: S.J.H.; Cornelia; A Lady of New Hampshire;
    Julia Parley.

    3; 7; 8(P); 12(P); 13; 14; 16(P); 28; 31; 35
    (b.1790); 38; 40; 41; 44; 50; 53; 62 (b.1795); 66;
    69(P); 70; 77; 79; 80; 88; 92; 93; 94; 96; 97;
    103; 110; 111; 126; 128; 135; 136; 145; 148; 149;
    150; 153; 154; 155 (b.1790); 156; 161; 166(P);
    173; 177; 178; 183; 195; 198; 199; 205; 210
    (Buell); 215; 216; 223; 226; 229; 233; 235; 239;
    240; 244(P); 248; 251; 253; 255; 257; 259; 260(P);
    261; 268; 277(P); 280; 281; 286; 287; 295; 298;
    300; 301; 307(P); 313; 315; 323; 334; 347; 352;
    361; 370; 379

Hall, Louisa Jane [Park] (1802-1892) Also wrote
    under: L.J.H.; L.J.P.; Mrs. Edward B. Hall.

    7; 13; 38; 77; 78; 145; 149; 155; 281

Hanaford, Phebe A[nn Coffin] (1829-1921)

    7; 13; 35; 58; 88; 149(P); 151(P); 152; 239;
    376(P)

Hardenbrook, Ellie Lee (b.1836)

    275

Harlan, Mary B. (fl.1853)

    7; 337

Harper, Frances E[llen] W[atkins] (1825-1911) Also
    wrote under: Effie Afton; Frances Ellen Watkins.

    7; 13; 14; 33; 46; 58; 61; 68; 84; 149; 181; 191;
    199; 206; 211; 239; 247; 306(P); 324(P); 372; 377

Harris, Miriam Coles (1834-1925) Also wrote under:
    Mrs. Sidney S. Harris.

7; 8; 13; 14; 28; 86; 88; 227; 321; 323

Haven, [Emily] Alice B[radley Neal] (1827-1863) Also
    wrote under: Cousin Alice; Clara Cushman; Alice G.
    Lee; Alice B. Neal.

    7 (d.1868); 8; 13; 23 (b.1828); 25 (Neal); 28
    (Neal); 44; 58 (Neal); 65; 76 (b.1828); 77(P); 78
    (Neal); 88; 92 (Neal); 120; 145 (Neal) (P); 149
    (Neal); 154 (Neal, b.1828) (P); 155 (b.1828); 160;
    199; 220(P); 226 (b.1828); 236 (Neal); 239; 244
    (Neal) (P); 260 (Neal); 305; 313 (Neal)

Hayden, Caroline A.   (fl.1855)

    28

Hayden, Sarah Marshall   (1825-1899)   Also wrote under:
    Mary Frazaer.

    28; 304

Haynes, Mrs. H.S.   (fl.1834)

    107

Hazlett, Helen   (fl.1859-1870)   Also wrote under: H.M.
    Tatem; M.H. Tatem.

    7; 13

Hentz, Caroline Lee [Whiting]   (1800-1856)   Also wrote
    under: Aunt Patty.

    7; 8; 13; 14; 19; 25; 28; 37; 38; 44; 46; 54; 58;
    63; 72; 73; 74; 76; 77; 88; 91; 96; 97; 98; 105;
    106; 118; 121; 128; 129; 130; 131; 132; 136; 139;
    143; 145(P); 149; 153; 154(P); 155 (b.1804);
    166(P); 167; 168; 181; 186; 187; 188; 199; 201;
    217; 224; 229; 237; 239; 242; 243; 251; 256; 257;
    260; 275; 277; 279; 281; 286; 287; 291; 292; 294;
    295; 298; 300; 301; 315; 316; 317; 318; 333; 341;
    349; 371

Hentz, Caroline Therese [married name Branch]   (b.1833)

    201; 275 (Branch)

Herndon, Mary E[liza Hicks]   (b.1820)   Also wrote
    under: Mrs. Reuben Herndon.

    7; 201

Hilbourne, Charlotte [S.]   (fl.1852-1863)

    305

Hildeburn, Mary J[ane Reed]   (1821-1882)

    7 (Reed); 155

Holmes, Mary Jane [Hawes]   (1825-1907)

        7; 8; 13; 25; 28; 37; 44; 54; 63; 66; 72; 73; 86;
        88; 91; 93 (b.1839); 94; 98; 103; 115; 118; 122;
        124; 126 (b.1839); 128; 131; 143; 153; 155;
        171(P); 172; 173; 186; 187; 188; 194; 199; 201;
        217; 224; 227; 229; 231; 236; 239; 242; 243; 251;
        255; 257; 259; 260; 277; 295; 302; 312; 316; 327;
        336; 337; 341 (b.1828); 376(P)

Homes, Mary Sophie [Shaw Rogers]   "Millie Mayfield"
    (b.1830)

    7; 155; 167; 201; 275; 276

Hooper, Lucy   (1816-1841)   Also wrote under: L.H.

    7; 13; 77; 78; 109; 145; 149; 155

Hornblower, Jane Elizabeth [Roscoe]   (1797-1853)   Also
    wrote under: Mrs. Francis Hornblower.

    28

Hosmer, Margaret [Kerr] (1830-1897) Also wrote under:
  An Old Teacher.

    7 (d.1889); 145; 155

Hoyt, Elizabeth Orpha [Sampson] "Aunt Libbie" (1828
  or 1834-1912)

    74

Hubbell, Martha [Stone] (1814-1856)

    7; 224

Hubbell, Mary Elizabeth "Lela Linwood" (1836-1856)

    361

Hunter, Bettie Keyes (b.1834)

    275

Jacobs, Harriet A. "Linda Brent" (ca.1813-1897)

    61 (b.1815?); 68; 122; 142; 157; 166 (1818-1896);
    206 (Brent); 211 (Brent); 231 (Brent); 271
    (b.ca.1815); 324; 372; 377 (Brent)

Jacobus, Rebecca (b.1832)

    121; 275; 276

Janvrin, Mary W [olcott] [married name Ellsworth] (1830-
  1870) Also wrote under: Mrs. L.L. Worth.

    7; 77

Jeffrey, Rosa [Griffith] Vertner [Johnson] (1828-
  1894) Also wrote under: Rosa; Rosa Vertner
  Johnson.

7; 8; 83; 88; 121 (Johnson); 128; 155; 201; 209;
249 (Johnson); 275; 276; 294; 317; 341; 376(P)

Jerauld, Charlotte A[nn Fillebrown]   (1820-1845)   Also
wrote under: Charlotte A. Fillebrown.

7; 13; 14; 38; 92; 94 (Fillebrown); 151(P)

Jervey, Caroline Howard [Gilman Glover]   (1823-1877)
Also wrote under: Caroline Howard; Mrs. Lewis
Jervey.

7 (Glover); 13; 77 (Glover); 83; 121 (Howard);
155; 201; 275; 276; 317

Judson, Emily Chubbuck   "Fanny Forester"   (1817-1854)
Also wrote under: Emily Chubbuck.

7; 8; 13; 14; 35; 54 (Forrester); 77(P); 78; 88;
92 (Chubbuck); 94 (Forrester, d.1853); 97
(Forrester); 126; 145(P); 149; 153 (Forrester);
154(P); 155; 207; 239; 245 (Chubbock); 255; 257
(Chubbuck); 260 (Forrester); 277; 295 (Chubbuck);
313; 315 (Chubbuck); 321; 323; 361 (Forester)

Ketchum, Annie Chambers [Bradford] (1824-1904)

7; 83; 155; 201; 275; 276; 294; 317; 323; 337; 341

Kilbourn, Diana Treat   (fl.1850)   Also wrote under: A
Lady.

47

King, [Susan] Sue Petigru [married name Bowen]   (1824-
1875)   Also wrote under: A Heartless Woman; An
Idle Woman.

7; 13 (Bowen); 60; 83; 155; 167 (Bowen); 201
(b.1826); 247; 275; 276; 281; 317; 359 (b.1826)

Kinney, Elizabeth C[lementine Dodge Stedman] (1810-
1889) Also wrote under: Mrs. W.B. Kinney; Mrs.
E.C. Stedman.

7; 8; 13; 86; 88; 154; 155; 277; 323; 369

Kinzie, Juliette A[ugusta Magill] (1806-1870) Also
wrote under: Mrs. John H. Kinzie.

7; 13; 199; 239

Kirkland, Caroline [Matilda Stansbury] (1801-1864)
Also wrote under: Mary Clavers; Aminadab Peering.

7; 8; 13; 14; 19; 25; 31; 34; 35; 44; 50; 62; 72;
77(P); 78; 86; 88; 91; 92; 119; 123; 124; 126;
137; 140; 145; 146; 149; 154(P); 155; 159; 160;
162; 166(P); 182; 196; 197; 199; 203; 204; 205;
220(P); 239; 251; 255; 259; 260; 269; 271; 272;
277; 286; 292; 310; 321; 323; 333; 354; 355; 362

Ladd, C[atherine] M. [Stratton] (1808-1899) Also
wrote under: Alida; Arcturus; Minnie Mayflower;
Morna.

88; 201; 275 (b.1810); 276 (b.1810)

Lamas, Maria (fl.1849)

305

Larcom, Lucy (1824-1893) Also wrote under: L.L.

3; 4; 7; 8(P); 13; 14; 23 (b.1826); 50; 58; 88; 93
(b.1826); 94; 103; 104; 109; 112; 126; 145; 146;
149; 155 (b.1826); 183; 184; 199; 210 (b.1826)
(P); 213; 215; 230(P); 239; 248; 252(P); 255; 260;
262; 267; 277; 288; 293 (b.1826); 323 (b.1826)/
328(P); 346; 358(P); 375(P); 376 (b.1826) (P);
377; 382; 384; 385

Lasselle, N[ancy] P[olk] (fl.1853-1859)

7; 305

Latham, Mrs. C.   (fl.1847)

287

Latimer, [Mary] Elizabeth Wormeley (1822-1904)
    Also wrote under: Mary Elizabeth Wormeley.

    7 (Wormeley); 8; 13; 14; 88; 128; 199; 201
    (Wormeley); 210; 303; 376(P)

Lawrence, Margaret [Oliver] Woods "Meta Lander"
    (1813-1901) Also wrote under: A Mother.

    7; 13

Lee, Eliza Buckminster   (ca.1788-1864)   Also wrote
    under: Miss Lee.

    7; 8; 13; 30; 35 (b.1794); 88; 94; 141; 152; 155
    (b.1794); 255; 281; 320

Lee, Hannah Farnham [Sawyer]   (1780-1865)   Also wrote
    under: A Friend; A Lady.

    7; 8; 13; 28; 44; 77; 78; 88; 92; 93 (1794-1864);
    145; 149; 154; 155; 217; 227; 257; 277; 281; 282;
    286; 305

Lee, Mary Elizabeth   (1813-1849)   Also wrote under:
    M.E.L.; A Friend.

    7; 13; 40; 59; 78; 121; 145(P); 154; 155; 201;
    226; 275; 294; 359

Le Grand, Julia [Ellen] [married name Waitz]   (1829-
    1881)

    279

Leslie, Eliza (1787-1858) Also wrote under: A Lady of Philadelphia; Eliza Lord.

7; 8; 13; 28; 38; 40; 44; 50; 77(P); 78; 88; 93; 126; 137; 140; 145(P); 146; 148; 149; 154; 155 (d.1857); 164; 178; 183; 197; 216; 220(P); 226 (d.1857); 236; 239; 240; 244(P); 251; 255; 259; 271; 277; 287; 323; 343; 347; 379

Lewis, Estelle Anna [Blanche Robinson] "Stella" (1824-1880) Also wrote under: Sarah Anna Lewis.

3; 7; 8 (Sarah Anna Lewis); 13; 14; 66 (Sarah Anna Lewis); 77(P); 78; 88; 93; 145; 154; 155; 201; 275; 277 (Sarah Anna Lewis); 303

Lippincott, Sara Jane Clarke "Grace Greenwood" (1823-1904) Also wrote under: Sara J. Clarke; Mrs. L.K. Lippincott.

7; 8; 10(P); 13; 14; 23; 35; 38; 52; 62; 77(P); 78 (Clarke); 88; 93; 94; 97 (Greenwood); 104; 108 (Greenwood); 109 (Greenwood); 124 (Greenwood); 141; 145 (Clarke) (P); 146; 149; 154 (Clarke); 155; 164; 171 (P); 175 (Greenwood) (P); 199; 210 (d.1905); 220(P); 239; 240 (Greenwood); 244; 253 (Greenwood) (P); 255; 259 (Greenwood); 260 (Greenwood) (P); 293; 295 (Greenwood); 313; 315 (Greenwood); 323; 347 (Clarke); 358 (Greenwood); 361 (Clarke); 375 (Greenwood); 376 (P)

Little, Sophia Louisa [Robbins] (b.1799) Also wrote under: Rowena.

7; 13; 145; 155; 231

Livermore, Elizabeth D[orcas Abbot] (fl.1855, d.1879)

74

Livermore, Mary A[shton Rice] (1820-1905)

3; 7; 8; 13 (b.1821); 35 (b.1821); 39(P); 40; 88; 93 (b.1821); 149(P); 151(P); 163; 199; 210; 239;

248; 252(P); 267; 280; 285; 326; 358(P); 368(P);
375(P); 376 (b.1821) (P); 382

Locke, Jane E[rmina Starkweather]   (1805-1859)   Also
wrote under: A Lady of Massachusetts.

7; 13; 14; 77; 145

Logan, Olive   (ca.1839-1909)   Also wrote under:
Chroniqueuse; Mrs. Wirt Sikes.

7 (Sikes, b.1841); 8; 13; 14; 74 (b.1838); 88; 155
(b.1841); 180(P); 239; 277

Longstreet, [Rachel Abigail] Abby [Peters] Buchanan
[Gildersleeve] (1834-1899)   Also wrote under:
Rachel Buchanan; Mrs. C.H. Gildersleeve.

7; 180 (Gildersleeve)

Loughborough, Mary Ann [Webster]   (1836-1887)   Also
wrote under: A Lady.

13; 201; 275

McAdoo, Mary Faith Floyd   (b.1832)   Also wrote under:
Mary Faith Floyd.

201; 275 (McAdo)

McIntosh, M[aria] J[ane]   (1803-1878)   Also wrote
under: Aunt Kitty; Cousin Kate.

7 (MacIntosh); 13; 25; 28; 41; 44; 46; 77(P); 78;
83; 98; 121; 128; 130; 136; 139; 145; 149; 154(P);
155; 167; 186; 187; 188; 201; 216; 217; 226; 239;
249; 275; 291; 295; 317 (b.1810)

McKeever, Harriet B[urns]   (1807-1886)

7; 155

McLeod, [Georgiana] Georgie A. Hulse (1835-1890) Also
   wrote under: Georgie A. Hulse.

   7 (Hulse); 83; 121; 155; 201; 275; 276

Manvill, Mrs. P.D. (fl.1807-1810)

   7; 118; 221; 257; 266

Marsh, Caroline [Crane] (1816-1901) Also wrote under:
   Mrs. George P. Marsh.

   7; 134

Martin, Margaret Maxwell (1807-1869)

   7; 83; 201; 275; 276

Martyn, Sarah Towne [Smith] (1805-1879)

   7; 8; 13; 88; 155; 208; 226; 361

Mason, Mary A[nn Bryan] (1802-1881)

   181; 237; 275; 356

Mathews, Julia A. (fl.1855) Also wrote under:
   Alice Grey

   7; 38

Maxwell, Maria (fl.1855)

   7; 133; 305

Mayo, Sarah C[arter] Edgarton (1819-1848) Also wrote
   under: Sarah C. Edgarton; Mrs. A.D. Mayo.

   7; 8; 13; 40; 58; 78; 88; 94 (d.1849); 145; 149;
   151(P); 155; 173; 216 (Edgarton); 322 (Edgarton)

Means, Selina E.   (b.1840)

    275

Milward, Maria G.   (fl.1839-1846)

    13

Mitchell, Agnes Woods   (fl.1842)   Also wrote under:
A.W.M.

    13

Moise, Penina   (1797-1880)

    8; 13; 59; 88; 239

Montaigne, M.C.   (fl.1855)

    305

Moore, Clara [Sophia] Jessup   (1824-1899)   Also wrote
under: Mrs. Bloomfield Moore; Clara Moreton; Mrs.
H.O. Ward.

    7; 13 (Bloomfield-Moore); 154; 210; 239; 313;
    376(P)

Moore, Mrs. H.J.   (fl.1855-1860)

    7; 13; 28; 217

Moragne, Mary [Elizabeth] [married name Davis]
(1815/16-1903)   Also wrote under: A Lady of South
Carolina; Mary E. Moragne Davis.

    7 (Morange); 154; 283

Morton, Sarah Wentworth [Apthorp]   (1759-1846)   Also
wrote under: Constantia; Philenia.

7; 8(P); 13; 14; 15; 17(P); 31; 44; 66; 72; 77;
87; 88; 89; 126; 147; 199; 212; 239; 255; 261;
277; 323; 343; 373; 382

Moulton, [Ellen] Louise Chandler (1835-1908) Also
   wrote under: L.C.M.; A Lady; Ellen Louise; Ellen
   Louise Chandler; Louisa Chandler.

   7 (Chandler); 8; 13; 14; 28; 35; 52; 65; 77; 88;
   126; 149; 153; 154 (Chandler); 155; 171(P); 199;
   210(P); 223; 239; 248; 252(P); 255; 267; 277;
   280(P); 293; 314; 323; 346; 358; 375; 376(P); 384

Mowatt, Anna Cora [Ogden] [married name Ritchie]
   (1819-1870) Also wrote under: An Actress;
   A Lady; Helen Berkeley; Henry C. Browning; Cora;
   Isabel; Charles A. Lee, M.D; Anna Cora Mowatt
   Ritchie.

   7 (Ritchie); 8(P); 9; 13 (Ritchie); 14 (Ritchie);
   19 (Ritchie); 28; 35 (Ritchie); 41; 44; 55; 70; 77
   (Ritchie) (P); 78; 83 (Ritchie); 88; 93 (Ritchie);
   101; 121 (Ritchie); 145(P); 149 (Ritchie); 155
   (Ritchie, b.1820); 161; 175(P); 199; 205; 239;
   243; 248 (Ritchie); 255; 267; 269; 272; 274; 275
   (Ritchie); 277; 305 (Ritchie); 317 (Ritchie,
   b.1818); 347; 357 (Ritchie) (P); 370; 376
   (Ritchie) (P)

Murray, Judith Sargent [Stevens] (1751-1820) Also
   wrote under: The Gleaner; Constantia.

   7; 13; 15; 17; 32; 81; 88; 89; 189; 193; 199; 214;
   239; 266

Myers, Sarah A[nn Irwin] (1800/02-1876)

   7 (b.1810); 155

Nichols, Mary S[argeant Neal] Gove (1810-1884)
   Also wrote under: Mary S. Gove; Mary Orme.

   7; 8; 12; 28; 78; 88; 239; 269 (Gove)

Orne, Caroline [Chaplin]   (fl.1834-1854, d.1882)   Also
     wrote under: B. Perley Poore.

     7; 154; 155

Otis, Eliza Henderson [Bordman]   (1796-1873)   Also
     wrote under: One of the Barclays; Mrs. Harrison
     Gray Otis.

     38; 101; 305; 319; 376

Palfrey, Sara H[ammond]   "E. Foxton"   (1823-1914)

     7; 77; 155

Palmer, Fanny Purdy   (b.1839)   Also wrote under:
     Mrs. W.H. Palmer.

     64; 65; 210

Parker, Jane Marsh   (1836-1913)   Also wrote under:
     Jenny Marsh Parker.

     7 (Jenny Marsh Parker); 8; 88; 155 (Jenny Marsh
     Parker); 255

Parsons, Mary H.   (fl.1840)

     287

Patterson, Mrs.   (fl.1797)

     266

Pearson, Emily C[lemens]   (fl.1852-1868)   Also
     wrote under: Ervie; Pocahontas.

     7; 38; 44; 46 (Pierson); 128 (Pierson); 191; 231
     (Pierson); 291; 380

Peirson, Lydia Jane [Wheeler]   (1802-1862)

7; 78; 145; 155

Phelps, Almira H[art] Lincoln   (1793-1884)
    Also wrote under: Almira H. Lincoln.

    7; 13; 14; 28; 78; 83; 88; 121; 132; 134; 139;
    145(P); 154; 155; 199; 201; 210; 239; 303; 315;
    317

Phelps, Elizabeth [Wooster] Stuart   (1815-1852)   Also
    wrote under: Mary Adams; Leigh North; H. Trusta.

    7; 8; 13; 14; 25; 28; 38; 88; 126; 143; 145; 149;
    153; 239; 255; 271; 277; 380

Piatt, Louise Kirby   "Bell Smith"   (1826-1864)

    7; 74

Pike, Mary Hayden [Green]   (1824/25-1908)   Also wrote
    under: Mary Langdon; Sydney A. Story.

    7 (b.1827); 8; 13; 28; 88; 128 (Langdon); 155
    (b.1827); 196; 198; 199; 228; 231; 239; 255; 291
    (Langdon); 378 (b.1827)

Pindar, Susan   (ca.1820-1892)

    7; 145; 155; 247

Pope, Eliza   (fl.1818)   Also wrote under: A Young Lady.

    266

Porter, [Lydia] Ann E[merson]   (1816-1898)   Also wrote
    under: Uncle Jerry.

    7; 154; 180; 226 (Emerson)

Prentiss, Elizabeth Payson   (1818-1878)   Also wrote
    under: Aunt Susan; Mrs. G.L. Prentiss; Elizabeth

under: A Lady of Virginia; A Mother; Mrs. William
C. Rives.

18; 201; 275; 357

Roberts, Sarah [married name Boyle] (1812-1869)

7; 323

Robinson, Therese [Albertine Louise Von Jakob] "Talvj"
(1797-1870) Also wrote under: Talvi; Ernst
Berthold; Mrs. Edward Robinson.

7; 28; 55 (Talvj); 77; 78; 88; 93 (d.1869); 145;
154; 155 (Mrs. Edward Robinson); 199

Roe, Elizabeth A. (fl.1855)

337

Rose, Henrietta (fl.1858)

28; 176; 304

Rosewood, Emma (fl.1845)

305

Rowson, Susanna [Haswell] (ca.1762-1824)

6; 7 (b.1761); 8; 9; 11; 15; 17(P); 22; 24; 28;
31; 32; 35; 44; 50; 66; 72; 77; 78; 81; 82; 87;
88; 89; 92; 103; 117; 118; 119; 126; 141; 145;
147; 150; 152; 153; 155 (b.1761); 166(P); 178;
179; 180(P); 193; 199; 203; 204; 205; 212; 214;
217; 221; 222; 227; 228; 229; 234(P); 239; 241;
243; 250; 251; 255; 257; 261; 265; 266; 272; 277;
278; 281; 284; 299; 306(P); 307(P); 323(P); 343;
348; 353; 360; 373

Royall, Anne [Newport] (1769-1854) Also wrote under:
A Traveller; Paul Pry; Mrs. R.

7; 8; 10; 13; 14; 87; 88; 91; 128 (Royal); 155;
167; 199; 201; 212; 239; 253; 255; 277; 305; 357;
370; 371; 379

Rush, Caroline E.   (fl.1850-1855)

13; 44; 46; 98; 128; 129; 130; 136; 167; 291; 334;
380

Rush, Rebecca   (fl.1812)   Also wrote under: A Lady of
Pennsylvania.

7; 13; 44; 126; 212; 222; 251; 255; 266

Russell, Martha   (fl.1854-1857)

7; 38

Sadlier, Mary Anne Madden   (1820-1903)   Also wrote
under: M.A. Madden; Mrs. James Sadlier.

7 (Madden); 88; 155 (Mrs. James Sadlier); 199;
239; 338

Sansay, Leonora [real name Mary Hassal]   (fl.1801)
Also wrote under: A Lady of Philadelphia.

81; 82; 266; 313 (Mary Hassall)

Savage, Sarah   (1785-1837)   Also wrote under:
Anonymous; A Lady.

7; 266; 281; 305

Sawyer, Caroline M[ehitable Fisher]   (1812-1894)

7; 40; 77; 78; 145; 149; 151(P); 239

Saxon, E[lizabeth] L[yle]   (1832-1915)   Also wrote
under: E.L.S; Annot Lyle.

275

Schoolcraft, Mary Howard   (fl.1852-1860)   Also wrote
    under: A Southern Lady; Mary Howard; Mrs. Henry R.
    Schoolcraft.

    7; 13; 44; 46; 98; 128; 129; 130; 136; 167; 201;
    228; 291; 299 (Howard); 334

Sedgwick, Catharine M[aria]   (1789-1867)   Also wrote
    under: Miss C.M.S.

    7; 8(P); 9; 12(P); 13; 14; 22; 25; 28; 29(P); 30;
    31; 35; 38; 40; 43; 44; 47; 50; 58; 62; 66; 67;
    70; 72; 73; 77(P); 78; 87; 88; 90; 92; 93; 94; 97;
    100; 101; 111; 114; 119; 120; 122; 126; 140; 141;
    145(P); 146; 147; 148; 149; 153; 154(P); 155; 162;
    166(P); 182; 183; 186; 187; 188; 192; 196; 199;
    200; 203; 205; 210; 212; 216; 217; 220(P); 225;
    226; 229; 233; 235; 239; 241; 247; 251; 255; 257;
    259; 261; 262; 263; 269; 271; 272; 277(P); 278;
    281; 282; 284; 286; 287; 295; 298; 299; 305; 314;
    319; 320; 321; 323(P); 331 (Mrs. Sedgwick); 332;
    333; 335; 343; 345; 346; 352; 353; 358(P); 363;
    373(P); 374; 375(P); 376; 377; 385

Sedgwick, E[lizabeth Buckminster Dwight]   (1791-1864)
    Also wrote under: Mrs. Charles Sedgwick.

    7; 216

Sedgwick, Susan [Anne Livingston] Ridley   (1789-1867)
    Also wrote under: An Unknown Author; Mrs. Theodore
    Sedgwick.

    7; 13; 126; 189; 216; 226; 255; 281

Shindler, Mary S[tanley] B[ruce] [Palmer] Dana   (1810-
    1883)   Also wrote under: Mary S.B. Dana.

    7; 13; 59 (Dana); 62 (Dana); 78; 83; 121; 145; 149
    (Spindler); 154; 155; 201 (Palmer); 226; 249
    (Dana-Shindler); 275; 276; 294 (b.1814); 341
    (d.1880); 359 (d.ca.1880)

Sigourney, Lydia H[oward Huntley] (1791-1865) Also
    wrote under: L.H.S.; A Lady; Lydia Huntley.

    3; 7; 8(P); 12(P); 13; 14; 16(P); 40; 41; 44; 50;
    52; 55; 57; 62; 66; 70; 77(P); 78; 80; 87; 88; 91;
    93; 94; 95; 96; 97; 103; 108(P); 110; 111; 126;
    137; 141; 145(P); 146; 148; 149; 153; 154; 155;
    173; 183; 196; 199; 200; 203; 210(P); 216; 217;
    220(P); 225; 226; 227; 229; 233; 236; 239; 251;
    254; 255; 257; 260; 262; 266; 271; 277(P); 286;
    287; 293; 295; 321; 323; 343; 345; 346; 352;
    358(P); 370; 373; 374; 375(P); 376(P)

Smith, Elizabeth Oakes [Prince] (1806-1893) Also
    wrote under: E; Ernest Helfenstein; Oakes Smith;
    Mrs. Seba Smith.

    5(P); 7; 8; 12(P); 13; 14; 28; 36; 40; 41; 44;
    48(P); 62; 66; 69(P); 70; 72; 77(P); 78; 86; 88;
    94; 96; 102; 124; 145(P); 149; 151; 153; 154; 155;
    160; 163; 173; 180(P); 226; 229; 239; 255; 260;
    277; 285; 295; 298; 305; 323; 331; 332; 342; 376;
    378

Smith, Margaret Bayard (1778-1844) Also wrote under:
    Mrs. Samuel Harrison Smith.

    7; 13; 14; 28; 78; 88; 103; 149; 239; 255; 305

Smith, Sarah Pogson (fl.1807-1837) Also wrote under:
    A Lady.

    13; 152

Snelling, Anna L. [Putnam] (d.ca.1859)

    7; 22; 91

Soule, Caroline [Augusta White] (1824-1903) Also
    wrote under: Aunt Carra.

    7; 13; 91; 149; 151(P); 196; 239; 305; 310

Southworth, E[mma] D[orothy] E[liza] N[evitte]   (1819-
    1899)

    7 (b.1818); 8(P); 13; 14; 18; 24; 25; 28; 31; 35
    (b.1818); 37; 38; 44; 54; 56; 66; 70; 72; 73; 77;
    78; 80; 83; 88; 93; 96; 98; 109; 115; 118; 121;
    122; 124; 126; 128; 131; 132; 139; 141; 143;
    145(P); 149; 150; 152; 153; 154; 155 (b.1818);
    166(P); 167; 168; 170; 172; 173; 179; 186; 187;
    188; 191; 195; 196; 198; 199; 201; 210; 217;
    220(P); 227; 229; 231; 232; 236; 239; 242; 243;
    251; 255; 256; 257; 260; 275; 277; 278; 286; 287;
    291; 294; 295; 301; 302; 308; 311; 312; 316; 317;
    318; 327; 353; 360; 365; 376(P)

Southworth, Mrs. S.A.   (fl.1854-1870)

    7; 44

Spencer, Bella Z[ilfa]   (1840-1867)

    7 (d.1865); 65; 94; 336; 337

Spofford, Harriet [Elizabeth] Prescott   (1835-1921)
    Also wrote under: Harriet Elizabeth Prescott.

    7 (Prescott); 8(P); 13; 14; 35; 64 (Prescott); 65;
    66; 67 (Prescott); 77; 88; 115; 126; 146; 149;
    155; 171(P); 199; 202(P); 207; 210; 223; 229; 239;
    251; 252(P); 255; 259; 262; 271; 272; 277; 280;
    293; 314; 321; 323(P); 346; 347; 358(P); 375(P);
    376(P); 377; 378

Stephens, Ann S[ophia Winterbotham]   (1810-1886)
    Also wrote under: Jonathan Slick.

    7; 13; 19; 25; 28; 38; 41; 44; 48(P); 54; 70; 72;
    77; 78; 86; 88 (b.1813); 93 (b.1813); 94; 96
    (d.1856); 131; 141 (Winterbotham); 143; 145(P);
    149; 153; 154(P); 155 (b.1813); 160; 180(P); 196;
    197; 199; 215; 217; 227; 229; 236; 239; 255
    (b.1813); 257 (b.1813); 269(P); 264; 269; 274; 277
    (b.1813); 278; 286; 295; 299; 305; 310; 316; 321;
    322; 323 (b.1813); 325; 327

Stephens, Harriet Marion [Ward] (1823-1858) Also
wrote under: Miss Rosalie Somers; Marion Ward.

7; 28; 191

Stoddard, Elizabeth Drew [Barstow] (1823-1902)
Also wrote under: Mrs. R.H. Stoddard.

7; 8; 13; 35; 64; 67; 88; 90; 102; 126; 191; 202;
203; 206; 238; 251; 255; 272; 293; 319; 321;
323(P); 376

Stowe, Harriet [Elizabeth] Beecher (1811-1896)
Also wrote under: The American Novelist;
Christopher Crowfield; Franklin; Henry
Henderson.

1; 2; 3(P); 5(P); 7(b.1812); 8(P); 9; 11; 12(P);
13; 14; 16(P); 23 (b.1812); 25; 28; 29(P); 31; 33;
35; 37; 38; 39(P); 41; 43; 44; 45; 46; 49; 50; 51;
52; 53; 55; 56; 57; 58; 62 (b.1812); 66; 67; 70;
71; 72; 74; 75; 77 (b.1812) (P); 78; 86; 88; 90;
92; 93 (b.1812); 94; 96; 99; 101; 103; 104; 108;
110; 113; 115; 117; 118; 119; 120; 122; 125; 126;
127; 128; 129; 132; 135; 136; 137; 141; 142; 143;
145; 146; 147; 148; 149 (b.1812); 150; 153; 154
(b.1812); 155 (b.1812); 156; 159; 161; 162; 164;
168; 171(P); 172; 173; 175(P); 177; 181; 183;
185(P); 186; 187; 188; 191; 192; 197; 198; 199;
200 (b.1812); 202(P); 203; 204; 205; 206; 210;
215; 220(P); 223; 224; 226; 227; 228; 231; 232;
234(P); 238; 239; 241; 246; 248; 251; 252(P); 254;
255; 257; 259; 260(P); 261; 262; 265; 268; 271;
272; 274; 277(P); 281; 282; 284; 286; 287; 292;
293(P); 295; 298; 300; 301; 302; 306(P); 307(P);
308; 309; 314; 319; 321; 323 (b.1812) (P); 324;
326; 328(P); 329(P); 333; 335; 337; 339; 340; 342;
343; 345; 346; 348; 349; 353; 356; 358(P); 360;
361; 362; 363; 364; 368(P); 370; 373(P); 375(P);
376 (b.1812); 377(P); 380; 381; 382; 383(P); 384;
385

Sweat, Margaret J[ane] M[ussey] (1823-1908)
Also wrote under: M.J.M.S.

5(P); 7; 48(P); 378

Talbot, Mary Elizabeth (fl.1830)

    181

Tenney, Tabitha [Gilman] (1762-1837) Also wrote
    under: Anonymous.

    7; 8; 13; 14; 17; 44; 66; 72; 77; 83; 88; 89; 92;
    126 (Tenny); 155; 166; 189; 212; 217; 221; 239;
    250; 251; 255; 257; 266; 277; 284; 323; 373

Terhune, Mary Virginia [Hawes] "Marion Harland"
    (1830-1922)

    3 (Harland); 7; 8(P); 13; 14; 18 (Harland); 23
    (b.1838); 25 (Harland); 28 (Harland); 35; 38; 60;
    66; 72; 77; 83; 86 (Harland); 88; 96 (Harland);
    115; 118; 121; 126; 128; 132; 135; 141; 145; 155;
    167; 170 (Harland, b.1831); 171 (Harland) (P); 172
    (Harland); 173 (Harland); 186; 187; 188; 199; 201;
    208; 210 (b.1831); 217; 218; 224; 229; 239; 242
    (Harland); 246; 247 (Harland); 248; 249 (b.1831);
    251 (Harland); 252(P); 255; 256; 257 (Harland);
    275; 277; 286 (Harland); 293; 294 (Harland); 295
    (Harland); 302 (Harland); 311; 315; 317 (b.1831);
    321 (Harland); 323; 347; 350; 353; 357 (Harland)
    (P); 358 (Harland) (P); 365; 369 (d.1923); 370
    (Hawes); 375 (Harland) (P); 376 (b.1831) (P)

Thayer, Mrs. J. (fl.1842-1847)

    7; 44

Thomas, Martha M[cCannon] (1818-1890)

    7 (b.1823); 74; 155; 201 (b.1823)

Thompson, Clara M. (fl.1854-1873) Also wrote under:
    Clara M. Thompson Logan.

    7; 13

Torrey, Mary Ide (1817-1869) Also wrote under: A

Tyler, Martha W. (fl.1855)

    7; 13; 36; 305

Upshur, M[ary] J[ane] [Stith] [married name Sturges]
    "Fanny Fielding" (b.1828)

    83; 155; 201 (Upshaw); 275

Vaughan, Mary C. (fl.1855-1865)

    7; 236; 247

Vickery, Sukey [married name Watson; mistakenly called
    Eliza Vicery in NATIONAL UNION CATALOG] Also
    wrote under: Fidelia; A Young Lady of Worcester
    County.

    13 (Watson); 221; 250 (Vicery); 266

Victor, Frances [Auretta] Fuller (1826-1902) Also
    wrote under: Frances Barritt; Dorothy D.; Florence
    Fane; Frances Fuller.

    7; 8; 13; 14; 74; 88; 145 (Fuller); 180 (Barritt)
    (P); 199; 239; 255; 270(P); 277; 310 (Barritt);
    376(P); 377

Victor, Metta [Victoria] Fuller (1831-1885) Also
    wrote under: George E. Booram; Corinne Cushman;
    Eleanor Lee Edwards; Metta Fuller; Walter T. Gray;
    Louis LeGrand; Rose Kennedy; Mrs. Mark Peabody;
    Seeley Regester; The Singing Sybil; Mrs. Henry J.
    Thomas.

    7; 8 (d.1886); 13; 14; 21; 28; 44 (Fuller); 46;
    74; 86; 125; 128; 145 (Fuller); 153; 155; 166(P);
    180(P); 191; 198; 199; 231; 232; 236; 239; 243;
    255 (d.1886); 257; 264; 277 (d.1886); 310; 327;
    337; 349 (d.1886); 376 (b.1851) (P)

Walker, Katherine [Kent Child] (b.1833) Also wrote
    under: K.K. Kind; Mrs. Edward Ashley Walker.

64; 65; 207; 323 (b.1842)

Walsingham, Mary [married name Crean]   (b.ca.1835)

    83; 201 (Walsington); 275 (Crean); 276 (Crean);
    317

Warfield, Catharine A[nn Ware]   (1816-1877)   Also wrote
under: A Southern Lady.

    7; 13; 60; 77; 83; 88; 121; 128; 145; 155
    (b.1817); 167; 180; 201; 209; 249 (d.1887); 275;
    276; 294; 316; 317; 341; 349

Warner, Anna B[artlett]   (1827-1915)   Also wrote under:
Amy Lothrop.

    1; 3; 7; 8; 13 (b.1824?); 25; 28; 52; 77; 88; 93
    (b.1820); 145; 153; 154 (Lothrop); 155; 159; 164;
    183; 192 (Lothrop); 199; 229; 239; 255; 257;
    260(P); 277; 293

Warner, Susan [Bogert] "Elizabeth Wetherell"   (1819-
1885)   Also wrote under: E.W.; S.W.

    1; 3; 6; 7; 8; 13; 14; 16(P); 19; 23 (b.1818); 25;
    28; 35; 37; 38; 41; 42; 43; 44; 52; 53; 57; 70;
    72; 73; 75 (Wetherell); 77; 88; 90; 92; 93; 94;
    96; 97; 99 (Wetherell); 104; 110; 115; 117; 118;
    122; 124; 126 (Wetherell); 132; 135; 143; 145
    (Wetherell); 149 (Elizabeth Warner); 152; 153; 154
    (Wetherell); 155 (b.1818); 156; 159; 164; 166(P);
    169; 179; 183; 186; 187; 188; 192; 194; 195; 199;
    217; 219; 223; 224; 226 (b.1818); 227; 229; 239;
    246; 248; 251; 255; 257; 260(P); 277; 281; 284;
    286; 293; 295; 309; 311; 321; 323; 333; 339; 342;
    343; 348; 352; 353; 360; 365

Warren, Caroline Matilda [married name Thayer]
(ca.1787-1844)   Also wrote under: Caroline
Matilda Thayer.

    7 (Thayer); 8 (Thayer); 13 (Thayer); 44; 72; 126;
    212; 217; 222 (Thayer); 250; 251; 255; 266; 272;

281 (Thayer)

Wells, Helena [married name Whitford] (ca.1760-ca.1824)

    7; 15 (d.ca.1809); 44; 72; 81; 89; 212; 255; 266; 272; 283

Westmoreland, Maria [Elizabeth] J[ourdan]   (b.1815)
Also wrote under: Mystery.

    7; 201; 275; 276

Weston, Maria D. [Gaines] (fl.1847-1866)   Also wrote under: An American Lady; Maria.

44

Whitaker, Mary Scrimzeour [Furman Miller]   (1820-1906)

    83; 155; 201; 275; 276; 359

Whitcher, Frances M[iriam Berry] (ca.1811-1852) Also wrote under: Aunt Maguire; Frank; Widow Bedott; Widow Spriggins.

    7 (b.1812); 8 (b.1814); 13 (b.1813?); 14 (b.1813?); 23 (b.1812); 50; 86; 88 (b.1814); 92; 126; 143; 144; 146; 153; 154 (Berry, b.1812); 155 (Whitaker, b.1812); 166; 197; 199; 224; 239; 245; 251; 255 (b.1814); 260; 274 (Berry, b.1814); 277 (b.1814); 321; 323; 333 (b.1814); 347; 354 (b.1814); 355 (Whicher)

White, Rhoda E[lizabeth Waterman] (fl.1853-1885) Also wrote under: Uncle Ben; Uncle Ben of Rouses Point.

    7; 13; 14; 305

Whitney, A[deline] D[utton] T[rain]   (1824-1906)

    7; 8; 13; 35; 53; 77; 88; 93; 94; 97; 104; 115; 126; 138; 143; 145; 146; 155; 165; 173; 183; 199;

Wood, Julia Amanda Sargent   "Minnie Mary Lee"   (1825-
1903)   Also wrote under: Mrs. Julia A.A. Wood.

   7; 85 (b.1830); 239; 376 (b.1826) (P)

Wood, [Sarah] Sally [Sayward Barrell Keating]   (1759-
1855)   Also wrote under: A Lady of Maine; A Lady
of Massachusetts; Sally Keating.

   5(P); 7; 8; 13; 14; 32; 44; 48; 72; 81; 88; 89;
   117; 126; 150; 153; 166(P); 212; 229; 239; 250;
   251; 255; 266; 272; 277; 321; 378

Worthington, Jane Taylor [Lomax]   (d.1847)

   7; 77; 121; 201; 275

Yale, Catherine B[rooks]   "Katinka"   (1818-1900)

   7; 35

INDEX TO AUTHORS AND EDITORS IN PART 1

INDEX TO TOPICS IN PART 1

Index

PSEUDONYMS/ALTERNATIVE FORMS OF NAME FOR AUTHORS IN PART 2

NAME	SEE
A., L.M.	Alcott
Actress, An	Mowatt
Adams, Mary	Phelps, Elizabeth Stuart
Adelaide	Bogart
Adelia	Farley
Adrienne	Creswell
Aesop	Blake
Afton, Effie	Harper
Alida	Ladd
American, An	Brownson
	Child
American Citizen, An	Green
American Lady, An	Read, Martha
	Weston
American Novelist, The	Stowe
Anonymous	Savage
	Tenney
Arcturus	Ladd

Ashley, Mary	Townsend, Mary Ashley
Aunt Alice	Graves, Adelia C.
Aunt Carra	Soule
Aunt Fanny	Barrow
	Gage
Aunt Friendly	Baker, Sarah S.
Aunt Hattie	Baker, Harriette
	Newell Woods
Aunt Kitty	McIntosh
Aunt Libbie	Hoyt
Aunt Maguire	Whitcher
Aunt Patty	Hentz, Caroline Lee
Aunt Susan	Prentiss
B., S.G.	Bagley
Barber, Catharine Webb	Towles
Barnard, A.M.	Alcott
Barritt, Frances	Victor, Frances Fuller
Bedott, Widow	Whitcher
Beecher, Mrs. Henry Ward	Beecher, Eunice
	White Bullard
Bennett, Martha Haines	
Butt	Butt
Berkeley, Helen	Mowatt
Berry, Frances M.	Whitcher
Berthold, Ernst	Robinson
Bleeker, Anna Eliza	Bleecker
Bloomfield-Moore, Mrs.	Moore, Clara Jessup

Booram, George E.	Victor, Metta Fuller
Bowen, Sue Petigru King	King
Branch, Caroline Therese	Hentz, Caroline Therese
Brent, Linda	Jacobs
Browne, Mattie Griffith	Griffith
Browning, Henry C.	Mowatt
Buchanan, Rachel	Longstreet
Buell, Sarah Josepha	Hale, Sarah Josepha
C., L.M.	Child
C., M.	Cummins
C., M.A.	Cruse
Canute, Judith	Campbell, Juliet H.L.
Carey, Alice	Cary, Alice
Carey, Phoebe	Cary, Phoebe
Carleton, Cousin May	Fleming
Caustic, Mrs.	Bullard, Anne Tuttle
Chandler, Ellen Louise	Moulton
Chandler, Louisa	Moulton
Chesebrough, Caroline	Chesebro'
Child, Mrs. D.L.	Child
Childs, Lydia Maria	Child
Chroniqueuse	Logan
Chubbock, Emily	Judson
Chubbuck, Emily	Judson
Clare	Clare, Ada

Clark, Rebecca Sophia	Clarke, Rebecca Sophia
Clarke, Sara J.	Lippincott
Clavers, Mary	Kirkland
Colvil, Edward	Putnam
Constantia	Morton
	Murray
Cooper, Miss	Cooper, Susan Fenimore
Cora	Mowatt
Cornelia	Hale, Sarah Josepha
Cousin Alice	Bradley
	Haven
Cousin Kate	McIntosh
Cowden, Mrs. V.G.	Cowdin
Crane-Seemuller, Anne Moncure	Crane
Crean, Mary Walsingham	Walsingham
Crossbones, Crabb	Townsend, Mary Ashley
Crowfield, Christopher	Stowe
Cummings, Maria	Cummins
Cunctare	Dodge, Mary Abigail
Cushman, Clara	Haven
Cushman, Corinne	Victor, Metta Fuller
Cutler, Mrs. P.Y.	Cutler, Lizzie Petit
D.	Cate
D., A.M.	Denison
D., Dorothy	Victor, Frances Fuller

D., M.A.	Denison
D., M.M.	Dodge, Mary Mapes
Dana, Mary S.B.	Shindler
Dana-Shindler, Mary S.B.	Shindler
Dashmore, Frank	Downing
Davis, Mary E. Moragne	Moragne
Denison, Mrs. C.W.	Denison, Mary Andrews
Dupuy, A.E.	Dupuy, Eliza A.
E.	Smith, Elizabeth Oakes
E., E.F.	Ellet
Edgarton, Sarah C.	Mayo
Edson, N.I.	Denison
Edwards, Eleanor Lee	Victor, Metta Fuller
Eldredge, Sara	Fern
Elenjay, Louise	Elemjay
Ella	Farley
Ellemjay, Louise	Elemjay
Ellinjay, Louise	Elemjay
Emerson, Ann	Porter
Emmet, Elizabeth	Comstock
Ervie	Pearson
Estelle	Bogart
Evans, Augusta J.	Wilson, Augusta Evans
F., H.	Farley
Fairfield, Flora	Alcott

Fane, Florence	Victor, Frances Fuller
Farnham, Mrs. T.J.	Farnham, Eliza W.
Farquharson, Martha	Finley
Female, A	Gales
Fidelia	Vickery
Fielding, Fanny	Upshur
Filia	Dorsey, Sarah Anne
Filia Ecclesiae	Beauchamp
Fillebrown, Charlotte A.	Jerauld
Fleming, Mary Agnes	Fleming, May Agnes
Floyd, Mary Faith	McAdoo
Ford, Mrs. Samuel Howard	Ford, Sallie R.
Forester, Fanny	Judson
Forrester, Fanny	Judson
Foster, Mrs. John	Foster, Hannah
Fowler, Mrs. L.N.	Fowler, Lydia Folger
Foxton, E.	Palfrey
Frank	Whitcher
Franklin	Stowe
Frazaer, Mary	Hayden, Sarah Marshall
French, Virginia L.	French, L. Virginia
Friend, A	Lee, Hannah Farnham
	Lee, Mary Elizabeth
Fuller, Frances	Victor, Frances Fuller
Fuller, Metta	Victor, Metta Fuller

G., H.B.	Goodwin, H.B.
Gildersleeve, Mrs. C.H.	Longstreet
Gleaner, The	Murray
Glover, Caroline Howard Gilman	Jervey
Goodwin-Talcott, Mrs.	Goodwin, H.B.
Gove, Mary S.	Nichols
Grahame, Nellie	Dunning
Gray, Walter T.	Victor, Metta Fuller
Green, Fanny	Green, Frances H.
Greene, Frances H.	Green
Greenough, Mrs. Richard S.	Greenough, Sarah Dana Loring
Greenwood, Grace	Lippincott
Grey, Alice	Mathews
Griffin, Mattie	Griffith
Griffith, Martha	Griffith, Mattie
Griffiths, Mattie	Griffith
H., A.W.	Cooke
H., L.	Hooper
H., L.J.	Hall
H., S.J.	Hale, Sarah Josepha
Hall, Mrs. Edward B.	Hall, Louisa Jane
Hamilton, Gail	Dodge, Mary Abigail
Harland, Marion	Terhune

Kelly, Caroline E.	Davis, Caroline E.
Kennedy, Rose	Victor, Metta Fuller
Kind, K.K.	Walker
Kinney, Mrs. W.B.	Kinney, Elizabeth C.
Kinzie, Mrs. John H.	Kinzie, Juliette A.
L., L.	Larcom
L., M.E.	Lee, Mary Elizabeth
Lady, A	Cooper, Susan Fenimore
	Evans
	Follen
	Kilbourn
	Lee, Hannah Farnham
	Loughborough
	Moulton
	Mowatt
	Savage
	Sigourney
	Smith, Sarah Pogson
	Torrey
	Tuthill, Louisa C.
Lady Chrysalis, A	Curtis
Lady of Maine, A	Wood, Sally
Lady of Massachusetts, A	Child
	Foster
	Locke
	Wood
Lady of New Hampshire, A	Hale, Sarah Josepha
Lady of Pennsylvania, A	Rush, Rebecca
Lady of Philadelphia, A	Botsford
	Leslie
	Read, Martha
	Sansay
Lady of South Carolina, A	Moragne
Lady of Virginia, A	Rives

Lady of the West	Collins
Lander, Meta	Lawrence
Langdon, Mary	Pike
Lanmere	Dorr
Layman, A	Eames
Lee, Alice G.	Haven
Lee, Charles A., M.D.	Mowatt
Lee, Minnie Mary	Wood, Julia Amanda Sargent
Lee, Miss	Lee, Eliza Buckminster
Lee, Patty	Cary, Alice
LeGrand, Louis	Victor, Metta Fuller
Leslie, Isabel	Dorr
Leslie, Madeline	Baker, Harriette Newell Woods
Lewis, Sarah Anna	Lewis, Estelle Anna
Lincoln, Almira H.	Phelps, Almira H. Lincoln
L'Inconnue	French
Linwood, Lela	Hubbell, Mary Elizabeth
Lippincott, Mrs. L.K.	Lippincott, Sara Jane Clarke
Logan, Clara M. Thompson	Thompson
Lord, Eliza	Leslie
Lorraine, A.M.	Collins
Lothrop, Amy	Warner, Anna B.
Louise, Ellen	Moulton

Lover of the Fine Arts, A	Brooks, Maria Gowen
Lyle, Annot	Saxon
Lynch, Anne	Botta
M., A.	Alcott
M., A.W.	Mitchell
M., L.C.	Moulton
M, Mrs.	Botsford
McAdo, Mary Faith Floyd	McAdoo
McDougall, Frances H. Green	Green
McElheney, Jane	Clare
McElhinney, Jane	Clare
MacElhinney, Julia	Clare
MacIntosh, M.J.	McIntosh
Madden, M.A.	Sadlier
Maria	Weston
Marsh, Mrs. George P.	Marsh, Caroline
Matilda	Eastman
May, Sophie	Clarke, Rebecca Sophia
Mayfield, Millie	Homes
Mayflower, Minnie	Ladd
Mayo, Mrs. A.D.	Mayo, Sarah C. Edgarton
Minister's Wife, A	Beecher
Moina	Dinnies
Morange, Mary	Moragne

Moreton, Clara	Moore, Clara Jessup
Morna	Ladd
Mother, A	Lawrence Rives
Myrtle, Mina	Curtis
Myrtle, Mollie	Bacon, Julia
Mystery	Westmoreland
Neal, Alice B.	Haven
Neely, Kate J.	Bradley
New England Bride, A	Gilman
New England Housekeeper, A	Gilman
North, Leigh	Phelps, Elizabeth Stuart
Occidente, Maria del	Brooks, Maria Gowen
Old Teacher, An	Hosmer
Olivia	Briggs
One of the Barclays	Otis
One of Themselves	Brownson
O'Quillo, Michael	Townsend, Mary Ashley
Orme, Mary	Nichols
Otis, Mrs. Harrison Gray	Otis, Eliza Henderson
P., L.J.	Hall
P., M.L.	Putnam
Packard, Clarissa	Gilman
Palmer, Mary S.B.	Shindler
Palmer, Mrs. W.H.	Palmer, Fanny Purdy

Parker, Jenny Marsh	Parker, Jane Marsh
Parley, Julia	Hale, Sarah Josepha
Parton, Sara	Fern
Peabody, Mrs. Mark	Victor, Metta Fuller
Peering, Aminadab	Kirkland
Penfeather, Anabel	Cooper, Susan Fenimore
Periwinkle, Tribulation	Alcott
Petit, Lizzie	Cutler
Peyre, Anna	Dinnies
Philenia	Morton
Pierson, Cornelia Tuthill	Tuthill, Cornelia
Pierson, Emily C.	Pearson
Pleasants, Julia	Creswell
Pocahontas	Pearson
Poore, B. Perley	Orne
Prentiss, Mrs. G.L.	Prentiss, Elizabeth Payson
Prescott, Elizabeth	Prentiss
Prescott, Harriet Elizabeth	Spofford
Pry, Paul	Royall
Queen of Bohemia	Clare
R., Mrs.	Royall
Rachel	Dinnies
Reed, Mary J.	Hildeburn
Regester, Seeley	Victor, Metta Fuller

Rhode Islander, A	Green
Rip, Henry	Townsend, Mary Ashley
Ritchie, Anna Cora Mowatt	Mowatt
Rives, Mrs. William C.	Rives, Judith Walker
Robinson, Mrs. Edward	Robinson, Therese
Rodman, Ella	Church
Rosa	Jeffrey
Rowena	Little
Royal, Anne	Royall
S., Miss C.M.	Sedgwick, Catharine M.
S., E.L.	Saxon
S., L.H.	Sigourney
S., M.J.M.	Sweat
S.S. Teacher, A	Browne, Sara H.
Sadlier, Mrs. James	Sadlier, Mary Anne Madden
Schoolcraft, Mrs. Henry R.	Schoolcraft, Mary Howard
Sedgwick, Mrs. Charles	Sedgwick, E.
Sedgwick, Mrs. Theodore	Sedgwick, Susan Ridley
Seemuller, Anne Moncure Crane	Crane
Shotwell, Nathaniel	Dodge, Mary Mapes
Sikes, Mrs. Wirt	Logan
Singing Sybil, The	Victor, Metta Fuller
Slick, Jonathan	Stephens, Ann S.

Smith, Bell	Piatt
Smith, Lucy	French
Smith, Mrs. Samuel Harrison	Smith, Margaret Bayard
Smith, Mrs. Seba	Smith, Elizabeth Oakes
Smith, Oakes	Smith, Elizabeth Oakes
Somers, Miss Rosalie	Stephens, Harriet Marion
Southern Lady, A	Schoolcraft Warfield
Southern Matron, A	Gilman
Spindler, Mary S.B. Dana	Shindler
Spriggins, Widow	Whitcher
Sproat, Eliza L.	Turner
Stacy, Joel	Dodge, Mary Mapes
Stedman, Mrs. E.C.	Kinney
Stella	Lewis
Stoddard, Mrs. R.H.	Stoddard, Elizabeth Drew
Story, Sydney A.	Pike
Susan	Farley
Tabitha	Chamberlain
Talcott, H.B. Goodwin	Goodwin, H.B.
Talvi	Robinson
Talvj	Robinson
Tatem, H.M.	Hazlett
Tatem, M.H.	Hazlett
Tenella	Clarke, Mary Bayard

W., E.	Warner, Susan
W., S.	Warner, Susan
Walker, Mrs. Edward Ashley	Walker, Katherine
Walsington, Mary	Walsingham
Ward, Marion	Stephens, Harriet Marion
Ward, Mrs. H.O.	Moore, Clara Jessup
Warner, Elizabeth	Warner, Susan
Watkins, Frances Ellen	Harper
Watson, Sukey Vickery	Vickery
Wetherell, Elizabeth	Warner, Susan
Whicher, Frances M.	Whitcher
Whipple, Frances Harriet	Green
Whitaker, Frances M.	Whitcher
Willis, Sara	Fern
Winterbotham, Ann S.	Stephens, Ann S.
Wood, Mrs. Julia A.A.	Wood, Julia Amanda Sargent
Woodbine, Jenny	Blount
Woodson, Eliza	Farnham
Wormeley, Mary Elizabeth	Latimer
Worth, Mrs. L.L.	Janvrin
Xariffa	Townsend, Mary Ashley
Young, Annie	Dupuy
Young Lady, A	Pope
Young Lady of Virginia	Collins

Young Lady of Worcester
   County, A   Vickery